GLOBALIZATION AND HEALTH

D1591066

JEREMY YOUDE
UNIVERSITY OF MINNESOTA DULUTH

ROWMAN & LITTLEFIELD
Lanham • Boulder • New York • London

Executive Editor: Susan McEachern
Editorial Assistant: Katelyn Turner
Senior Marketing Manager: Amy Whitaker

Credits and acknowledgments for material borrowed from other sources, and reproduced with permission, appear on the appropriate page within the text.

Published by Rowman & Littlefield
An imprint of The Rowman & Littlefield Publishing Group, Inc.
4501 Forbes Boulevard, Suite 200, Lanham, Maryland 20706
www.rowman.com

6 Tinworth Street, London SE11 5AL, United Kingdom

Library of Congress Cataloging-in-Publication Data

Names: Youde, Jeremy R., 1976– author.
Title: Globalization and health / Jeremy Youde.
Other titles: Globalization (Lanham, Md.)
Description: Lanham : Rowman & Littlefield, [2020] | Series: Globalization | Includes bibliographical references and index. | Summary: "It's a cliché to say that diseases do not respect national borders, but the realities of this aphorism present serious and significant challenges to the global community. Health and disease are intimately connected with the movement of people, goods, and ideas that are emblematic of globalization. This book will examine the various dimensions of the intersections between globalization and health, calling attention to the challenges these relationships present and the opportunities for cross-border collaboration and solidarity"— Provided by publisher.
Identifiers: LCCN 2019020429 (print) | ISBN 9781538121818 (cloth) alk. paper | ISBN 9781538121825 (paperback) alk. paper | ISBN 9781538121832 (ebook)
Subjects: MESH: Global Health | International Cooperation
Classification: LCC RA441 (print) | LCC RA441 (ebook) | NLM WA 530.1 | DDC 362.1—dc23
LC record available at https://lccn.loc.gov/2019020429
LC ebook record available at https://lccn.loc.gov/2019980287

♾️™ The paper used in this publication meets the minimum requirements of American National Standard for Information Sciences—Permanence of Paper for Printed Library Materials, ANSI/NISO Z39.48-1992.

For Steve McCrea and Orean Yahnke

CONTENTS

Acknowledgments

Even if there is only one name listed on the cover, any book is necessarily a group effort—and this book is no different. My deepest thanks to my colleagues in the Department of International Relations in the Coral Bell School of Asia Pacific Affairs in the College of Asia and the Pacific at the Australian National University where I wrote this book. Your thoughtful feedback, encouragement, and well-timed coffee breaks were absolutely vital in helping me to think about this topic. Friends and colleagues from the Global Health Section of the International Studies Association have also proven absolutely invaluable, and the two anonymous reviewers saved me from making egregious mistakes (though any that remain are wholly my responsibility). Perhaps most importantly, my partner Ben has stood by me for years, even when we've been on opposite sides of the world.

The staff at Rowman & Littlefield have been marvelous partners in this enterprise. I'd especially like to thank my editor, Susan McEachern. Not only did she first approach me about writing this book, but our shared love of yellow labs meant that every meeting we had would invariably turn into an opportunity to share dog pictures with each other. That's how you know you are in good hands. Katelyn Turner and Alden Perkins both went above and beyond in turning my manuscript into an actual book that you can hold in your hands.

Finally, I dedicate this book to two amazing teachers—people who saw a little nerd come into their classrooms and gave him the support to become the big nerd I am today. Steve McCrea taught me in junior high and high school, and he instilled in me the value of pursuing my seemingly esoteric interests. Even more importantly, he introduced me to Monty Python. Orean Yahnke was my first- and third-grade teacher, and she sparked a love of learning and research in me. I can only hope this book is better than the report I wrote for you about marsupials in first grade, Mrs. Yahnke.

ABBREVIATIONS

ACT UP   AIDS Coalition to Unleash Power
AIDS   acquired immune deficiency syndrome
ARVs   antiretroviral drugs
ASEAN   Association of South East Asian Nations
BMGF   Bill & Melinda Gates Foundation
BSE   bovine spongiform encephalopathy
CBD   Convention on Biological Diversity
CDC   Centers for Disease Control and Prevention
DAH   development assistance for health
FCTC   Framework Convention on Tobacco Control
FENSA   Framework of Engagement with Non-State Actors
GDP   gross domestic product
GHSA   Global Health Security Agenda
GISN   Global Influenza Surveillance Network
GISRS   Global Influenza Surveillance and Response System
GPA   Global Program on AIDS
H1N1   influenza A (H1N1)
H5N1   influenza A (H5N1)
HIV   human immunodeficiency virus
IHME   Institute for Health Metrics and Evaluation
IHR   International Health Regulations
IHR (1983)   International Health Regulations (1983)
IHR (2005)   International Health Regulations (2005)
IPRs   intellectual property rights
ISR   International Sanitary Regulations
LGBT   lesbian, gay, bisexual, and transgender
MDGs   Millennium Development Goals

MERS	Middle East respiratory syndrome
MOU	memorandum of understanding
MSF	Médecins Sans Frontières/Doctors Without Borders
NAFTA	North American Free Trade Agreement
NAMRU-2	Naval Medical Research Unit-2
NCDs	noncommunicable diseases
NGO	nongovernmental organization
NIH	National Institutes of Health
PAHO	Pan American Health Organization
PEPFAR	President's Emergency Plan for AIDS Relief
PHC	primary health care
PHEIC	Public Health Emergency of International Concern
PIPF	Pandemic Influenza Preparedness Framework
PRC	People's Republic of China
SARS	severe acute respiratory syndrome
SDGs	Sustainable Development Goals
SDHs	social determinants of health
SMTA	standard material transfer agreement
TAC	Treatment Action Campaign
TRIPS	Agreement on Trade-Related Aspects of Intellectual Property Rights
UCL	University College London
UN	United Nations
UNAIDS	Joint United Nations Program on HIV/AIDS
UNGA	United Nations General Assembly
WHA	World Health Assembly
WHO	World Health Organization
WTO	World Trade Organization

INTRODUCTION

As I write this, it has been one hundred years since the world was caught in the grip of worldwide influenza pandemic. The virus took advantage of the movement of troops, the transportation networks, and the mixing of different groups of people in the midst of World War I to reach nearly every part of the world (Youde 2017). Crosby notes, "Nothing else—no infection, no war, no famine—has ever killed so many in as short a period. . . . Single-handedly the flu thrust the year of 1918 back into the previous century" (2003: 311). The outbreak sickened a quarter of the Earth's population, killing at least twenty million and reducing life expectancy in the United States by twelve years (Price-Smith 2009: 57–58). More soldiers died of influenza than died in battle, and the pandemic had far-reaching social, political, and economic consequences. It was the ties that facilitated the movement of people and goods across borders so quickly that allowed the influenza outbreak to flourish.

A century later, the collapsing of space and time emblematic of globalization are having their own effects on the health of the world's citizens. There may not be a single epidemic ravaging the globe at this moment, but there is unmistakable evidence that viruses, bacteria, and other causes of ill health piggyback on the movement of people and goods to further their spread. Globalization's benefits may increase our risk of getting sick from new diseases. The fact that I can fly from Australia to the United States in about fourteen hours is incredibly convenient for me, but it is also incredibly convenient for microbes. Viruses do not need passports; they take advantage of ours. That may sound ominous, but it need not inspire fear. The same processes that may increase our vulnerability also allow us to keep an eye on diseases and build solidarity with others. Globalization can reinforce power imbalances, but it can also provide us with the tools to challenge health inequities.

This book aims to help explain the connections between global health and globalization. It highlights how these linkages include both infectious and noncommunicable diseases. It describes the institutional structures that have developed in an effort to keep people safe. It shows how globalization may have made it easier for illnesses to cross borders, but also expanded the opportunities for joint transnational action to address health problems. It examines the power dynamics at play in understanding the links between health and globalization and how globalization can both reinforce and challenge those inequities. In these ways, it seeks to offer a nuanced perspective on the various ways in which globalization and global health influence and are influenced by each other. It aims to "locate global health in the context of changing world orders" (Oni et al. 2019: e302) so as to figure out what is going right and what needs to be fixed in this globalized world.

PLAN FOR THE BOOK

The book begins by clearly describing how and why globalization and global health are related to each other. The first two chapters lay out the theoretical connections between health and globalization. Chapter 1 focuses on the globalization side of this relationship. It defines the term, shows how these definitions are related to health, and notes how the globalization of health complicates our traditional understandings of state sovereignty. The globalization of health has even changed how we talk about these sorts of issues. Chapter 2 uses three health conditions—smallpox, severe acute respiratory syndrome (SARS), and overweight/obesity—to highlight the connections between health and globalization in practice. The efforts to eradicate smallpox brought the international community together, but globalization means that a disease that has not naturally circulated for nearly forty years remains prominent on the global security agenda. SARS is a brand-new human illness that appeared without warning, spread rapidly as people crossed borders, and then disappeared. It shows the importance of keeping track of outbreaks, as well as the difficulties that go along with trying to foster cooperation among different actors to stop a disease's spread. Rates of overweight and obesity have increased substantially in all parts of the world, but that has nothing to do with viruses circulating. Instead, this rise in a noncommunicable disease is connected to changes in trade and agricultural policies facilitated by globalization.

The next four chapters apply the interplay between globalization and health to distinct policy realms. Chapter 3 looks at some of the institutions of global health governance that have emerged. In particular, it highlights the broad definition of institution to move beyond a state-centric approach. Instead, it shows that the global health space continues to diversify to include a growing range of formal and informal institutions—and that this diversification is a potential source of both strength and weakness. Chapter 4 examines how activists have harnessed globalization's ability to shrink time and space to push for better health policies. This includes building an international human immunodeficiency virus (HIV)/acquired immune deficiency syndrome (AIDS) movement that links the Global North and the Global South, challenging the global intellectual property rights regime to improve access to pharmaceuticals, and campaigning to introduce taxes on sugary beverages. Globalization allows for geographically distant people to come together in a shared sense of purpose and to exchange ideas about strategy and tactics. Chapter 5 focuses on the idea of viral sovereignty. Indonesia invoked this idea in 2006 when it stopped sharing samples of human cases of H5N1 influenza with an existing global laboratory network. This action forced the global community to reckon with issues of pharmaceutical access, disease surveillance, and the respective balance between national sovereignty and international cooperation—ideas that are at the heart of contemporary global health governance. Chapter 6 takes up the importance of disease surveillance. The ease with which people and goods can cross borders makes it all the more important that the international community can identify disease outbreaks before they get too large, but surveillance raises a host of objections. There are international treaties that mandate disease surveillance structures, but they come with no financial support to bolster their operations. Brief examinations of H1N1 influenza, Ebola, and Zika illustrate both the importance of surveillance and how the existing systems can fall short.

The final chapter, chapter 7, concludes the book by looking forward. What issues are currently being overlooked? What issues deserve greater attention? What are the concerns that global health governance will need to grapple with in the near future? A greater recognition of how gender is marginalized within the study of globalization and health, an appreciation of how human health is intricately linked to animal and environmental health, and the emergence of political leaders who question the value of multilateralism and foreign aid all pose potential challenges to the global health system that has developed.

CHAPTER 1

THE GLOBALIZATION OF HEALTH

How does a virus that originates in camels cause an infectious disease outbreak in humans in South Korea? That's globalization at work. Middle East respiratory syndrome (MERS) is a viral respiratory illness first discovered in Saudi Arabia in 2012. People infected with MERS frequently experience fever, coughs, shortness of breath, and pneumonia, and some also experience diarrhea and vomiting. As of early 2019, more than twenty-two hundred people have come down with MERS, and more than one-third of them have died. There is no specific treatment for MERS yet, and scientists believe that the virus originates in dromedaries—though it is not clear how the virus makes the leap from camels to humans.

Because the virus originates in camels, it makes sense that areas with lots of camels would have a higher proportion of MERS cases—and that is what we have seen. The vast majority of cases have appeared in Saudi

Arabia. Which country has the second-highest number of cases? South Korea. South Korea is a land of many things, but it is not known for its large camel population. Despite this, South Korea saw nearly two hundred MERS cases between May and July 2015. Why would MERS emerge there? In a word, globalization. A Korean citizen unknowingly caught MERS while he was traveling in the Middle East, and he inadvertently brought the disease back with him when he returned home. Shortly after his trip, he developed respiratory problems. He sought treatment at a few different health clinics in Seoul but could not get a proper diagnosis and saw little improvement. Eventually, doctors admitted him to the hospital on May 15, 2015. Shortly thereafter, some of his family members exhibited the same symptoms, as did nearly thirty people who had visited the same health clinics as the traveler (Wong et al. 2015: 398). Because health care workers had little reason to suspect that a camel-borne virus would appear in Korea, they failed to implement proper infection control procedures. The virus exploited the fact that it was in a new population with no previous exposure to MERS, and it spread. Nearly two weeks later, a Korean man who traveled to China introduced MERS to that country (Su et al. 2015). Even in the absence of camels, MERS was able to spread internationally—and far beyond the Middle East—because of the ease and speed with which people can cross borders. A virus can hitch a ride to spread into new parts of the world, and this has profound implications for the international community. This book aims to tease out the relationships between health and globalization.

Ask five different people what they think when they hear the word "globalization," and you are likely to get five different answers. That is not necessarily a surprise. Globalization is one of the most contested and debated terms in international relations. As Stiglitz emphasizes, "Almost overnight, globalization has become the most pressing issue of our time, something debated from boardrooms to op-ed pages and in schools all over the world" (Stiglitz 2002: 4).

Globalization embodies a range of contradictions. It is simultaneously divisive and homogenizing. It can reinforce inequities and power imbalances, but it can also provide the tools necessary to challenge those imbalances. Globalization's supporters see it as a hopeful, positive development in the modern world—something that will allow millions to escape poverty, increase opportunities, and allow goods, people, and information to circulate easily for the greater good.

In this view, globalization benefits the international community. Its detractors, though, link globalization to an array of ills. Rather than being a tool for improving the lives of all, they argue that globalization represents the triumph of a specific form of Western liberal capitalism that serves only to benefit the Global North. Instead of opening opportunities, globalization stifles diversity and forces states to adopt a narrow range of policies. It leads to homogenization, marginalization, and exploitation, and it foments a wide range of social ills that harm the majority of people.

Despite its pervasiveness, globalization is often difficult to fully comprehend. Richardson and colleagues capture its ambiguity: "Globalization is everywhere and nowhere: a pervasive, powerful force that shapes the trivial and transcontinental alike, but remains elusive and complex—a process whose precise definition is fleeting and whose causes and effects defy easy explanation" (Richardson, Callaghan, and Wamala 2015: 557). It is this almost ethereal quality that makes understanding the role of globalization and its relationship to issues of health so difficult to encapsulate in a single tidy package.

Part of the reason for all the debate over what globalization means is that it involves so many different dimensions. For some people, globalization is primarily an economic process. For others, it involves cultural changes. Others still might focus on the political elements. What is interesting, though, and will become apparent throughout this book is that all of these different dimensions of globalization touch on health and health outcomes. The economic, cultural, and political changes brought about by globalization have their own unique effects on global health and the ability of people around the world to live healthy lives.

Globalization is neither unambiguously good, nor unambiguously bad, for health. Its growth has undoubtedly had negative effects on global public health, be it through increased exposure to pollution, the ease and speed with which new diseases can cross the globe, the environmental changes that alter animal habitats, or the changes in food production and consumption that contribute to increased rates of noncommunicable diseases. At the same time, globalization has also fostered the development of transnational movements that have brought much needed attention to previously neglected diseases and increased the access to life-extending drugs. Globalization is a complicated, nuanced process, and that reality is no less apparent in the global health space.

WHAT IS GLOBALIZATION?

At its core, globalization refers to "heightened transnational inter-connections and interdependencies, propelled by intensified global trade, production, and finance, new information and communication technologies, and looming crises of the global commons" (Reus-Smit and Dunne 2017: 30). This definition, which fits squarely within the mainstream of international relations, links up with five key elements (McGrew 2014: 227):

- *Intensification.* Globalization suggests that linkages between physically distant peoples are becoming increasingly close and have an interdependent quality. "Local happenings," Giddens writes, "are shaped by events occurring many miles away and vice versa" (Giddens 1990: 21). In this way, distant social relations have a greater effect, whether intentionally or not. Social, political, and economic relations become more intense, even across great distances.
- *Integration.* This is often used in the economic sense to suggest that financial and trade relations are becoming closer and more tied together (Gilpin 2001: 364), but this idea goes beyond commercial interactions and relations. Other realms of political and social relations are also becoming increasingly integrated as an outgrowth of the intensification of relationships across borders.
- *Deterritorialization.* Globalization means that sovereign borders are no longer as important as they once were. This does not imply that borders are irrelevant; rather, it emphasizes that political, social, and economic issues cross borders. Scholte argues that the result of this deterritorialization is "the growth of relations between people" (Scholte 2000: 46) rather than solely being about interstate relations and interactions.
- *Elevation.* Policies that had once belonged solely to the domain of sovereign state governments are increasingly being elevated to the transnational level. Policymakers need to consider the international environment, and there are greater calls for shared policy-making at the international level because states cannot effectively address problems solely on their own (Hirst and Thompson 1999).

- *Expansion.* Not only are economies becoming increasingly integrated, but a growing range of goods, services, and policies are experiencing the same sort of integration (Garrett 2000: 941). This refers not just to consumer products and financial services, but also to a range of public goods like education and health care.

These five key elements feature a range of globalization's economic, cultural, and political dimensions, and they are distinct from earlier periods "in both the *intensity* and the *extent* of international interactions" (Clark 1997: 1; emphasis in the original). Contemporary globalization is about "the widening, deepening, and speeding up of worldwide interconnectedness in all aspects of contemporary social life, from the cultural to the commercial, the financial to the spiritual" (Held et al. 1999: 2).

A key question in the debates over globalization is how far beyond economics the concept travels. Nearly every definition of globalization includes economic elements, but some definitions equate globalization *solely* with economic policy changes. Gilpin defines globalization as "increasing interdependence of national economies in trade, finance, and macroeconomic policy" (Gilpin 1987: 389). Wade describes "the globalization consensus" as consisting of liberalizing trade and finance, increasing market integration across borders, reducing the role of the state in regulating the economy, and making it easier for hostile corporate takeovers to occur (Wade 2009: 142–43). These frameworks equate globalization with neoliberalism, which is itself a contested term (Harvey 2007; Mirowski 2014). Along similar lines, Cox (1996) describes globalization as more of an ideology loosely connected to neoliberalism and an emphasis on technocratic solutions to problems of economic development. These approaches do not necessarily deny the social and political elements of globalization; rather, they relegate them to second- or third-order consequences of globalization. It is because of the increased economic market integration that more people are crossing borders, and this emphasis on reducing state involvement in the economy that globalization encourages governments to scale back their various social policies. This suggests that economic considerations need to be dominant when considering how and why globalization and health have become increasingly intertwined.

Other definitions of globalization give greater weight to cultural, social, and political elements, urging a more holistic understanding of globalization. They emphasize that the social, cultural, and political elements better reflect how most people actually experience globalization in their daily lives. Few of us trade currencies in international markets or set national macroeconomic policy, but we can all listen to K-Pop or eat a banh mi much more easily now than in the past.

Globalization leads to a temporal shift. Castells, for example, talks about how globalization allows for the world "to work as a unit in real time on a planetary scale" (Castells 1996: 92), whereas Kobrin (1997) focuses on how the flow of information and technology drives globalization. Giddens discusses how globalization brings about a decoupling or "distanciation" between time and space (Giddens 1990: 64), and Mittelman describes globalization as compressing space and time (Mittelman 1996).

Other academic work on globalization highlights the social, cultural, and political dimensions more forcefully. Robertson, for instance, defines globalization as "both the compression of the world and the intensification of consciousness of the world as a whole" (Robertson 1992: 8). This latter part of the definition sets him apart from the other definitions discussed, as it suggests globalization includes an element of communal thinking. Along similar lines, Albrow speaks of globalization as the "diffusion of practices, values, and technology that have an influence on people's lives worldwide" (Albrow 1997: 88). Guillen defines it as "a process leading to greater interdependence and mutual awareness (reflexivity) among economic, political, and social units in the world, and among actors in general" (Guillen 2001: 236). To this end, Guidry, Kennedy, and Zald (1999) and Keck and Sikkink (1998), among others, speak of globalization as facilitating an opportunity for cross-border collaboration, awareness, and advocacy on issues like the environment, human rights, and feminism. In these ways, globalization is not just about markets—it is also about people's senses of who they are and how they relate to distant others.

Globalization is also closely linked with migration, and people moving across borders raises a host of questions and concerns about health effects. The International Organization for Migration counts more than one billion people currently living outside the region where they were born, and a quarter of that group lives outside their countries of origin (International Organization for Migration 2017: 2). Some of these people have voluntarily moved for new jobs or to pursue schooling. Others have been forced from their homes due to conflict, drought, or climate change. Regardless of the reason for moving, an analysis of migration patterns shows that migrants are moving to an increasingly diverse array of countries (Czaika and de Haas 2015). This means that more countries are confronting the human realities of globalization's ease of movement across borders. Migration has proven a potent political issue, particularly in recent years, with nationalist political parties campaigning on fears that migration will dilute a country's culture, harm its economy, or lead to increased crime (Harteveld, Kokkonen, and Dahlberg 2017; Munck 2008).

At the same time, it is important to recognize that globalization is not a one-way street. Rather than the simple top-down imposition of specific practices or politics, we frequently see how the forces of globalization can take on local elements. It gets shaped by local customs, habits, and practices. Rushing emphasizes, "Human lives and histories are anchored in specific places, and place continues to mediate social life and affect life choices"—even in the face of globalization (Rushing 2004: 79).

Despite its seeming ubiquity, globalization does not affect all areas of the world equally. "Globalization is a fragmented, incomplete, discontinuous, contingent and in many ways contradictory and puzzling process," observes Guillen (2001: 238). There may be an overall increase in foreign direct investment, for example, but that raw statistic overlooks the wide variations. Between 1982 and 2008, foreign direct investment inflows increased from fifty-nine billion dollars to $1.697 trillion (United Nations Conference on Trade and Development 2009: 3). After dipping briefly as a result of the global financial crisis, foreign direct investment exceeded pre-crisis levels by 2011 (United Nations Conference on Trade and Development 2012). Analysts note, though, that this incredible increase in foreign direct investment reflects an increasing degree of concentration. Investors are investing more money, but they are placing those funds in fewer places. Large "mega-deals," typically associated with corporate mergers and acquisitions and concentrated in a small number of cities, can artificially inflate the totals (Thun 2014: 285). Raw figures rarely reflect these nuances, though, and give a misleading picture of the extent of globalization's spread.

Globalization is a conscious process driven by choices made by various actors, though it can have unintended consequences. There is no "natural" state of globalization. Instead, the specific form of globalization that exists in the modern world has been selected as part of a political process. It is no more "natural" than any other facet of political, economic, and social life. If globalization has reduced a certain set of policy options or empowered a particular group of actors, that arrangement is "no accident" (Pauly 1997: 4). This understanding reinforces the notion that globalization can represent a form of power. If we understand the policies that support and advance the goals of globalization as the result of conscious choices made by political and economic leaders, then we can understand how the intersection of power and globalization could either ameliorate or exacerbate power dynamics. It could serve to reduce disparities, or it could make them worse.

Defining globalization is not simply an academic exercise; it directly engages policymakers and world leaders. Indian Prime Minister Narendra Modi has described globalization as the antithesis of isolationism and protectionism. Speaking at the World Economic Forum in 2018, he called economic protectionism both ill-advised and flying in the face of globalization's natural progress. Speaking of globalization's opponents, Modi told the assembled delegates, "Their wish is not only to save themselves from globalization, but to change the natural flow of globalization" (Bansal 2018). German Chancellor Angela Merkel talks about globalization as a force that can and should improve everyone's lives and that fosters cooperation. By pooling resources and working together, she argues, globalization can foster win-win outcomes (Reuters 2017). Chinese President Xi Jinping links globalization with multilateral agreements, international trade deals, and cross-national investment. While acknowledging that globalization needs to go further to be more open, balanced, and beneficial, Xi told the delegates to the 2017 APEC Summit in Vietnam that globalization is "an irreversible historical trend" that can benefit developing countries (AFP 2017).

Not all world leaders embrace globalization. Venezuela's Hugo Chávez made opposition to globalization and the governments and institutions that supported it one of the hallmarks of his tenure (Ellner 2002). Jeremy Corbyn, the leader of the opposition Labour Party in the United Kingdom, has decried "the predatory excesses of a globalized free-for-all" and argued that globalization has led to a "failed economic system [that] is delivering falling living standards and rising inequality" (Elgot 2016). Most prominently, when he was on the campaign trail, Donald Trump railed against "globalization [that] has made the financial elite who donate to politicians very, very wealthy . . . but it has left millions of our workers with nothing but poverty and heartache" (Jackson 2016). Since assuming office, Trump has withdrawn the United States from both the Trans-Pacific Partnership and the North American Free Trade Agreement (NAFTA) because he sees those agreements as emblematic of globalization weakening the United States.

Much like political leadership, public attitudes toward globalization are mixed. A 2016 YouGov poll commissioned by *The Economist* found a distinct split in affinity for globalization between the West and emerging markets. Less than half of the respondents in the United States, United Kingdom, and France agreed that globalization is "a force for good." In contrast, more than 70 percent of respondents in Thailand and Indonesia and more than 90 percent in Vietnam agreed. The survey finds a relationship between people believing globalization is a force for good and the percentage increase in a country's per capita gross domestic product at purchasing-power parity—with higher increases in per capita leading to stronger support for globalization (*Economist* 2016). These economic indicators interact powerfully with cultural ideas, though. One study of attitudes toward NAFTA found that noneconomic interests, such as belief in nationalism, attitudes toward immigration and immigrants, and attitudes toward job protection, outweighed economic considerations in understanding support for the agreement (Merolla et al. 2005). Similarly, a survey in seventeen developed and developing countries found that attitudes toward the free market, consumerism, and modern life outweighed economic attitudes and partisanship in explaining attitudes toward globalization (Edwards 2006).

LINKING HEALTH AND GLOBALIZATION

Globalization and health are directly connected. "Many of the social, economic, and environmental problems that benefit the opportunistic microbial world are caused or exacerbated by globalization in other contexts," writes Fidler (1997: 33). Understanding the relationships between health and globalization matters because they inform how the international community frames and conceptualizes health. If globalization's effects on health are primarily economic in nature, then that has distinct effects on which issues receive attention, the sorts of interventions supported, and the actors who have significant roles in crafting responses. If, on the other hand, globalization matters for health on a wider range of issues, that may open up greater possibilities for addressing a broader cross-section of health concerns—and/or give states in the Global North more of an opportunity to intervene in the Global South and violate the sovereignty of those states.

Globalization increases commercial and travel ties between formerly distant lands, and that provides an excellent opportunity for microbes to move to new places. In 2018, Qantas Airways debuted its longest international flight—a nine-thousand-mile, seventeen-hour flight from Perth to London for a journey that once took twelve and a half days to complete (*Telegraph* 2018). That means that a person can literally get to the opposite side of the world in less time than it would take to watch all of the *Star Wars* movies. Humans are not the only travelers that can take advantage of the speed and relatively low cost of moving to the other side of the world in less than a single day. Microbes and parasites can take advantage of trade, tourism, migration, increasing population density, environmental degradation, and inequities in the international distribution of resources to cross into new territories—and potentially infect new people (Price-Smith 2009: 5). In these ways, the same means for improving our lives through the opportunities that globalization presents also provides the means for threatening human health.

The connections between globalization and health lead to questions of whether health is a public good. Public goods are goods that provide widespread benefit—with two key defining characteristics:

- Their consumption is *nonrivalrous*—my enjoyment of the good does not diminish anyone else's ability to consume the good, and
- Their benefits are *nonexcludable*—no one can effectively be denied the good (Ostrom and Ostrom 2015: 4–6).

Market-based systems do not provide public goods in sufficient quantity, meaning that governments or other public authorities need to get involved. Think about a lighthouse. Its job is to provide light to help with navigation and prevent ships from crashing into the shore. That is an incredibly important function with a public benefit, as none of us want to see lots of ships running aground—but it's not one well-suited to market mechanisms. The light from the lighthouse is nonrivalrous in its consumption; you and I can both use the light as we steer our ships without the amount of light decreasing. The light is also nonexcludable; there is not really a practical way to prevent a ship from using the light once it is produced. For these reasons, there is not much of a profit to be made for a private company providing lighthouses—so public authorities need to step in to provide this public good.

Similar dynamics are at play with the globalization of health. We already know that globalization means that there is a high degree of interconnectedness among people and states due to economic trade, travel, and personal mobility. We also know that diseases can take advantage of those connections in order to spread farther and faster than would otherwise happen. Disease epidemics can have devastating effects on personal well-being, life expectancy, economies, and political systems—negative outcomes that we would generally want to avoid. Because disease outbreaks can happen anywhere and at any time, though, it is not enough for a single country to deal with a disease solely on its own; the threat of disease being reimported remains and forces the state to be ever vigilant. Trying to exclude a state from benefiting from better health is impractical, and there is not a finite amount of health to go around. As a result, there is an increasing international consensus to recognize health as a global public good (Youde 2010: 44–48). Because the presence of a disease anywhere represents a potential threat everywhere, health is considered a particular kind of public good—a weakest-link public good (Barrett 2007). This means that the effectiveness of providing that public good is only as strong as where it is provided least. Globalization means that we need more cooperation on health in order to achieve a measure of protection.

Calling global health a public good is one thing; putting this idea into practice is more difficult. One of the world's biggest health successes is the eradication of smallpox, officially declared by the World Health Organization (WHO) in 1980. Smallpox killed millions of people annually, and even countries that had eliminated the dreaded disease from their borders had to remain vigilant because of the constant threat of reintroduction. The United States, for example, eliminated smallpox from within its borders in 1929, but the disease re-emerged in 1946 when a soldier returning home from Japan inadvertently reintroduced it in Seattle, causing fifty-one cases and sixteen deaths. The following year, a traveler from Mexico checked into a hospital in Manhattan with smallpox. Before he died, he infected twelve other people—and caused a panic that required more than six million people to get vaccinated (Fenner et al. 1988: 331–32). Because of this ongoing threat and the recognition that addressing smallpox in individual states was insufficient, the WHO convinced the international community that it was in its collective interest to eradicate the disease from natural circulation. Excluding people from getting vaccinated against smallpox would undermine the goal, and vaccinating one person did not prevent another person from getting vaccinated. By recognizing how the interconnectedness of the world put everyone at risk of smallpox and reconceptualizing smallpox eradication as a public good, the WHO eradicated a disease for the first time ever. This was a great success.

On the other hand, there was a move in the 1970s to recognize primary health care (PHC) as a public good. PHC means that everyone has access to essential health services to support a basic level of health. This idea crystallized in 1978 when nearly every country in the world signed the Alma-Ata Declaration. Named for the Soviet city where it was drafted (now known as Almaty, Kazakhstan) at a conference co-sponsored by the WHO and the United Nations Children's Fund, the declaration promised "Health for All by 2000" and demanded that wealthy states take an active role in financing health services in the poorest countries. As you may have already guessed, the Alma-Ata Declaration did not achieve its goals. It quickly found itself caught up in the Cold War politics of the day, a worldwide economic recession that decreased foreign aid budgets, and the emergence of more conservative, neoliberal politicians in leading countries (Hall and Taylor 2003). PHC thus did not become a global public good—a fact reflected in the current variations in access to essential health services around the world to this day.

The two examples exemplify the difference between the rhetoric of global public goods and their actual provision. People and governments may talk about health as a global public good, but are they willing to provide the support necessary to make it a reality? Putting health as a global public good into practice demands both political will and economic capacity from the international community—and that so far appears to be a tall order. Indeed, this raises questions about whether calling health a global public good is better thought of as trying to guarantee a human right to health. While a human right to health may seem intuitive, Wolff identifies the key dilemma in this debate, "On the one hand, the reasons for asserting a human right to health seem overwhelming. On the other, a universal human right to health seems impossible to satisfy in the current conditions of the world" (Wolff 2012: xv).

The economic, social, and political changes brought about by globalization have direct effects on health, too. Take migration, for instance. We saw earlier how globalization has led to more and more people moving away from their home regions—whether voluntarily or otherwise. That has prompted fears in some quarters about how migration might change political and economic situations. These worries extend to population health, too, with accusations that migration leads to higher rates of infectious disease in receiving states (Belluz 2018a). A comprehensive meta-analysis of studies on migration and health shows, though, that "the risk of transmission from migrating populations to host populations is generally low" (UCL-Lancet Commission on Migration and Health 2018: 2613). A bigger issue is whether migrants have access to health care services in the receiving state, as that has a large effect on health outcomes (Heywood and Lopez-Velez 2018; Huynen, Martens, and Hilderink 2005). These realities do not necessarily alter the political dynamics and debates over migration and whether globalization makes it too easy for people to cross borders.

Health can also be a site for the intermingling of different practices brought together by globalization. Jennings describes how Western biomedical practices, traditional healers, and Chinese medicine operate simultaneously—with patients frequently availing themselves of all three systems—in Dar es Salaam. The emergence of Western and Chinese medical practices in Dar es Salaam has not eliminated traditional practices; rather, these different systems co-exist. He writes, "Healing within Tanzania—within Africa—consists of these multiple agents: coexisting and competing systems granted legitimacy through use" (Jennings 2005: 459). In their examination of human immunodeficiency virus (HIV)/acquired immune deficiency syndrome (AIDS) projects funded by international donors in Africa, Anderson and Patterson (2017) demonstrate how local actors frequently exert agency to shape these global responses in ways that make sense for the communities in which they operate. HIV/AIDS programs in Zambia and the United States may both provide antiretroviral drugs, but they will look very different because of the local conditions. The role of faith-based organizations and existing church/state relationships alter the form and practice of health service delivery, though programs in both countries ultimately have the same goal (Patterson 2011, 2018).

The linkages between globalization and health are not solely limited to infectious disease. The spread of noncommunicable diseases is directly connected to dietary changes, increased rates of smoking, and easier access to alcoholic and sugary beverages. Many of these changes result from international trade regulations that make it easier for multinational corporations to sell these products in an increasing number of countries. These same corporations work to weaken public health regulations—often in the name of consumer choice or freedom—and resolve any tensions between free trade and public health in favor of the former. These realities exacerbate the disparities between rich and poor in ways that reflect the broader inequalities that globalization has brought to the international political economy (Harman 2012: 7).

Noncommunicable diseases are also connected to globalization through more indirect means. Lung cancer is the most common form of cancer and the leading cause of cancer-related deaths in China. Not only are China's lung cancer rates rising, but they are doing so faster than in Western states. Part of the increase is due to relatively high rates of cigarette smoking, but the other major risk factor is the increasing level of air pollution (Chen et al. 2015). Lung cancer has increased by 50 percent over the past decade in Beijing alone, with increased air pollution identified as the leading cause (Carney 2016). That increase in air pollution, though, is connected to China's embrace of globalization. As the country has assumed a more important role within global economic production structures, environmental protections have not kept pace. There has also been a wave of pollution-producing factories moving from countries like the United States to China, thanks to the combination of "globalization and outsourcing of pollution" (Lim 2007). Globalization facilitates economic policy changes that lead to environmental changes, which in turn have profound health consequences. These sorts of indirect connections between globalization and noncommunicable diseases complicate efforts to craft effective interventions that can help to reduce the lung cancer rate, and they show

how economic decisions seemingly unrelated to health-related matters can have a large effect on population health.

Globalization also has links with increasing rates of urbanization, and urbanization has clear and distinct connections to health. Urbanization is one of the twenty-first century's defining characteristics, and developing countries are urbanizing at the fastest rates (Spencer, J. 2015). More and more people see urban areas—either in their own countries or abroad—as offering the personal and professional opportunities they seek (or at least hope for). The United Nations estimated in 2005 that more than half of the world's population lived in urban areas. In North America, the region with the highest level of urbanization, more than eight in ten people lived in an urban area. Latin America and sub-Saharan Africa are the two regions where the percentage of the population living in urban areas is still below 50 percent, but both of those regions have experienced urban growth rates of more than 25 percent between 1990 and 2005 (Spencer, J. 2015: 8–9). Richardson, Callaghan, and Wamala describe this shift in population patterns as "the largest rural-to-urban migration in history" (Richardson, Callaghan, and Wamala 2015: 567). These moves toward concentrating a country's population increasingly within cities is not solely the result of millions and millions of individual decisions; national governments have also introduced various policies that encourage and incentivize these moves (Henderson 2005). While the human, financial, and ecological costs associated with urbanization may eventually outweigh the prospective economic benefits (Bloom, Canning, and Fink 2008), rightsizing urbanization policies is extremely difficult in the most ideal political and economic environments and requires a degree of control and forethought that few governments possess.

The massive growth of urban areas thanks to globalization increases health challenges for a number of reasons. First, the higher population density makes it easier for an infectious disease outbreak to take root and propagate itself (Tarwater and Martin 2001). Second, urban growth generally proceeds much faster than the expansion of sanitation infrastructure, leading to increases in water-borne illnesses and other infectious diseases (Neiderud 2015). Third, moves to urban areas can change eating and nutrition patterns, which can change a person's susceptibility to noncommunicable diseases (Goryakin, Rocco, and

Suhrcke 2017). Fourth, inadequate housing stock and increased social disparities in rapidly urbanizing areas that can provide additional opportunities for infectious disease vectors like mosquitoes to take up residence and spread illnesses (Alirol et al. 2011). Fifth, urban areas experience higher rates of air pollution and other environmental risk factors that raise a person's chances of developing certain cancers and other noncommunicable diseases (Islam et al. 2014). Finally, urban areas are associated with motor vehicle accidents, which are rapidly becoming one of the leading causes of death worldwide (WHO 2015).

Globalization does not simply put pressures on health by facilitating the spread of disease. Harrison points to globalization's effects on the global health regulatory architecture. He ominously warns that "the pressure which globalization places on sanitary regulations" is perhaps the most important, yet underappreciated, concern. It is not simply that globalization challenges these regulations; it is that it does so in an uneven manner (Harrison 2012: 248). This leads to growing policy inconsistency, which can open up more opportunities for health problems to emerge and potentially encourage a race-to-the-bottom mindset among regulators. It could also stiffen the resolve of multinational corporations to pressure national governments and intergovernmental organizations to reduce regulations—especially if they perceive those regulations as introducing unfair interruptions to commercial regulations.

Globalization may contain emancipatory possibilities in the health realm, too. From a cosmopolitan perspective, all human beings are of equal moral worth and therefore deserve to have their demands for adequate human health satisfied. Principles of care and treatment dependent upon a person's geographic location or country of residence are, by this framework, arbitrary because those conditions are essentially a matter of luck. If it is true that globalization "has 'stretched' the need for cooperative relationships beyond the state" (Brown and Paremoer 2014: 87) because of the interdependence necessary to realize global health goals, then health and globalization provide a framework that facilitates this cosmopolitan vision. While it does not guarantee that people all around the world will have their demands for adequate human health realized, globalization can introduce a sense of obligation to the equation. Those who benefit from globalization have a concomitant duty to reform the global health system and help others to benefit from the system, too (Parekh 2003). In other words, because globalization brings people closer together, it makes them more aware of disparities and provides an impetus for working to reduce or eliminate those inequities.

One of the most vexing elements of the intersection of globalization and health is how the processes that increase vulnerability to the spread of disease are not necessarily linked to conscious action. The ease of movement facilitated by globalization has given rise to discussions of "super-spreaders"—individuals responsible for a disproportionate percentage of cases of an infectious disease. For example, research on the Ebola outbreak in West Africa suggests that 2 to 3 percent of those infected with the disease were responsible for more than 60 percent of the cases (Lau et al. 2017). This terminology frequently brings with it an element of blame for the disease's spread and suggests some degree of culpability. This can have negative consequences, as it blames a person or group for a disease's spread rather than understanding the underlying social conditions that allowed the disease to spread in the first place. This was evident in the emergence of one of the first new infectious diseases of the modern era, HIV/AIDS. For years, Gaetan Dugas, a French-Canadian flight attendant for Air Canada, has been blamed as "Patient Zero," responsible for spreading the virus throughout North America. In his history of the early days of the AIDS epidemic, *And the Band Played On*, journalist Randy Shilts described Dugas in nearly pathological terms, painting a picture of someone who took perverse pleasure in infecting others with a deadly virus:

> It was around this time that rumors began on Castro Street about a strange guy at the Eighth and Howard bathhouse, a blond with a French accent. He would have sex with you, turn up the lights in the cubicle, and point out his Kaposi's sarcoma lesions. "I've got the gay cancer," he'd say. "I'm going to die and so are you." (Shilts 1987: 165)

The problem with the story of Gaetan Dugas as an HIV super-spreader is that it is not true. Dugas is not singlehandedly responsible for HIV's spread throughout North America. In fact, the only reason that he is called Patient Zero is because a journalist misread a contact tracing report listing Dugas as patient O—so labeled because Dugas was from "outside Southern California" (McNeil 2016b). Research has demonstrated that the virus entered the United States in the 1960s and 1970s in waves; it was not a singular event (Worobey et al. 2016). As the myth of Patient Zero grew, though, government officials used it to justify their own inaction. There was no need for them to address the issue if it was just a matter of a few people behaving poorly. Instead of motivating a response, it reinforced existing prejudices—particularly toward gay men—and discouraged rational policymaking (Howard 2016).

What makes Dugas interesting to the story of HIV/AIDS in North America is not anything that he specifically did. Rather, it is how he symbolizes the technological and mobility changes of the early days of contemporary globalization that facilitated the spread of a new virus. It is not the behavior of a so-called super-spreader that is of importance; it is how illnesses can exploit the niches opened by the social, economic, and political changes brought about by globalization to establish themselves. At the same time, these ideas about super-spreaders tie into larger questions of blame and how it is apportioned when diseases take advantage of those niches. The fact that viruses take advantage of the opportunities available to them through globalization does not prevent people from blaming others for causing the outbreaks (Wald 2008). The people blamed are often marginalized or considered distant others—even though it is precisely the fact that these distances have rapidly shrunk that has made it possible for the outbreak to occur in the first place.

GLOBALIZATION, HEALTH, AND THE STATE

The importance of cross-border cooperation to address health issues is not unique to the late twentieth and early twenty-first centuries. Governments have long recognized that effective infectious disease control necessitated international cooperation. What has changed in recent times, though, is the ease with which health issues cross borders and the increased urgency associated with addressing these concerns (Fidler 1997: 17–18). In addition, the move from conceptualizing these issues as global rather than international illustrates how these responses to health issues have expanded beyond the sole realm of sovereign governments to include nongovernmental organizations, private businesses, and philanthropic organizations.

These ideas directly challenge the typical conceptions of sovereignty. Krasner identifies four different ways in which sovereignty is used in international relations:

- *Domestic*—the exercise of public authority within a state;
- *Interdependence*—the ability of public authorities to control trans-border movements;
- *International legal*—the mutual recognition of states and other governmental entities; and
- *Westphalian*—the exclusion of foreign actors from the exercise of domestic authority structures (Krasner 1999: 9).

These different forms of sovereignty matter for understanding the relationship between globalization and health because the demands of addressing cross-border health issues may require a shift in our understanding of how they operate. Sovereignty has ostensibly been the bedrock of international relations since the Treaty of Westphalia. This has had two effects: making the state the primary unit within international relations and privileging the idea that states can make decisions for themselves about appropriate policies. The health challenges posed by globalization challenge both the primacy of the state as an actor and the appropriateness of states being able to make policy autonomously.

Fidler uses the severe acute respiratory syndrome (SARS) epidemic of 2002–2003 to question the interplay of sovereignty, globalization, and health. For many months after the disease was first detected, it was clear that SARS was spreading rapidly throughout China, but the government denied and downplayed this fact. Rather than accepting this response at face value, though, the WHO mobilized an aggressive response that publicly challenged and chastised the Chinese government's inaction. Fidler cites this energized response by the WHO as evidence that SARS was the first "post-Westphalian pathogen" because traditional Westphalian approach sovereignty lost out to the imperatives of a global response (Fidler 2003). Traditionally, responses to disease outbreaks found themselves limited by the need to respect Westphalian sovereignty. The international community could suggest or encourage governments to take certain actions, but the state retained the ultimate authority to determine what sort of policies it implemented within its own borders. SARS challenged this assumption on two different levels. First, it showed that the WHO and other actors would be willing to violate the niceties of state sovereignty when a crisis situation demanded it—and that the international community would generally support this action. Second, it highlighted how much the response to a disease outbreak could be hampered by a recalcitrant government. The Chinese government's refusal to acknowledge the presence of SARS within its borders or to cooperate with international authorities set back the efforts to contain this new pathogen significantly (Huang 2004). The weakness of the Chinese government's deployment of domestic sovereignty in responding to SARS put both Chinese citizens and others around the world in danger, thus necessitating a broader response that prioritized more of a notion of shared sovereignty.

For Fidler, SARS was not unique because of the ease with which the virus crossed international borders; the outbreak was unique because of the international community's willingness to violate traditional notions of state sovereignty to effectuate a response (Fidler 2003: 486). The Westphalian public health system did not require addressing the domestic policies of the state or penetrating the state's sovereign domain. It was largely restricted to a focus on the points at which an infectious disease might cross an international border. This system placed few demands on the state and largely allowed it to determine how it wanted to engage with the rest of the world. It also suggested that health was a relatively low priority for a state's foreign policy and did not rise to the level of an existential threat. By contrast, post-Westphalian public health drew on the changes wrought by globalization to recognize that the previous system was broken and failing to respond to the microbial threats the world now faced. As a result, global health governance needed to shift to a stance that placed greater emphasis on disease as a key security threat, broadened the range of potentially worrisome infectious diseases, broadened the range of actors involved in responding to disease threats, and took the cliché that viruses do not respect borders seriously (Fidler 2003: 487–88). It contains a normative element with regards to what proper global health governance entails and demands that the state actively engage with the global community in order to stop the spread of infectious diseases that could potentially become epidemics. "The Chinese government's actions during the SARS outbreak," he writes, "cost the country dearly because it acted Westphalian in a post-Westphalian world" (Fidler 2003: 490).

The intersection between China, Taiwan, and the WHO during the SARS epidemic shows the tensions between different understandings of sovereignty in responding to global health concerns. The Chinese government in Beijing has long adopted a hard line against international organizations engaging with the Taiwanese government. If an international organization were to allow Taiwan to join as a full member with voting rights, it could be taken as evidence of the Taiwanese government's legitimacy and independence (Yahuda 1996). The political imperative of the People's Republic of China (PRC) has thus limited the WHO's ability to engage with Taiwan, despite efforts by the Taiwanese government to gain membership. In the midst of these geopolitical tensions, Taiwan had the third highest number of SARS cases behind the PRC and Hong Kong, which the WHO counted separately from the PRC (WHO 2003a). China may not have wanted to allow any sort of engagement between Taiwan and the WHO that could confer a degree of legitimacy on the Taiwanese government, but the SARS epidemic could not effectively be addressed unless the WHO responded to the 218 cases of the disease within Taiwan. In May 2003, the Chinese government allowed a WHO delegation to travel to Taiwan to address the spread of SARS. While this action may appear insignificant, it marked "the first visit by any representatives of a UN-affiliated organization since China took Taiwan's seat on the world body 30 years ago" (Watts 2003: 1709). China thus asserted its sovereignty by positioning itself as the only authority that could allow the WHO to operate in part of what it saw as its territory, but Taiwan also saw the WHO's operations as an implicit recognition of its sovereignty because it was engaging directly with an intergovernmental organization. The imperatives of addressing a public health crisis challenged the existing debates around sovereignty, borders, and political control. This suggests that the requirements for addressing global health in a globalized world could force governments to abandon their traditional stances.

While the response to SARS may have given rise to optimism about globalization's ability to challenge the traditional imperatives of sovereignty, its aftermath highlights the limitations of globalization and demonstrates that its advances can be countered by governments. Fidler may have expressed optimism that SARS would move the world more toward a post-Westphalian view of sovereignty, but his expectations outstripped practical realities. Ricci (2009) disputes claims that the world has entered a post-Westphalian or globalized status, calling them overstated and premature. The state is complicit in global health governance decisions, he argues, so it is making choices about when and under what circumstances it is willing to share power with other entities or abdicate some of its traditional responsibilities. More actors may be getting involved in global health politics, but they are not necessarily *replacing* the state. Davies (2008) points out that WHO's authority may have increased during the SARS outbreak, but that this expansion did not happen independently of state support or acquiescence. There may be a greater willingness by states to recognize the validity of nonstate sources of authority and information within global health governance, but she argues that states must consent to this—and they could withdraw their consent at any point (Davies 2012a).

WHO's expanded role during the SARS crisis bring their own sets of questions with it. The WHO's actions during SARS in China may have addressed some public health needs, but these very actions reflected authoritarian and autocratic policies that lacked international legal grounding (Kreuder-Sonnen and Zangl 2015). Price-Smith calls the expanded role of the WHO during SARS more of an aberration than the precedent for far-reaching changes (Price-Smith 2009: 156). Indeed, the recent history of Sino-Taiwanese relations around global health gives little evidence of improved cooperation. The Chinese government permitted Taiwan to attend the WHO's annual World Health Assembly (WHA) between 2009 and 2016—but only as a nonvoting observer and only if it was designated Chinese Taipei (Jennings 2017). In 2017, though, the PRC vociferously objected to Taiwan's participation in the WHA—and other international meetings—in an effort to thwart pro-independence Taiwanese politicians (Huang 2017).

Despite these challenges to the state, its primacy, and the role of intergovernmental organizations in responding to global health challenges, people still look to the state for health services. Even with all of the attention paid to the globalization of health, states are still the bodies who do the most and are seen as the most responsible for addressing basic health needs (Harman 2012: 28–31). Globalization thus forces us to confront awkward and unresolved paradoxes. We speak of a global health governance system, but this system is still overwhelmingly state-centric. We continue to look to the state to address our health needs, but it is increasingly unable to do so. There are moves to challenge our traditional understandings of sovereignty in all of its forms, but we resist challenging sovereignty too explicitly. The globalization of health thus seems to encourage us to look beyond the state while simultaneously leading us to cling to the state.

CONCLUSION

Globalization may be controversial and contested, but its effects on nearly every element of international relations—including health—is undeniable. Globalization calls into question some of the traditional understandings of how health affects countries, which factors promote cooperation on cross-border health issues, and what sorts of responses are considered important. It shifts the discussion from one focused on *international* health, with its state-centric emphasis, to *global* health and its attendant holistic view.

Globalization may open a number of opportunities in the health space. It can promote greater awareness of health issues around the world. It can broaden the range of issues considered important for the international community. It can integrate technology into various health programs in order to stop disease outbreaks before they expand too far. For example, telemedicine has become increasingly important in rural parts of the United States like Appalachia (Richardson, Fry, and Krasnow 2013) and Iowa (Kaspar 2014), and doctors in Rwanda can order supplies and blood products by text message and have them delivered by drones (McVeigh 2018). At the same time, globalization raises serious questions about the future of the global health agenda. Globalization can exacerbate the divisions between the Global North and the Global South, narrow the global health agenda to focus only on those issues that fit into particular frames, and ignore the role of issues like human rights and privacy. Bollyky notes, "The world has gotten dramatically better at lengthening life spans and reducing child suffering in poor places, but the improvements in much of everything else that matters to people's well-being have failed to keep pace" (Bollyky 2018: 173). It is this tension that is at the heart of the interplay between globalization and health.

This chapter has focused primarily on building up the theoretical case for linking globalization and health. The next chapter digs more into the empirical evidence to show how globalization has real health effects on human lives.

CHAPTER 2

GLOBALIZATION AND HEALTH IN PRACTICE

We know that there will be disease outbreaks and epidemics in the future. We don't know when they happen, where they will occur, or which disease will emerge. We don't even know if it will be a disease that we have seen before. These are simply facts of life, and they become even more pressing in the face of globalization. Health and globalization have an interdependent relationship, but we cannot always anticipate how that relationship will play out. The previous chapter focused on understanding globalization and how its key attributes and dimensions operate. This chapter aims to describe the practical effects of this interdependence.

Disease and globalization are fellow travelers. In some cases, this relationship is very literal; pathogens tag along with people, animals, and goods moving across borders to inadvertently introduce a disease into a new area. In other cases, the relationship between is more indirect.

Changing international trade rules may allow multinational corporations to introduce foodstuffs, alcohol, and cigarettes into new markets, but these economic and social changes interrupt existing food systems or lead to an increase in rates of noncommunicable diseases (NCDs). These companies are not necessarily looking to make people sick, but they are selling products whose use has ill effects on the communities where they are introduced.

To examine the practical manifestations of globalization and health, this chapter will concentrate on three health conditions: smallpox, SARS, and overweight/obesity. All three have had cross-national effects, and those effects have been magnified by globalization. In each case, the various elements of globalization have combined to facilitate the condition's spread. Perhaps more importantly, globalization also had major implications for how the international system has responded—or failed to respond.

SMALLPOX: FIGHTING THE SPECKLED MONSTER

At first glance, smallpox may seem irrelevant to globalization. The disease no longer circulates freely, and no one has contracted smallpox since the movie *Grease* was originally in theaters. Linking smallpox and globalization almost seems like talking about contemporary birdwatching by focusing on the dodo.

Thinking about smallpox in terms of globalization, though, uncovers three important connections. First, smallpox's spread often mirrored the movement of goods and peoples. These same sorts of relationships get supercharged by globalization. Second, the effort to eradicate smallpox required international cooperation and a shared effort to reframe smallpox eradication as a global public good. It offers insights for fostering such cooperation in the current era. Third, smallpox figures prominently in contemporary debates about bioterrorism. These fears are closely linked with globalization and the flows of people and information. Globalization's intensification makes it all the more important that we learn the lessons from past experiences with infectious diseases that readily cross borders.

Smallpox was one of the most feared diseases in human history. It seemingly struck at random and killed indiscriminately. More than a quarter of those infected died, and survivors often bore disfiguring scars for the rest of their lives. In 1888, a medical textbook offered a chilling description of the disease: "Smallpox, by reason of the malignant nature of its poison, and the general susceptibility to it of individuals of all ages, races, classes, and conditions, is the most loathsome and fatal disease known to man" (cited in Kinney 1981: 334).

Smallpox is spread by the *Variola* virus. There are two main variants of the virus—variola major and variola minor. Both forms of smallpox spread in the same way, and both can now be prevented through vaccination, but their virulence varies. Variola major caused approximately 90 percent of all smallpox cases and killed 30 percent of the people it infected. Variola minor was both less common and less fatal, with a mortality rate of less than 1 percent (Aberth 2011: 74). It is unclear how the disease made its way into the human population, but no other animals carry or transmit smallpox. This fact would later prove crucially important for the efforts to wipe it out.

It took a while for smallpox to incubate before it made people sick. During the first week or two after infection, smallpox would replicate inside a person's body. The first symptoms to appear were a high fever, chills, and nausea. The fever would generally subside in two to four days, giving way to the characteristic rash (Aberth 2011: 75). The rash would begin as spots before becoming raised lesions filled with fluid. These lesions would then turn into pustules within a week or so. The pustules would then become scabs, falling off the body over the next week or two (Oldstone 2010: 72). A person would remain infectious until all of the scabs fall off—and those scabs could infect others if they get into bedding or clothes. If a person survived the infection, they may end up with skin pitted with deep scars, and roughly one-third of survivors became blind (Barquet and Domingo 1997: 636). There was no treatment for smallpox; health care workers could only treat symptoms as they appeared—and hope for the best.

The archaeological record provides evidence of smallpox's long history. The mummified head of the Egyptian pharaoh Ramses V, who died in 1156 BCE, bears evidence of smallpox infection, and records from China describe a disease much like smallpox as far back as 1122 BCE (Riedel 2005a: 21). There are also Hindu temples built at roughly the same time dedicated to the worship of a deity of smallpox (McNeill

1998: 157). Historical evidence shows that the disease spread to all corners of the world, often tracking commercial or military movements. Oldstone observes,

> By 1000, smallpox epidemics had been recorded in populated areas from Japan to Spain and throughout African countries on the southern rim of the Mediterranean Sea. The eleventh to thirteenth centuries abounded with the movement of people to and from Asia Minor during the Crusades (1096–1291) and of African caravans crossing the Sahara to West Africa and the port cities of East Africa, carrying smallpox as well as goods. (Oldstone 2010: 59)

Riedel notes, "The Arab expansion, the Crusades, and the discovery of the West Indies all contributed to the spread of the disease" (Riedel 2005a: 21). In the 1700s, more than four hundred thousand Europeans died annually from smallpox (Behbehani 1983: 458). During the twentieth century alone, smallpox killed somewhere between three hundred million and five hundred million people (Theves, Biagni, and Crubexy 2014: 210).

Smallpox had tangible political effects, too. The first stages of the decline of the Roman Empire coincided with a smallpox epidemic that killed between 3.5 million and seven million people (Barquet and Domingo 1997: 635). When smallpox killed Queen Anne's only son in 1700, it spelled the end of the House of Stuart and made possible the emergence of the House of Hanover that ruled the United Kingdom between 1714 and 1901. The disease also upended the Hapsburg Dynasty and killed royal leaders throughout Europe during the late seventeenth and eighteenth centuries. Perhaps most dramatically, the introduction of smallpox to the Americas utterly devastated local populations and allowed European powers to conquer wide swaths of territory with relative ease (Price-Smith 2009: 46–48). Within fifty years of smallpox's appearance, the population of central Mexico dropped an estimated 90 percent (McNeill 1998: 212–13).

Because there was no treatment for the disease, the best strategy to combat smallpox was to prevent it in the first place. The first efforts at this were known as variolation. Variolation deliberately infects a person with a mild case of smallpox in order to give them immunity to the disease in the future—assuming that they survived. References to this technique date back to 590 BCE in China (Bollet 2004: 76).

Lady Mary Wortley Montague, an English aristocrat and smallpox survivor, is credited with popularizing variolation throughout Europe. In 1717, she moved to Constantinople when her husband was appointed ambassador. While there, she saw local women practicing variolation. Despite resistance from Western medical authorities, she demanded that her five-year-old son be variolated—and he remained healthy. Upon the family's return to England in 1721, she also had her four-year-old daughter variolated in front of the physicians of the royal court to prove its efficacy. The results were so impressive that Charles Maitland, the embassy surgeon in Constantinople who had variolated Montague's son, received permission to try the treatment on prisoners and orphans to confirm its usefulness. When none of the prisoners or orphans fell ill after being exposed to smallpox, the Princess of Wales asked to have two of her daughters variolated, and the practice gained public acceptance (Riedel 2005a: 22). Shortly thereafter, in the United States, Cotton Mather, an influential Puritan minister and author, popularized the practice after learning about it from one of his slaves (Glenn 2004).

Unfortunately, while variolation sought to give people only a mild form of smallpox, it was hard to control the disease's virulence. As a result, the efforts to stop smallpox could inadvertently cause an outbreak. This fact encouraged the search for a more effective technique to prevent smallpox. One idea for doing so derived inspiration from milkmaids. Milkmaids frequently contracted cowpox when they came into contact with the udders of infected cattle. Cowpox and smallpox are members of the same genus, but cowpox is not fatal to humans and the milkmaids who contracted it never seemed to catch smallpox. Edward Jenner, a naturalist and doctor, noticed this correlation and sought to determine whether cowpox could safely prevent smallpox. In a now famous experiment, Jenner extracted fluid from a cowpox pustule on Sarah Nelmes's hand on May 14, 1796, and inserted it into two half-inch incisions on the arm of James Phipps, a healthy eight-year-old boy. Two months later, Jenner took fluid from a smallpox pustule and introduced it into cuts on Phipps' arm, but Phipps never contracted the disease. Two years later, after doing additional experiments, Jenner published his successful results. He decided to call his procedure vaccination, based on the Latin words for cow (*vacca*) and cowpox (*vaccinia*) (Barquet and Domingo 1997: 639–40). While Jenner did not necessarily know *why* vaccination worked because germ theory of disease remained unknown, he knew that he had found something important.

Despite Jenner's efforts, vaccination was not immediately embraced. When Jenner first wrote up his results, the British Royal Society, of which Jenner was a member, rejected the paper for being too revolutionary and at odds with established knowledge. Some members of the medical establishment found the idea of injecting a person with material from a diseased animal repulsive and unsafe (Tucker 2001: 25–27). Some religious leaders objected that vaccination thwarted God's will by preventing a disease (Henderson 1997: 120). Over time, though, vaccination gained public favor as it demonstrated its efficacy. Thomas Jefferson even wrote to Jenner to congratulate him that "future generations will know by history only that the most loathsome smallpox existed and by you has been extirpated" (Barquet and Domingo 1997: 641).

Vaccination campaigns caused smallpox rates to decline dramatically throughout the nineteenth and twentieth centuries. By the 1940s, endemic smallpox had all but disappeared from North America and Europe (Behbehani 1983: 485). Unfortunately, it was not uncommon for travelers to accidentally reintroduce smallpox into countries from which it had been eliminated, forcing governments to scramble to prevent outbreaks from occurring. For example, when a Mexican businessman came down with the disease in New York in 1947, the US government had to vaccinate 6.4 million people over the span of a month to prevent a smallpox outbreak (Sepkowitz 2004). While North America and Europe worried about the reimportation of smallpox, the rest of the world still faced widespread endemic smallpox and its high mortality rates. Few held out much hope for being able to do much more than control the disease. Smallpox was "perceived as a disease of the poor, lower classes, and thus [was relegated] to the status of a neglected, inevitable disease" (Hopkins 1989: 2). As long as smallpox continued to circulate anywhere in the world, all countries remained at risk of the disease and thus had to maintain a high degree of vigilance. The only way to change this situation was to eradicate the disease—something that had never been done before.

Eradication has a specific epidemiological meaning. *Eradication* means permanently reducing the number of human cases worldwide to zero through deliberate interventions. In other words, the disease is no longer circulating anywhere in the world. By contrast, *elimination* means reducing the number of human cases to zero in a particular geographic region through deliberate interventions. Malaria has been eliminated from the United States because the parasite no longer circulates within its borders, but it is still present in Africa and Asia. *Controlling* a disease refers to decreasing the number of cases to a locally acceptable level. We expect to see a certain number of cases of seasonal influenza each year because we have taken steps to control it like encouraging people to get a flu shot (Dowdle 1999). Not all diseases are good candidates for eradication. Biologically, there needs to be an extremely effective vaccine or treatment, ease of diagnosis, and the ability to control the means of transmission (Garrett 1994: 41). Economically, there needs to be a reconciling of the potential costs and benefits of such a campaign and whether the resources could be better used for other programs. Socially and politically, there needs to be a broad support for the program and a willingness to commit to it over the long term (Dowdle 1999). These factors help explain why eradication campaigns for diseases like polio (Abimbola, Malik, and Mansoor 2013) and Guinea worm (Molyneux and Sankara 2017) have seen greater success and are generally more plausible than the eradication campaigns against malaria (Greenwood 2009).

The impetus for a smallpox eradication campaign emerged in the 1950s. Brock Chisholm, the World Health Organization (WHO) Director-General, officially proposed an eradication campaign in 1953, but a study committee declared the plan unrealistic (Fenner et al. 1988: 366). Five years later, the Soviet Union proposed a global five-year eradication campaign with the WHO providing technical assistance and staff training and national governments doing the actual vaccinating themselves (Tucker 2001: 80–81). The following year, the World Health Assembly (WHA) approved a resolution to support this smallpox eradication campaign. In the midst of the heightened geopolitical tensions of the Cold War, all sides found common ground in eradicating smallpox. The costs of an aggressive and successful smallpox eradication campaign, the Soviets argued, would be less than ongoing national vaccination campaigns, and technical advancements made the smallpox vaccine easier to distribute and more effective (Packard 2016: 145).

The smallpox eradication campaign took longer than the five years initially proposed by the Soviets, but its successes encouraged ongoing support. A smallpox eradication program in Central and West Africa eliminated the disease from twenty countries in less than four years and proved that neither poverty nor weak infrastructure were insurmountable challenges (Hopkins 1989: 8). When smallpox was eliminated from Asia in 1975, the disease remained endemic in only three countries—Ethiopia, Kenya, and Somalia. Aggressive vaccination efforts wiped out smallpox in Ethiopia and Kenya by the middle of 1976, but Somalia proved a more difficult challenge. Five cases appeared in Mogadishu in September 1976, and those quickly blossomed into more than three thousand cases. Complicating matters, poor infrastructure and the nomadic travels of afflicted groups made it hard to conduct vaccinations. The vaccination campaigns adapted and persisted despite these tough circumstances, fearful that a failure in Somalia would undermine all of the efforts over the previous decades. On October 26, 1977, Ali Maow Maalin, a Somali hospital cook, came down with variola minor—and became the last person in the world to contract smallpox through natural circulation.

After two years with no new natural cases of smallpox anywhere in the world, the WHO officially declared smallpox eradicated on December 9, 1979. The WHA in 1980 passed a resolution affirming that the world "had won freedom from smallpox" because of international cooperation (Bazin 2000: 173). After twenty-two years, deliberate human intervention wiped out one of the most feared infectious diseases, and it had widespread benefits for humanity. Economically, Barrett estimates that for every dollar spent to get rid of the disease, the world saved nearly $160. He argues, "I would venture to guess that smallpox eradication was probably the greatest global public investment in human history" (Barrett 2013: 5). Politically, the eradication campaign demonstrated the ability of seemingly intractable foes to bridge their differences to work together on issues for the collective good. Socially, the campaign managed to overcome religious and ethnic differences and ongoing civil conflicts to provide vaccination to people around the world regardless of ability to pay.

Though smallpox no longer circulates naturally, the virus itself still exists. In the same resolution where the WHA declared smallpox eradicated, it accepted the recommendations of the Global Commission for the Certification of Smallpox Eradication that up to four WHO collaborating laboratories should hold on to their stocks of the variola virus for research purposes. Eventually, all known variola samples ended up in one of two labs: the Centers for Disease Control and Prevention (CDC) in Atlanta and the Research Institute for Viral Preparations in Moscow. In 1986, the WHO Committee on Orthopoxvirus Recommendations unanimously called for these remaining samples to be destroyed. While there were repeated recommendations to destroy all remaining variola stocks throughout the 1990s, scientists and policymakers resisted these calls (Koplow 2003: 146–48).

Why would the international community hold on to a virus that it worked so hard to eradicate? One strand of argument focuses on the ethics of destroying the variola virus. Koplow argues that the virus "is part of nature's grand scheme, with a unique role in our own history and environment, and we should be loath to extinguish it, absent the most compelling justification" (Koplow 2004: 4). Drawing analogies to environmental and animal rights law, Koplow asserts that we should not destroy the virus simply because we can; rather, we have an ethical obligation rooted in our humanity to avoid causing the wholesale destruction of any form of life (or quasi-life).

Even more directly related to questions of globalization, some experts worry that we will be more vulnerable to bioterrorist and bioweapons attacks without smallpox virus samples. They raise three concerns. First, they doubt that the only variola stocks are actually in Atlanta and Moscow. In 1973, the Soviet Union established Biopreparat. Presented to the world as a state-owned pharmaceutical company for developing vaccines, Biopreparat was actually a military-funded offensive biological weapons program (Enemark 2017: 8–9). In 1992, Biopreparat's deputy director, Ken Alibek, defected to the United States and told American authorities that Soviet government officials considered smallpox their number one strategic weapon and possessed at least twenty tons of a liquid variola agent that could be attached to intercontinental ballistic missiles (Koplow 2003: 72–73). Osterholm and Schwartz claimed that Iraq and North Korea also retained undeclared variola stocks for offensive capabilities (Osterholm and Schwartz 2000: 17). More recently, scientists cleaning out an old lab at the National Institutes of Health outside of Washington in 2014 discovered a number of vials labelled "variola." Tests revealed that the vials did indeed possess smallpox DNA, though it was not clear whether there was enough to potentially cause transmission (Harris 2014). The possibility that the smallpox virus exists outside of the two internationally approved lab facilities raises the possibility that the disease could reappear. It also heightens fear that rogue actors or terrorist groups could acquire smallpox virus samples and use publicly available information and a relatively low level of knowledge about biology to create their own weapon (Thompson 2017; Whitley 2003). The CDC classifies smallpox as a Category A bioterrorism threat—the highest category because of its "possibility of use and . . . impact on public health" (Riedel 2005b: 13). While other analyses have found that smallpox is far more difficult to weaponize than commonly assumed and largely unavailable to terrorist organizations (Leitenberg 2002; Pennington 2003), the fear remains a potent one for government policymakers.

Second, they worry that the world is unprepared if smallpox were to return. The WHO stopped recommending routine smallpox vaccination in 1979, and some countries discontinued routine smallpox vaccination even earlier, meaning that the vast majority of people alive today have no immunity to the disease—and that the overwhelming majority of medical personnel have no experience diagnosing or treating smallpox. It is unclear how many doses of smallpox vaccine are currently available or how effective those vaccines are. In the immediate aftermath of 9/11, the US government restarted its smallpox vaccination program for military and government personnel deployed to high-risk areas, but the program saw a high number of adverse reactions to the vaccine (including a few deaths) and provoked widespread opposition (Guillemin 2005: 181). When the US government created Project BioShield in 2004, it acquired twenty-eight million doses of a smallpox vaccine, but this is nowhere near enough for the entire country and their efficacy in the midst of an actual outbreak remains unproven (Enemark 2017: 171–72). The fear is that without the actual smallpox virus itself, scientists will be unable to develop new vaccines or treatments, leaving the world at even greater risk.

Third, they note that the virus' continued existence allows us to continue to learn from it. Caplan worries, "Eradication . . . means replacing prophylaxis and vigilance with indifference and trust" (Caplan 2009: 2193). As synthetic biology continues to advance, the chances that someone would be able to recreate the smallpox virus on their own increases. More worrisome, "through gain-of-function techniques, terrorist-employed scientists might be able to modify or enhance their new variola virus so that we are not protected by our current vaccine" (Osterholm and Olshaker 2017: 134). Gain-of-function refers the idea that genetic mutation or manipulation can change how genes express themselves. In other words, scientists could alter a virus in such a way to make it more lethal, easier to spread, or harder to detect. If we lack the virus itself for research purposes, then we risk ceding the scientific knowledge advantage to those who might want such information for evil purposes.

SARS: FROM UNKNOWN ORIGINS TO GLOBAL HEALTH EMERGENCY

In their review of the political responses to SARS in Asia, So and Pun bluntly state, "It is well known that SARS is a product of globalization. Otherwise, it could not possibly spread so fast to so many countries in such a short time" (So and Pun 2004: 5). Its outbreak posed a range of challenges. It was a brand–new disease. States varied widely in their willingness to cooperate with other governments and international organizations to stop SARS. The disease's spread directly mirrored international travel patterns. It intersected with questions of sovereignty. It raised serious questions about the power of intergovernmental organizations and helped further massive reforms in the global health governance system. Perhaps most bafflingly of all, once the outbreak ran its course, it disappeared and (at least as of early 2019) has not caused any natural human infections since then.

SARS is a highly contagious viral respiratory illness that spreads person-to-person through coughs and sneezes. Without treatment, each person with SARS can spread the disease to three to four other people on average (Wallinga and Teunis 2004). The initial symptoms of SARS are indistinguishable from many other respiratory illnesses. Patients experience a fever, headache, shivers, a dry cough, shortness of breath, and occasionally diarrhea. As the infection worsens, it can turn into pneumonia—and that requires more intensive medical care. Indeed, before SARS got its name, doctors described the illness as atypical pneumonia (WHO 2003b). As of 2018, there is still no vaccine or treatment for SARS; doctors instead focus on supportive care by trying to reduce fever and provide ventilation as needed (Jiang, Lu, and Du 2012).

The origin of SARS remains undetermined. Most scientists believe that the disease is zoonotic—that is, it entered the human population from animals—but they do not yet know for certain its origin. Suspicion initially fell to civets, leading Chinese government officials to order widespread culling of the weasel-like mammal in 2003 (Parry 2004). More recently, Chinese scientists have linked the outbreak to a colony of horseshoe bats (McKie 2017).

This new disease first appeared in November 2002 in Guangdong, a province along China's southeastern coast that borders Hong Kong. Disease surveillance systems picked up media reports of unusual respiratory illnesses in Guangdong, and the WHO requested additional information from the Chinese government in early December. The government reported it was merely an influenza outbreak (Heymann 2006: 351). In January 2003, more reports about an atypical respiratory illness appeared, this time noting "unusual increases in antiviral drug sales by a pharmaceutical company based in Guangdong" (Weir and Mykhalovskiy 2010: 88). When the WHO received reports about more than one hundred deaths from an unknown infectious disease on February 10, it again contacted the Chinese government for more information. Officials told the WHO that the outbreak was under control and claimed there was no need for WHO's involvement (Heymann 2006: 351). We now know that these unknown respiratory illnesses were actually the first human cases of SARS. On March 10, they officially gave the disease the name SARS and established a common diagnostic checklist for identifying potential new cases (Kamps and Hoffmann 2003: 15–16).

Over the course of the outbreak from November 2002 to July 2003, the WHO identified 8,098 cases of the disease in thirty-seven different countries. Of these, 774 people died (WHO 2003a). Over the next year, there were a few scattered cases of the disease, and a few laboratory researchers accidentally fell ill, but widespread person-to-person transmission did not occur. On May 19, 2004, the WHO officially declared China to be free of SARS, and there have been no known human cases of the disease since then (Centers for Disease Control and Prevention 2004).

SARS' dramatic spread—and its intensification, expansion, and deterritorialization—can be traced back to a specific place on a specific date. In this case, Room 911 at the Hotel Metropole in the Kowloon section of Hong Kong on February 21, 2003, is the epicenter of the globalization of SARS. On that day, Dr. Liu Jianlun checked in to the hotel in order to attend a family wedding. Liu was a medical doctor in Guangdong, and he had had been treating cases of this atypical pneumonia (Wong 2004). Shortly after checking in, Liu began to feel ill, and his condition rapidly worsened. He soon went to the hospital, where he died on March 4. Unfortunately, the other hotel guests staying on the same floor fell ill themselves over the next few days. These other guests were Singaporean, Canadian, Chinese, and an American bound for Vietnam. Over the next few days, they all boarded planes to their intended destinations—and, in that simple act of international air travel, managed to spread SARS far beyond China. The first cases of SARS outside of China appeared in Vietnam on February 26, 2003, and the disease soon appeared in more countries. Within four months of Dr. Liu's hotel stay, more than four thousand cases and 550 deaths of SARS outside China and Taiwan could be traced back to the Hotel Metropole's ninth floor (Fleck 2003: 625).

Dr. Liu did not set out to deliberately infect others. The virus took advantage of his movements and those of the other people on his floor to extend its geographical spread and flout international borders. In this way, SARS became a global issue in a way that no one could have anticipated. While Liu is frequently described as "Patient Zero" or a "super-spreader" (Dutton 2009), that language implies a degree of intentionality rather than recognizing that these sorts of occurrences happen because of the economic, social, and political changes introduced by globalization.

The response by various governmental institutions to the SARS outbreak speaks to how actors tried to manage globalization. The Chinese government, for example, actively sought to suppress information about SARS and initially denied that there was a problem. When asked by international officials about the outbreak, Chinese officials repeatedly replied that it was under control (Price-Smith 2009: 141). During a fact-finding mission by the WHO during the outbreak, one hospital in Beijing loaded thirty-one patients with SARS into ambulances and drove them around the city to hide them from WHO officials. Another hospital moved approximately forty patients with SARS to a different facility while WHO personnel were conducting their investigation. In both instances, hospital personnel claimed that they were ordered to take these actions by government officials (Pomfret 2003). Lower-level government bureaucrats also had strong incentives to distort information about SARS as it went to higher officials because they feared that any problems found within their jurisdictions could cause them to lose their jobs or be passed over for future promotions (Huang 2003: 11). The government prohibited public discussion of the disease, and it maintained that it did not need assistance from international organizations or other groups.

Despite these strenuous efforts at the domestic level, the Chinese government could not prevent information and rumors about SARS from getting out. Bear in mind, this outbreak occurred before the advent of social media. There was no Facebook, Instagram, or Twitter, yet information about this new disease still found ways to get around official government newspaper, television, and radio stories. A survey found that nearly 41 percent of urban residents in China had heard about the disease even though the government officially denied its existence. Much of this information came via text messages, which became so ubiquitous that government officials in Guangzhou felt compelled to hold a press conference to refute them (Huang 2003: 12). The ability of information—both reliable and unreliable—to circumvent official government channels is one of the hallmarks of globalization, as communication flows make it easier to challenge official narratives. On the flip side, though, that also means that it can be harder to correct misinformation.

While the Chinese government denied the existence of SARS, the WHO instead implemented an incredibly aggressive response. This was all the more remarkable because the organization technically lacked the international legal authority to override national sovereignty. At the time, the International Health Regulations (IHR)—an international treaty that governs how states should respond to infectious disease outbreaks and that will be discussed in greater detail in chapter 3—only required states to report human cases of cholera, yellow fever, and plague. SARS fell outside the IHR's mandate and thus severely limited the WHO's ability to mount a response. If the Chinese government did not want to report cases of SARS or cooperate with the WHO, that was entirely within its legal rights. Its actions reflected its Westphalian sovereignty, even at a time when international borders were proving irrelevant to containing the spread of a new pathogen (Fidler 2003: 490).

When disease surveillance systems first picked up reports of deaths due to an unknown infectious disease in China, the WHO approached the Chinese government for more information. This happened on multiple occasions, and in each instance, government officials told the WHO that they did not require any assistance. The WHO escalated its involvement when it issued a global health alert about a severe atypical pneumonia that placed health workers at particular risk on March 12, 2003. Three days later, it issued a rare emergency advisory, recommending postponing any nonessential travel to Hong Kong and Guangdong—the epicenters of the outbreak (Curley and Thomas 2004: 21–22). The WHO later added Toronto to its travel advisory after a cluster of more than 250 SARS cases appeared there (Christensen and Painter 2004: 36).

During the outbreak, the WHO played three roles—all of which reflected the intersection of globalization and health. First, it acted as an epidemic intelligence coordinator. With reports coming in about a potential new disease, it brought some sense of order to the information and perform follow-up activities. This role became particularly important after February 28, 2003, when Dr. Carlos Urbani, a WHO epidemiologist working in Vietnam who later died of SARS himself, concluded that the atypical pneumonia cases developing around Asia were likely a brand-new disease and connected to each other (Kamradt-Scott 2015: 89–90).

Second, the WHO served as a policy advisor. Rather than simply reporting what other states were doing in response to SARS, the WHO issued ongoing policy recommendations and technical guidance. While it could not compel states to adopt its recommendations, many did because the WHO was uniquely placed to collect information from networks of epidemiologists, scientists, and frontline health care workers. It was in this context that the WHO recommended that airlines conduct temperature checks and health questionnaires to identify potential carriers and that health care workers take specific precautions to protect themselves from infection. It even issued travel advisories, though this led some to criticize the WHO for overstepping its boundaries (Christensen and Painter 2004: 39; Kamradt-Scott 2015: 91–93).

Third, and perhaps most powerfully, the WHO acted as a critic of government actions. It publicly named and shamed governments that tried to hide cases, failed to introduce effective containment methods, or shunned international cooperation. At the height of the outbreak, WHO officials were giving daily press conferences that both shared their policy recommendations and called out laggard states. The willingness to engage and cooperate with the WHO had direct effects. Both Vietnam and China had local transmission of SARS in late March and early April 2003, but only the latter was included on the travel advisory. Kamradt-Scott argues this is because Vietnamese officials had responded "forcefully and rapidly to the threat" of SARS, while China "continued to decline to fully cooperate with the organization's request to send a team of investigators" (Kamradt-Scott 2015: 95–96). WHO officials repeatedly and publicly called out Chinese officials for failing to provide adequate information and implement effective control measures. WHO Director-General Gro Harlem Brundtland even went so far as to declare, "It would have been much better if the Chinese government had been more open in early stages" (cited in Kamradt-Scott 2015: 97).

The combination of domestic and international pressures did eventually force the Chinese government to change its tactics. On April 4, the head of China's Center for Disease Control publicly apologized for failing to keep the Chinese public and international community informed about the outbreak. Less than a week later, Jiang Yanyong, a prominent member of the Communist Party, publicly accused the government of covering up the outbreak in Beijing (Price-Smith 2009: 141–42). Minister of Health Zhang Wenkang and Beijing Mayor Meng Xuenong were both subsequently fired for not stopping the outbreak— the first of more than 120 who lost their jobs or were disciplined for their lax responses. After the WHO publicly chastised the Chinese government for its failures on April 16, Chinese officials responded by declaring a national war on SARS (Price-Smith 2009: 142). On April 17, the government mobilized a large public campaign against SARS, publicly releasing the number of cases in each province and making government officials responsible for aggressively addressing the SARS outbreak within their jurisdictions. Tens of thousands of people were quarantined, and eighty million people in Guangdong were mobilized to clean the streets in an effort to kill the virus. The party even created a two billion yuan (approximately US $242 million) fund for SARS prevention and control to upgrade facilities and make free treatment available to SARS patients (Huang 2004: 11–13).

SARS had a particular relationship to the deterritorializing aspects of globalization. On the one hand, the spread of the disease once again reinforced the idea that national borders are insufficient to stop the spread of a virus. Even when countries introduced travel restrictions and the WHO suggested that people avoid venturing to SARS-infected areas, the disease still spread. On the other hand, SARS had its most dramatic effects in "global cities" like Hong Kong and Toronto. A global city is "a place which emphasizes cosmopolitanism and move-ment, where transnationalism is as much the rule as locality" (Galley 2009: 133). The same globalizing forces that make these cities dynamic and vibrant places put them at risk, and their role within the modern economy in some ways transcends their physical location.

The SARS outbreak had widespread economic effects, reflecting globalization's inherent interconnectedness. The tourism and service sectors bore the brunt of the economic effects as people delayed travel or avoided going out in public. Passenger traffic at the Hong Kong airport was down 70 percent in April 2003 from its April 2002 levels, and approximately 30 percent of its daily flights were canceled. This cost the airport at least $3.5 million per day in lost revenue. Restaurant receipts and retail sales throughout the city both declined roughly 10 percent, and hotel occupancy dropped more than 60 percent (Heymann and West 2015: 98–100). The Asian Development Bank estimates that SARS cost the Chinese economy alone $6.1 billion, or 0.5 percent of its GDP. The service sector was particularly hard hit, with its economic productivity down 6.8 percent in the second quarter of 2003 (Price-Smith 2009: 144). In Canada, Ontario went into recession in 2003 with a drop of real GDP of 0.7 percent in the second quarter and 2.5 percent in the third—an outcome that the government blamed squarely on the SARS outbreak in Toronto. Aside from the economic losses, Ontario's Health Minister said that SARS increased the costs to his department nearly one billion dollars through the end of June 2003 (Price-Smith 2009: 145). Singapore, which had 238 cases of SARS, saw its economic growth rate dip to only 1.1 percent in 2003—significantly lower than its neighbors, with the effects concentrated in the travel and tourism sectors. This sharp, sudden effect due to SARS "dramatized Singapore's vulnerability to sudden fluctuations in the global movement of goods and people" (Latif 2004: 228).

The political dynamics of globalization are part of the legacy of SARS, too, as it induced significant changes at the domestic and international levels. Internationally, the SARS outbreak strengthened the WHO's reputation. The organization received high marks for its effective response and reaffirmed its legitimacy and authority within global health governance (Fidler 2005: 354). This is precisely why Fidler described SARS as "first post-Westphalian pathogen." The outbreak, he argued, demonstrated to the international community that traditional understandings of sovereignty were far too weak to be effective in the face of globalization and the ease with which disease can travel around the world. Instead, addressing infectious disease outbreaks necessarily required that states subvert their individual interests to cooperate at the international level (Fidler 2003). While Fidler's arguments may have proven overly optimistic, they do reflect the changing nature of health policy in a globalized system.

SARS also had a range of domestic political effects in various countries. These were perhaps most obvious in China, where the government went from recalcitrance to active partnership in short order. The Chinese government used its eventual ability to stop the spread to demonstrate its capability and bolster its performative legitimacy (Freedman 2005). The outbreak made public health a more prominent issue within the Chinese government and increased its willingness to engage with external actors on an issue that it had traditionally seen as wholly domestic (Chan, Chen, and Xu 2010). The outbreak also raised political questions for Canada, as it demonstrated weaknesses within Ontario's public health system and caused concern about the relationship between provincial and federal public health officials. It inspired the creation of the federal Public Health Agency, a cabinet-level office directed by a chief public health officer and reporting to the minister of health. The Public Health Agency's mandate is to facilitate cooperation between the federal government and provincial public health systems in order to avoid a repeat of the confusion that emerged during the SARS outbreak (Price-Smith 2009: 146–48).

SARS' emergence and spread also intersected with assumptions and prejudices—particularly directed toward the Chinese. There was an aura of otherness and exoticism in the discussions about how the disease may have jumped from animals to humans. One early news report emphasized, "Preliminary studies suggest it jumped species from the civet, a member of the cat family, or the raccoon dog, both of which are delicacies in the cuisine of southern China" (Fleck 2003: 626). A report from *Newsweek* stressed, "Pigs, ducks, chickens, and people live cheek-by-jowl on the district's primitive farms. . . . The clincher is that these farms sit just a few miles from Guangzhou, a teeming city that mixes people, animals, and microbes from the countryside with travelers from around the world" (cited in Wald 2008: 5). *New Scientist* concurred, writing that the "deadly SARS virus" came from "three exotic animal species being sold live in a Chinese food market" (Bhattacharya and MacKenzie 2003). This focus on dietary exoticism cast the residents of Guangdong as Others and contributed to a sense that their actions bear responsibility for introducing it to the rest of the world. It was a "manifestation of a deep-seated stereotype of the Chinese as unhygienic people living in crowded places, and eating as well as living in proximity to dirty animals" (Hung 2004: 33).

Public and private decisions further marginalized Chinese persons and communities in the midst of the outbreak, regardless of their connection to SARS. The University of California, Berkeley, disallowed students from SARS-infected regions, like China, Hong Kong, Taiwan, and Singapore, from attending its summer programs. Anecdotal reports in New York, London, and San Francisco suggested significant drop-offs in patronage at Chinese restaurants, and Chinese tourists reported being denied accommodation in hotels and restaurants (Leong 2003: v–vii). Western media outlets spoke of a "Chinese plague" or "Oriental plague," and the *Wall Street Journal* went so far as to call for the international community to cut off contact with China for the duration of the epidemic (Hung 2004: 27–29).

Political leaders frequently emphasized that the negative effects their communities were feeling were not the result of the actual danger itself, but rather from the public perceptions being fomented by breathless negative press attention. Media reports about the outbreak frequently featured images of Asians wearing white masks "served to increase fearfulness" because the images appeared weird and out of character (Harrison 2012: 260). Toronto Mayor Mel Lastman complained, "It's not the disease that's doing the damage—it's public perception about SARS that's hurting Toronto's tourism industry" (cited in Strange 2007: 220).

NONCOMMUNICABLE DIS
COMPLEX LINES OF CAU:

Even though infectious disease outbreaks get the bulk of international attention, NCDs kill more people every year. According to the WHO, the three most common causes of death—heart disease, stroke, and chronic obstructive pulmonary disease—and five of the ten leading causes of death are NCDs (WHO 2016c). The increases in NCDs are not simply a trade-off with infectious disease rates. Instead, "death and disability from NCDs in low- and lower-middle-income countries is increasing faster than the rate of decline from communicable diseases" (Council on Foreign Relations 2014: 10). They are also rising faster among younger populations and causing a greater loss of working years and life. The Council on Foreign Relations suggests that the increasing rates of NCDs and the worsening treatment outcomes in developing countries could contribute to political instability in the worst affected countries (Council on Foreign Relations 2014: 15).

Before going further, let's highlight the differences between infectious (or communicable) and noncommunicable (or chronic) diseases. A communicable disease is something that passes from person to person by means of an infectious agent like a virus or bacteria. Influenza, HIV, and cholera have very different effects on the body, but they are all infectious diseases. No one gets sick with them unless and until an infectious agent is introduced into the body—and a person's immune system may very well fight off that infection in order to prevent you from getting sick (Skolnik 2016: 25). An NCD, on the other hand, emerges through a complex interplay of personal, societal, political, and environmental factors and tends to be of a long duration. As a result, they can be complex to treat (DeLaet and DeLaet 2012: 69). NCDs include conditions like heart disease, diabetes, and stroke. While people in the same community or even same family may be more prone to an NCD, that is not because of a virus or bacteria moving directly from one person to another.

Despite the seeming contrast between them, links exist between some communicable diseases and NCDs. Hepatitis C is a liver disease caused by a virus that spreads through contact with contaminated blood, making it a communicable disease. That said, hepatitis C is linked to increased risk for liver cancer (an NCD). Over the long term, hepatitis C can cause cirrhosis, or scarring of the liver. As these scars grow, the liver tries to heal itself by creating new cells to replace the damaged ones. This process, though, increases the chances the liver will inadvertently create cells with a mutation that can lead to cancer (Andrade et al. 2009). Similarly, human papillomavirus (HPV) is a communicable disease and the most common sexually transmitted infection, and many people who contract it will have no symptoms. Problems can occur, though, when HPV causes abnormal cell growths which in turn can become cancerous. Nearly all cases of cervical cancer and the vast majority of cancers of the anus, vagina, and vulva are due to HPV, leading the WHO to recommend HPV vaccination as part of routine vaccinations in all countries (WHO 2017b). In these cases, it is not that NCDs spread from person to person; rather, infectious diseases cause complications that allow an NCD to emerge.

Treating NCDs in resource-poor settings can pose particular challenges. In 2007, the WHO predicted a 17 percent increase worldwide and 27 percent increase in Africa alone in deaths from NCDs over the next decade. A total of 70 percent of those living with diabetes, 65 percent of patients with hypertension, and 75 percent of people with chronic obstructive pulmonary disease are in developing countries (Maher et al. 2009: 2). These are substantial increases, and they would pose a problem for a country's health system in the best of circumstances. The combination of weak primary health care systems and uncertain access to necessary supplies undermines the opportunity for people to receive the treatment that they need. As a result, NCD rates are rising, but treatment outcomes are worsening (Council on Foreign Relations 2014: 11). NCDs have no easy fixes. They can be difficult to diagnose, complex to treat, and long-term in nature. We do not necessarily understand the dynamics that give rise to NCDs in the first place, and that makes treatment and monitoring far more difficult than something like influenza. Unfortunately, NCDs have not inspired the same sense of urgency and attention as infectious diseases. In 2017, development assistance for health for NCDs totaled $825 million out of more than thirty-seven billion dollars for global health aid—less than one-tenth of the amount pledged for HIV/AIDS (Institute for Health Metrics and Evaluation 2018: 124–25).

The international framing of NCDs and how states should respond to them has proven inconsistent and contradictory. One frame emphasizes human rights and how the rise in NCDs undermines the right to health, a second frame focuses on economics and how NCDs contribute to personal and national poverty, and a third frame prioritizes individual responsibility. The policy recommendations that emerge from these competing frames are not necessarily consistent. Health as a human right suggests that the state has an obligation to ensure access to medicines, but an economic rationale means that interventions should be based on a cost/benefit analysis—and an individual responsibility frame removes the state from any sense of obligation (Patterson 2018: 130–33). Such inconsistency gives a government little incentive to tackle the issue.

At one point in time, rising NCD rates were taken as proof of a country's increased level of development. This is the idea of the epidemiological transition (Omran 1971). Omran argued that economic development prompts long-term shifts in morbidity and mortality within a society, with NCDs causing a higher proportion of illness and death as a country becomes wealthier. He described three mortality patterns: the Age of Pestilence and Famine (high rates of mortality and low life expectancy due to infectious disease outbreaks), the Age of Receding Pandemics (infectious disease becomes less common, leading to longer lives and population growth), and the Age of Degenerative and Man-Made Diseases (people die primarily of NCDs, life expectancy grows, and population growth moderates). Building on this, Morand (2004) proposed that countries move between different phases of the epidemiological transition when their citizens achieve certain income thresholds and accumulate a degree of capital. As such, the epidemiological transition posits rising NCD rates as signs of progress because it means that people are living long enough to fall victim to cancer, heart disease, or stroke.

More recently, the assumptions of the epidemiological transition have come under criticism. Santosa et al. (2014), for example, criticize this line of thinking for ignoring the social determinants of health (SDH) for the changing patterns of societal health and life expectancy. They also find that the demographic experience of many low- and middle-income countries deviates significantly from the expectations of the epidemiological transition. This is unsurprising, they assert, because the theory itself was premised on the experience of industrialized states—experiences unlikely to be replicated in other contexts. Another line of criticism highlights the failure of epidemiological transition theory to consider the societal divisions that mean different groups experience health benefits at very different rates (Gulliford 2003). The model provides no guidance for evaluating the efficacy of various health interventions, meaning that the transition seems more like an inevitability rather than the effect of affirmative government policies (Carolina and Gustavo 2003). There is also the problem of re-emergent infectious diseases—conditions like tuberculosis that we thought were under control but are actually becoming more virulent due to antibiotic resistance. The epidemiological transition, by contrast, suggests that once a society conquers infectious disease, the problem will not reappear (Armelagos, Brown, and Turner 2005).

The increases in NCD deaths highlight globalization's economic, social, and political changes. As noted earlier, NCDs spread through complex interactions between trade policies, environmental changes, consumerism, and personal lifestyle choices. In 2017, *The New York Times* released an investigative series called "Planet Fat," examining the connections between global trade policy, dietary changes, and increasing obesity rates. It described how multinational food and restaurant companies have increasingly targeted low- and middle-income countries as new markets, encouraged by free trade policies and economic incentives. While these companies have seen large increases in profits in these countries, the countries themselves are witnessing substantial increases in rates of obesity, diabetes, and other NCDs (*New York Times* 2017). Globalization is what makes these sorts of changes possible. To tackle NCDs effectively, we need to consider the underlying structural conditions like poverty, malnutrition, trade changes, and environmental degradation that give rise to them in the first place (Benson and Glasgow 2015: 181).

This is where the importance of the SDHs comes into particular focus. SDHs are "the conditions in which people are born, grow, work, live, and age, and the wider set of forces and systems shaping the daily conditions of life" (WHO 2018e). The anthropologist and medical doctor Paul Farmer notes, "All of the forces that bring a patient to a doctor (or keep a patient from a doctor), all of the processes leading to sickness and then to diagnosis and treatment, are related to a series of large-scale social factors" (Farmer 1999: 10–11). The political, economic, and social systems inflict harm on people, but we tend to overemphasize individual agency in health-related decisions. If we fail to consider SDHs, then NCDs look like the result of poor personal choices rather than reflections of larger structural forces.

The public health community has long understood how structural conditions can condition an individual's health outcomes. In 1842, Edwin Chadwick, the secretary of Britain's Poor Law Commission, outlined how inadequate housing, poor sanitation, dirty water, and the presence of slaughterhouses and factories near impoverished neighborhoods all contributed to higher disease rates and lower life expectancies among the poor (Tesh 1989: 28–32). Despite this recognition more than 150 years ago, public health during the twentieth century emphasized "single factor models that emphasize clinical solutions to health problems, leading to narrowly defined, technology-based medical and public health interventions . . . promot[ing] technology-drive, 'vertical' campaigns targeting specific diseases, with little regard for the large social contexts of illnesses" (Ruckert and Labonté 2014: 270).

More recently, the WHO has prioritized the importance of understanding the SDHs for promoting population health, and they have integrated these ideas into the action plans for achieving the SDGs. The challenge with the SDHs is that they rarely provide a direct, linear path that allows us to understand how a given life condition gives rise to a specific health problem. They operate over long lengths of time, making it harder to work them into our models or devise easy solutions (Barnes and Parkhurst 2014: 162–63). Giving someone penicillin to clear up an infection is straightforward; changing the economic system to ensure that people have an income high enough to ensure secure housing is far more difficult—even if it would ultimately be more beneficial for improving health in the long term.

The rise in NCDs is linked to globalization through a number of channels. Take, for example, the rise in overweight and obesity around the world. The WHO defines overweight for an adult as a body mass index—a measure of the relationship between a person's height and weight—higher than twenty-five and obesity for adults as a body mass index higher than thirty. Overweight and obesity are linked with a number of health conditions that decrease years of productive life and cause premature death, such as heart disease, diabetes, osteoarthritis, and some forms of cancer. Over the past forty years, the number of people who are overweight and obese has nearly tripled. More than 1.9 billion adults were classified as overweight in 2016, and more than 650 million were obese. This translates to nearly 40 percent of the world's adult population, and most of the world's population now lives in countries were overweight kills more people than underweight (WHO 2017c).

Understanding the rise in overweight and obesity is complicated, in part because it depends on one's level of analysis. At one level, overweight and obesity increase as people engage in less physical activity and eat more energy-dense and high-fat foods. People make their own decisions about what food to eat, whether they exercise, and how they want to move through the world. The four major factors that WHO has identified as contributing to the increase in NCDs like obesity are tobacco use, unhealthy diet, physical inactivity, and the harmful use of alcohol (Glasgow and Schrecker 2015: 280)—all of which are seemingly based on individual decisions. Outside of the occasional college party, few people are forced to drink to excess, smoke cigarettes, or eat loads of unhealthy food. As a result, getting healthier means individuals need to make better choices.

The problem with this approach is that it abstracts individuals from the larger contexts in which they exist and make decisions. This sort of individualization treats poor health as "individual shortcomings, products of poor individual choices, to be remedied by emphasizing individual responsibility . . . social and structural analyses are displaced in favor of individual solutions to individual problems valorizing individual choice and markets" (Fudge and Cossman 2002: 21–22). Placing the blame for rising obesity rates primarily on the individual relies on assumptions about agency, economic opportunity, and personal choice that are simply not applicable for many people. People generally do not make conscious choices to make themselves less healthy.

That means that we need to understand the increases in overweight and obesity in context, and that is where we see globalization's importance in changing NCD rates more starkly. Government policies have dramatically altered agricultural practices, which in turn has large effects on the foods available to consumers. The US government has long subsidized the production of corn and oilseed derivatives that go into cheap, energy-dense, and high-calorie foods (Nestle 2013), and the European Union's Common Agricultural Policy has led to a reduction in fruit and vegetable consumption and an increase in saturated fat intake (Lloyd-Williams et al. 2008). At the same time, the embrace of trade liberalization within a neoliberal economic framework means that governments are more likely to promote international trade regulations that make it easier for food manufacturers to sell cheap, energy-dense, and high-calorie foods without restriction (Hawkes et al. 2012). These less healthy foods crowd out healthier alternatives in the marketplace. Economic modeling demonstrates that under free trade agreements, food-importing countries see increases in their obesity rates because they find themselves subject to rules that favor food exporters and lack the ability to alter the agreement to promote better health (Miljkovic et al. 2015).

The experience of Pacific Island countries illustrates the interplay among globalization, trade policies, and obesity. Obesity rates increased among Pacific states during the latter half of the twentieth century, coinciding with changes in international agricultural trade policies (Ulijaszek 2002). Now, nine of the ten countries with the highest obesity rates are in the Pacific. The Cook Islands leads the world rankings, with 50.8 percent of the adult population obese in 2014 (Senthilingam 2015). More than 90 percent of the adult population in Tonga is overweight or obese, which has contributed to a five-year drop in average male life expectancy between 2006 and 2010 and a near-tripling of the rate of diabetes (Narula 2016). WHO studies find a direct correlation among dietary changes, the increased importation of manufactured food, and rising obesity rates in the region (Parry 2010). World Trade Organization (WTO) policies have privileged food manufacturers producing foods of low nutritional quality. Food-exporting countries like Australia, New Zealand, and the United States have been accused of "food dumping" in Pacific Island countries, undercutting locally produced foods with cheap high-fat products like mutton flaps, corned beef, and chicken backs. In 2002, the Samoan Health Minister noted that the country should ban such foods in order to bring its obesity epidemic under control, "but the government is looking at joining the World Trade Organization . . . so if we banned these products, it will interfere with policies of WTO" (cited in Hughes and Lawrence 2005: 300).

On an economic level, the changes in food availability and the effects of those dietary shifts on population health in Pacific Island states are a direct result of new economic policies and pressures. Those policies also have strong political elements, as evidenced by the Samoan health minister's comments. Countries seek the economic benefits that come with international trade, but doing so means that they must cede some of the policies that they would have previously used to protect the population's health—and government leaders recognize that privileging their domestic interests would cause the larger international political and economic structures to shut them out. The changes in food importation and availability also have social effects, as they alter community norms around diet. Fast food and imported food products may take on an image of a status symbol, or their price may undercut locally grown products. In these ways, governments lose a degree of sovereign control—at the cost of worsening health outcomes. Deterritorialization takes hold as global policies deprive states of the ability to make nuanced policies that reflect their unique situations. As states integrate into a globalized economy and undergo an intensified alteration to their previous practices, they face new health challenges.

Because NCDs have traditionally been framed as resulting from individual decisions, there has historically been far less global effort to address the problem in a cooperative manner. Since 2011, international society has taken more proactive steps to address the cross-border implications of rising NCD rates with mixed results. That year, the United Nations General Assembly (UNGA) hosted the High-Level Meeting on the Prevention and Control of Noncommunicable Diseases. This was only the second time that the UNGA had devoted a high-level meeting to a health issue; the first focused on HIV/AIDS (Afshin et al. 2014: 179). The resulting Political Declaration on the Prevention and Control of NCDs highlighted the need to tax alcohol and tobacco, regulate unhealthy food additives, and develop a framework for monitoring programs. Critics lamented that the agreement did not go far enough and that it was too willing to engage with the very industries that caused the problems in the first place (Marrero, Bloom, and Adashi 2012: 2037). Subsequent UN-sponsored meetings, such as its 2012 sustainable development conference called Rio+20, called NCDs "one of the major challenges for sustainable development in the 21st century" (cited in

Clark 2013: 510). UNGA has also sponsored two follow-up meetings on NCDs, one in 2014 and one in 2018.

While these high-level meetings attract attention and lead to the development of international agreements about how best to respond, they still reveal the lower position of NCDs on the global health agenda. The meetings have not fundamentally changed how development assistance for health donors allocate their funds. NCD programs receive 2 percent of total global development assistance for health, even though they account for approximately 60 percent of worldwide disease burden (Institute for Health Metrics and Evaluation 2018: 59). NCDs have also thus far failed to provoke the same sort of political pressure on governments to address them. They lack the moral urgency and contagion fears that accompanied HIV/AIDS. They do not have the same connection to national and international security. They have not attracted grassroots political mobilization or celebrity action. They are also coming on the international scene at a time where the increases in development assistance for health have stopped and funding has plateaued or even dropped slightly (Marrero, Bloom, and Adashi 2012). This poses a serious challenge for the ability of NCDs to cut through the global health political agenda. It also demonstrates that the mere fact that a health condition is exacerbated by globalization does not automatically mean that those same globalizing processes will foster an effective means for addressing the problem.

CONCLUSION

The emergence, growth, and persistence of globalization has had direct effects on the health of individuals around the world. Viruses and bacteria have taken advantage of the movement of goods and people across borders to expand into new territories. The spread of NCDs also illustrates how globalization can also dramatically alter health conditions by changing the economic, political, and social relationships that create the contexts in which people experience health and disease. At the same time, globalization and the interconnections it promotes can provide the impetus for cross-national cooperation to address collective health challenges.

On an economic level, globalization contributes to spread of disease in a number of ways. As more goods and people cross borders, there are more opportunities for illnesses to hitch a ride. The economic logic of globalization can also alter the sorts of trade that occurs and change the sorts of policy options that states may have in order to protect themselves. Contemporary global health governance recognizes this tension between economic interests and health concerns, and most international health policies seek to ensure that their recommendations do not unnecessarily impede international commerce. This makes sense from a globalization perspective, as much of globalization is premised on the idea that international trade is a good thing and that there should be few impediments to it. From a public health perspective and the idea of keeping a population safe from illness and disease, though, prioritizing relatively porous borders may not be in a state's interest.

Relatedly, on a political level, international policy and the institutions designed to maintain it provide a political rationale for promoting free trade and making sure that goods can cross borders easily. A state that wants to challenge these practices may find itself frozen out of international life. It is politically difficult for states to accept only some of the policy imperatives of globalization, so they have to make a statement about the relative costs and benefits of participating in globalization—and those costs and benefits may include changes to the collective health status of a state's population.

On a social level, globalization's challenges to the health status of a population may reflect the underlying cleavages within a society. The inequalities that exist in a given society may contribute to or exacerbate the conditions that make people more or less prone to certain illnesses and diseases. Globalization may also mask the social cleavages that have a direct bearing on an individual's ability to maintain their health. Telling people that they should eat better or take their medicine assumes that they have the ability to take those actions. If healthy food is not available or is too expensive, or if clinics have unreliable supplies of medicine or are inaccessible by public transport, then these social determinants override an individual's choices.

The five dimensions of globalization play distinctive roles in understanding the linkages illustrated by this chapter. The physical distance between peoples is no protection against the spread of disease and ill health, highlighting how globalization has *intensified* relations. Not only can disease agents travel easily, but the underlying conditions affecting the SDH show little regard for national boundaries. The increased *integration* of economies, political systems, and social relationships expands the range of connections that can allow for disease to spread. At the same time, this same integration means that national governments have fewer policy options at their disposal to change conditions because integration takes more and more policy decisions out of the realm of national politics. This speaks to the *deterritorialization* aspects of the relationship between health and globalization. It is not the case that states have no ability to control their borders; rather, it highlights the interdependence inherent in addressing any of these health issues. A country cannot address the increase in heart disease on its own because the situations that have given rise to the increase in the first place are complex, nonlinear, and inherently transnational. We see the *elevation* of these issues because the spread of both infectious diseases and NCDs is intimately connected to economic, political, and social issues operating at the international level. Because these issues operate at a higher level than the state, it can also be more opaque to understand how and where a government might intervene to improve the situation. Finally, the increasing degree of goods, services, and capital crossing international borders at an ever-increasingly rapid pace illustrates how globalization has fostered the *expansion* of issues—and how that expansion has had direct effects on global health.

Similarly, this chapter shows how globalization's effects on health raise issues for our traditional conceptions of sovereignty. While we traditionally think of sovereignty as a state's right to make its own policies and govern itself, health problems practically necessitate some sort of shared, collective response. That can complicate our ability to marshal an effective response to an infectious disease outbreak. At the same time, the economic and social changes that globalization has brought about have empowered a set of actors—multinational corporations—who have some ability to exist outside the control of a single sovereign state. If the US government wants to institute new rules that restrict KFC from opening new restaurants in Ghana in an effort to improve health in that country, what is to prevent KFC from simply moving its legal headquarters to another country that will not impose such restrictions? This, too, challenges our traditional understanding of the power dynamics at play in an international system that prioritizes Westphalian sovereignty—and we will see this conflict play out throughout our exploration of the relationship between globalization and health.

The first two chapters have focused on how health and globalization are linked to each other. The next chapters shift the analytical gaze, paying more attention to the systems and structures that operate in this globalized space. Globalization does not operate in a vacuum; it is supported and promoted by a web of international institutions, practices, and policies that gives it its unique contours. For all of the influence that these systems and structures can have on the health of people all around the world, these effects are not always the result of conscious decisions—and the fact that they matter for global health may be largely unanticipated. There is also the question of whether our international institutions and policies have kept up with the realities of the situations we face in our increasingly globalized world. Does the structure of the WHO still make sense today, especially when groups like the Bill & Melinda Gates Foundation spend almost the same amount on global health as the WHO each year? Has globalization made transnational health activism more effective, or do these movements get lost in the noise of the ever-increasing access to information? These are the sorts of questions that the next few chapters will address.

Chapter 3

Institutions and the Globalization of Health

If you are reading this book, there is a very good chance that you have spent at least a little bit of time in a library. You need access to information in order to pass your classes, so the university must find a way to help you with that. The university could just throw a whole bunch of books in a pile and encourage a *Lord of the Flies*–style competition to get the books you need, but most universities instead create and support libraries. Libraries are a key institution to making universities operate—and not just because librarians are amazing human beings. They make books, journals, and a variety of other material available. They facilitate the research that your professors do. They provide a space for groups to collaborate. They make it possible for you to borrow books for a specified period of time. They set up formal rules, policies, and procedures that facilitate your learning and give you a space for intellectual discovery.

Not all of the rules that make the library operate are written down, though. At my undergraduate college, it was an unwritten rule in Burling Library that the higher the floor you were on, the less noise was tolerated. You could speak with a normal voice on the first floor, and no one would bat an eye. On the fourth floor, though, you could expect to receive death glares if you turned a page too loudly. This was not an official college policy, but it was a widely shared expectation—and you could expect to deal with some consequences from your classmates if you violated it. Everyone knew how they should act, even if the "rules" were not written down anywhere. This practice is also an institution because it is part of a shared expectation that makes it possible for the library to work for students and for students to find the library a useful space.

It is this combination of formal and informal institutions that make social, political, and economic life happen—and that is just as true for international issues like globalization and health as it is for a college library. Globalization as currently practiced is supported by a wide variety of institutions, including international organizations like the World Trade Organization, conferences like the World Economic Forum, international financial institutions like the World Bank and International Monetary Fund, multinational corporations like Apple and Nestlé, and informal institutions like the dominant international economic norm of neoliberalism (Litonjua 2008).

Global health does not happen without formal and informal institutions, either. This chapter focuses on the institutions that facilitate the intersection between globalization and health. These institutions have, in some cases, emerged directly as a result of the recognition of how globalization alters how we conceptualize health and who is responsible for it. In other cases, institutions have struggled to adapt their structures and operational procedures to the current environment that the intersection of globalization and health present. It begins by defining two key terms—*institutions* and *global health governance*. After defining key terms, the chapter will focus on four key institutions in global health governance: the World Health Organization (WHO), the Bill & Melinda Gates Foundation (BMGF), the International Health Regulations (IHR), and development assistance for health (DAH). These four institutions represent a range of formal and informal global health institutions. WHO is a traditional intergovernmental organization with a distinct mandate to address cross-border health issues. BMGF is a philanthropic organization that has become a major player in global health thanks to its enormous wealth, but faces questions about its legitimacy and authority to act. The IHR is the leading international legal treaty addressing global health issues, and it combines legal requirements with normative suasion to shape the behavior of states and nonstate actors. Finally, DAH provides the money necessary to make this system operate and represents some of our collective ideas about addressing health issues in other countries. In all four cases, though, these institutions seek to decrease uncertainty in the political, economic, and social realm. They have different tools available to them, but they all aim to make cooperation on cross-border health issues possible.

DEFINING INSTITUTIONS

Institutions give social life meaning and structure—and this is particularly true at the international level. Institutions are "an expression of the element of collaboration among states in discharging their function—and at the same time a means of sustaining this collaboration" (Bull 1995: 71). March and Olsen describe institutions as an enduring collection of rules and practices that order life and are larger and more resilient than any single individual. They provide "constitutive rules and practices prescribing appropriate behavior for specific actors in specific circumstances" (March and Olsen 2006: 3). By establishing certain patterns of practice and expectations, they both reflect the norms that exist within international society and foster the relationships that make international life possible (Holsti 2004: 18–22).

These definitions point to one of the most important facts about institutions; namely, that both formal and informal institutions operate and exert unique influences within international relations. We often equate institutions with formal structures, and it is easy to think of how these formal institutions structure life. The Roman Catholic Church, the US Congress, and the United Nations (UN) are all examples of formal institutions because they are purposely created, operate according to written rules, and contain mechanisms to enforce their regulations. They have buildings and staffs. They make and enforce rules, and they operate with some degree of recognized or accepted legitimacy and authority. This gives international life a measure of order and predictability (March and Olsen 2006: 4).

These sorts of formal structures are not the only types of systems that give international life some order. Informal institutions are "socially shared rules, usually unwritten, that are created, communicated, and enforced outside of officially sanctioned channels" (Helmke and Levitsky 2004: 727). They are habits and practices whose existence help us to realize common goals, but they are not necessarily rooted in a specific formal organization (Bull 1995: 71). As such, they operate as "historically constructed normative structures" that can foster cooperation (Alderson and Hurrell 2000: 27). Norms would be types of informal institutions. A norm is "a standard of appropriate behavior for actors with a given identity" (Finnemore and Sikkink 1998: 891). Norms are not necessarily codified, and they lack formal enforcement mechanisms, but they still help to regulate how we act. Most of social life—whether we are talking about individuals or states—is guided by norms, and most international actors tend to follow norms most of the time (Cortell and Davis 2000). There is no law, for example, that wealthy states should provide foreign aid to developing countries, but this is something we expect—and something we notice when states fail to abide by this norm.

Clearly defining the various types of institutions is important for two reasons. First, it shows how and why a broad range of actors are involved in the intersection of health and globalization. The WHO, for example, may have a formal constitutional mandate to address cross-border health concerns, but that does not mean that it is the only institution involved in these issues—The World Bank, Médecins Sans Frontières, and BMGF are all incredibly important for understanding how the global health system operates. We need to understand these relationships in order to fully comprehend global health action (or inaction).

Second, so much of international cooperation on global health operates according to informal institutions and norms. There is very little international law that directly establishes rules about global health obligations and few formal mechanisms to punish noncompliant states. The WHO cannot send a government to jail if it does not contribute funds to address an international health outbreak. Despite these realities, we still see a relatively robust set of structures, organizations, and institutions that support global health and promote a vision of how contributing to global health is part of responsible international citizenship on the part of states (Youde 2018).

GLOBAL HEALTH GOVERNANCE

These different types of institutions come together to form the global health governance structures that facilitate global health action. Global health governance is "the use of formal and informal institutions, rules, and processes by which states, intergovernmental organizations, and nonstate actors to deal with challenges to health that require cross-border collective action to address effectively" (Fidler 2010: 3). It "integrates scientists, medical practitioners, philanthropists, governments, and international institutions with grandmothers in local communities and self-styled celebrity advocates" (Harman 2012: 2). While it is not a government and therefore lacks the power to impose its will on others, it provides a series of ideas, principles, and norms that most of the key actors accept most of the time—and the globalization narrative is central to how global health governance has evolved over time (McInnes and Lee 2012: 101).

Informal institutions play a prominent role within global health governance. Formal institutions can only do so much to alter the global health landscape. Lawrence Gostin, perhaps the world's most prominent scholar of global health law, admits, "Law has inherent limitations in its ability to solve the complex health challenges the world faces" (Gostin 2014: 71). He identifies three key reasons for international law's limitations in the globalization of health. First, global health governance lacks an explicit hierarchy. The WHO is incredibly prominent, but it is not necessarily "above" other organizations and cannot force them to do anything. Second, global health governance draws on a wide range of fields, including agriculture, development, human rights, the environment, and trade—to say nothing of public health, medicine, and laboratory science. Combining this diverse range of fields under a single legal framework proves nearly impossible. Finally, global health seeks to navigate a wide range of economic, social, and political crosscurrents. In trying to navigate all of these different realms, informal institutions can provide a degree of flexibility and open avenues for including a wide range of voices.

None of this is to say, of course, that formal institutions lack a role within global health governance. Informal institutions may provide some measure of flexibility and give a sense of order to much of the global health realm, but formal institutions obviously put much of global health governance into practice. They can organize responses to emergency situations, provide training, deploy resources, and maintain ongoing operations. Global health governance combines the operational heft of formal institutions with the normative imperatives of informal institutions in a variety of ways—and with varying degrees of success.

THE WORLD HEALTH ORGANIZATION

The WHO was established April 7, 1948, as one of the UN's specialized agencies with its headquarters in Geneva. When delegates assembled to create the UN, there was strong support for creating an organization to deal with international health. Under the terms of its constitution, the WHO's objective is "the attainment of by all peoples of the highest possible level of health" with a mandate to "act as the directing and coordinating authority on international health work" (WHO 1948: 2). Membership in the WHO is nearly universal. UN member-states join the WHO by accepting its Constitution in accordance with their domestic legal procedures. States that are not members of the United Nations can apply for membership and will be accepted with a majority vote in favor, and territories that do not have responsibility for conducting their own international relations can join as associate members. At the beginning of 2019, the WHO had 194 member-states—all of the UN members with the exception of Liechtenstein, and with the addition of the Cook Islands and Niue (WHO 2018b).

Organizationally, the WHO operates through four main structures. First, the World Health Assembly (WHA) is the annual meeting of all of the WHO members each May. This body adopts the WHO's budget and sets its agenda. Second, the Executive Board consists of thirty-four health experts selected from member-states for three-year terms who advise the WHA and implement its decisions. Third, the Secretariat oversees the organization's day-to-day operations. Heading the Secretariat is the director-general, who is elected for a five-year term (renewable once) to serve as the WHO's leader and public face. The director-general combines professional health expertise with political diplomacy in engaging world leaders on global health issues. Finally, six regional health organizations carry out much of WHO's programmatic work, but they retain a high degree of autonomy to implement their own programs. Each WHO member-state is also a member of one of the regional organizations. While the regional health organizations all possess programmatic autonomy, there are significant variations among them in terms of their leadership, funding, and power (Wenham 2017).

Only states can join the WHO, and the organization has struggled with how to engage with nonstate actors. Under the terms of the WHO Constitution, the Executive Board can enter into "official relations" with nongovernmental organizations, business associations, philanthropies, and other groups "that have had and continue to have a sustained and systematic engagement" with the WHO (WHO 2018d). These relationships give recognized nonstate actors the opportunity to participate in sessions of various WHO bodies and to make statements to those bodies when invited to do so. Groups accorded official status receive these rights for a renewable three-year term, but WHO can terminate this relationship earlier if it sees fit. While this model has provided an avenue for engagement between the WHO and nonstate actors, it does so wholly on the WHO's terms and has lacked transparency about how it chooses to engage with outside groups.

At the sixty-ninth WHA in 2016, the WHO adopted the Framework of Engagement with Non-State Actors (FENSA) as part of a deliberate strategy to collaborate with a wider array of actors through more transparent means. FENSA states that the WHO remains the coordinating authority on international health matters, but it recognizes that collaborating with nonstate actors can help it to implement its policies. Any sort of engagement needs to demonstrate a clear public health benefit, conform to the WHO's mandate, respect the WHO's membership structure, support an evidence-based approach to global public health, protect the WHO from any sort of undue influence, not sully the WHO's reputation for integrity, avoid conflicts of interest, and be based on transparency, accountability, and mutual respect (WHO 2016a). This was designed to move the interactions between the WHO and nonstate actors from mere participation to active collaboration (Rached and Ventura 2017: 2).

Putting these ideas into practice has proven far more difficult. Member-states generally supported FENSA when it passed in 2016, but a number of nonstate actors have raised concerns that the wording allows business and industry groups to gain undue influence over the WHO's messages on key health issues. FENSA does not distinguish between public and private sector groups, leading to fears that powerful private interests could take too large a role (Buse and Hawkes 2016: 446). In particular, critics worry about the prospect of regulatory capture by food, alcohol, pharmaceutical, and tobacco industries or that corporate actors would engage with the WHO solely as a means to improve their images (Khayatzadeh-Mahani, Ruckert, and Labonté 2017; Miller and Harkins 2010).

Despite its prominence, the WHO is not a wealthy organization. For the 2018/2019 biennium, the WHO's budget totals $4.42 billion. This represents a slight increase—about eighty million dollars—over its 2016/2017 budget (WHO 2017d: 5). This means that the annual budget for an intergovernmental organization that has a global constitutional mandate to coordinate and direct cross-border health efforts is roughly the same as what Americans spend annually on alkaline batteries (Statista 2018). As a result, the WHO is not a funding agency. Governments can turn to the WHO for technical assistance or advice on best practices with health care systems, but they generally need to look elsewhere for the cash to put those ideas into practice.

The WHO raises funds through two different sources, and this combination of funding plays a direct role in understanding its operations. The first funding source is its regular budgetary funds or assessed contributions. These are essentially membership dues, based on a formula that includes factors like population and size of the economy. The second funding source is extrabudgetary funds or voluntary contributions. States, nonstate actors, and individuals provide these funds to the WHO of their own free will.

These two streams of money are treated very differently. The WHO has total control over how it wishes to allocate its assessed contributions within its budget, but voluntary contributions are different. Most, though not all, voluntary contributions are tied to specific purposes or programs. As a result, the WHO does not have budgetary authority over how to allocate them; the donor makes those decisions. Over time, voluntary contributions have become a larger percentage of the WHO's overall budget. In 1970, voluntary contributions totaled 20 percent of its budget. The 1990/1991 biennium was the first budget where voluntary contributions made up more than half of the overall funding. For the 2006/2007 budget, the WHO got 72 percent of its funding from voluntary sources (Lee 2009: 39–41). The 2018/2019 budget continues the same trend. Assessed contributions will total $956.9 million, reflecting a 3 percent increase in annual dues. Voluntary contributions will total $3.465 billion (WHO 2017e: 7). Voluntary donations come from only a small group of donors, and this group includes nonstate actors. The top twenty sources of voluntary contributions are responsible for more than 80 percent of the total figure (Clift and Rottingen 2018).

The shift toward more voluntary contributions decreases the WHO's own degree of agency and control. Rather than letting the organization determine its priorities, the donors take the decision out of the WHO's hands, and donor priorities do not necessarily align with the WHO's priorities. It also provides an entry point for nonstate actors to exert a high degree of influence over the WHO. Nonstate actors cannot join the WHO, but they could use their donations to drive the WHO's agenda (Graham 2017: 18–19). In addition, this process confuses lines of responsibility for the WHO because it complicates the principal-agent relationship. In international organization theory, states (the principals) delegate certain responsibilities to an intergovernmental organization (the agent) because the organization has greater expertise or can devote attention to the issue that the principals cannot or are not interested in (Nielson and Tierney 2003: 245). This relationship gets increasingly complicated and confusing if there are multiple principals or if the principals do not all share the same perspective. If an organization has to satisfy a growing number of principals who have very direct control over its operations because of the funding structures, then the WHO loses autonomy while trying to balance potentially competing demands (Graham 2015). At a time when the WHO is expected to take on an increasing array of cross-border health issues because of globalization, its ability to operate is increasingly constrained, particularly if it does not enjoy a high reputation among its principals or it loses its claim to specialized and unique expertise. Health may be a more important issue on the global agenda, but that has not translated into greater freedom for the organization.

The funding structures complicate the WHO's ability to respond to crises. In early 2014, the first cases of Ebola were reported in Guinea, Liberia, and Sierra Leone. Not only was this the first time that we had seen an Ebola outbreak crossing national borders, but it was also occurring in states with weak health systems and no previous experience with Ebola. Those states turned to the WHO for help, but the WHO has neither operational reserves nor emergency funds. The director-general does have discretion to make minor adjustments to budgetary allocations determined by the WHA, but that only allows for a change of 5 percent. Because the WHO itself controls a relatively small portion of its budget, most of the programmatic and financial decisions conform to the demands of donors. Indeed, shortly before the Ebola outbreak, the WHA passed the WHO's 2014/2015 biennial budget, which included a seventy-two million dollar cut (7.9 percent) for infectious diseases and a $241 million cut (51.4 percent) for outbreak and crisis response (WHO 2014b: 8)—the very sorts of programs that would be important for responding to an Ebola outbreak, but ones that lost out because they did not accord with donors' programmatic priorities.

To facilitate quicker responses to outbreaks in the future, the WHO created an emergency reserve fund in 2015. The Contingency Fund for Emergencies holds up to one hundred million dollars to give the WHO the money necessary to mobilize an immediate response to disease outbreaks (Murphy 2015). Three years after its launch, the Contingency Fund for Emergencies had received just shy of sixty-one million dollars in contributions and distributed roughly fifty-two million dollars for responses to various health emergency situations. The initial outlays include money for Zika, yellow fever, Marburg virus, and humanitarian emergencies like the Rohingya crisis. The Contingency Fund for Emergencies is wholly funded through voluntary contributions, so its continued existence depends entirely upon the willingness of the WHO member-states and other contributors to give money for this purpose. In its first three years, Germany and the United Kingdom provided more than half of the Fund's total funding, and fourteen other countries (but no nonstate actors) contributed to the Fund, too (WHO 2018a). Long-time observers of the WHO like Laurie Garrett have argued that the Contingency Fund for Emergencies is potentially useful, but that its creation masks the larger problems about the WHO's lack of budgetary control. In order to make the WHO more effective, she argues, member-states have to be willing to increase—and pay—their annual assessed contributions (Garrett 2016). Additionally, if donors directed their voluntary contributions to the WHO's core budget, it would allow the organization to determine more of its budget and better reflect the WHO's priorities (Clift and Rottingen 2018).

In many ways, the problems bedeviling the WHO reflect larger concerns about the connections between globalization and health. As globalization increases the risk of an infectious disease outbreak spreading across national borders, the WHO's ability to respond quickly is increasingly important. We look to the WHO to do more, yet it struggles for the resources to carry out its remit. It is expected to take action in more places, but its states-based membership system means that traditional notions of Westphalian sovereignty prevail and raise questions about whether and when there may need to be shared sovereignty when domestic sovereignty fails to provide protection. Its place within global health governance is increasingly shared with non-state actors. The WHO is operating in a world that better recognizes the connections between health and globalization, but its underlying structure is still firmly rooted in a Westphalian system where member-states constrain its ability to act.

THE BILL & MELINDA GATES FOUNDATION

Before 2000, Bill Gates was primarily known as the cofounder of Microsoft and one of the original tech billionaires. When he stepped down as Microsoft chief executive officer in 2000, he announced he would devote his energies full-time to the BMGF. Building on smaller philanthropic organizations that he had established in the 1990s, BMGF has become a massive player in international development and global health. It is one of the largest funders of global health programs, and its wealth gives it a distinct influence over the global health agenda. At the same time, BMGF has faced serious questions over its legitimacy and authority to act internationally and in whose interests it is working.

BMGF is the world's wealthiest philanthropic organization. At the end of 2017, the foundation's endowment totaled $50.7 billion. That same year, it provided $4.7 billion in direct support to grantees—an increase of one hundred million dollars from the 2016 levels (BMGF n.d.). Much of its funding goes toward health-related initiatives. BMGF's Global Health program made $1.267 billion in grants in 2017. That was not the entirety of the foundation's global health support, though. Of the $1.776 billion in grants through BMGF's Global Development program, about two-thirds of the funds went toward health-related projects like polio eradication, vaccine delivery, family planning, nutrition, water and sanitation, and family planning (BMGF 2018).

Gates's involvement in philanthropy pre-dates the creation of BMGF, but his earlier efforts were fairly modest. He created the William H. Gates Foundation in 1995 with an endowment of ninety-four million dollars, and his father ran the organization out of a home office. In 1997, he created the Gates Library Foundation with an initial gift of two hundred million dollars to donate computer software to libraries. That same year, Ted Turner, the American media mogul who had pledged one billion dollars to the United Nations, chastised Gates for not donating more of his vast wealth to charitable causes (McGoey 2015: 116–17). Around the same time, Gates reportedly read a story in *The New York Times* about 3.1 million people, most of them children, dying of diarrheal diseases annually (Kristof 1997). Gates clipped the story out of the paper and passed it along to his father with a note, "Dad, maybe we can do something about this" (Desmond-Hellman 2015). That newspaper story started the process that put global health at the heart of the world's wealthiest philanthropy.

BMGF's wealth comes from two sources: Bill and Melinda Gates, and Warren Buffett. When Gates merged two of his earlier philanthropies together in 2000 to create BMGF, he also committed sixteen billion dollars of his wealth to support the new organization (McGoey 2015: 117). Warren Buffett came into the picture in 2006. At the time, he was the second-wealthiest person in the United States with an estimated net worth of forty-six billion dollars. On June 26, 2006, Buffett announced that he would give thirty-one billion dollars in Berkshire Hathaway stock to BMGF through a series of annual contributions. Buffett's donation came with the stipulation that his funds must be used to increase the foundation's grant-making capabilities. As a result, Buffett's donation doubled BMGF's annual philanthropic outlays (O'Brien and Saul 2006).

BMGF's financial contribution to global health is incredible. By 2015, the foundation had contributed $32.9 billion for disease prevention, immunization, and vaccination (Mathiesen 2015). In 2000, it pledged fifty million dollars over five years in conjunction with Merck Foundation to work with the government of Botswana to create a program to provide HIV-positive persons with antiretroviral drugs (ARVs) (Patterson 2018: 45). It has been a major funder of the Global Polio

Eradication Initiative, and it is among the leading funders of malaria and tuberculosis research. Its involvement with anti-malaria programs has led to a 25 percent decrease in malaria cases and a 42 percent drop in malaria deaths between 2004 and 2016 (Osterholm and Olshaker 2018: 101–02). Beyond its direct financial support, BMGF has spurred national governments to give more for global health. Peter Piot, the former director of the Joint United Nations Program on HIV/AIDS, credits BMGF for effectively shaming donor states into giving more for global health (Piot 2015: 65). BMGF has also succeeded in bringing additional philanthropic resources to global health issues, with the foundation and former New York mayor Michael Bloomberg jointly pledging five hundred million dollars to bolster anti-tobacco efforts in developing countries (Ledford 2008).

BMGF's funding also supports other global health governance institutions. Between 2000 and 2017, it has been one of WHO's largest sources of voluntary contributions at more than $2.4 billion (Huet and Paun 2017). It has pledged $1.6 billion to the Global Fund to Fight AIDS, Tuberculosis, and Malaria since its founding, pledging up to six hundred million dollars for the 2017 to 2019 period alone (Global Fund to Fight AIDS, Tuberculosis, and Malaria n.d.). It has also contributed $1.5 billion to Gavi: The Vaccine Partnership, an international partnership focused on developing and distributing vaccines in developing countries (Youde 2016: 210).

Gates and BMGF argue that they can bring unique insights to global health by drawing on their business and technical expertise. They also assert that they can be more adaptable and flexible in responding to changing needs precisely because they are not beholden to shareholders or voters. This includes being able to invest in global health priorities in which states are unwilling or unable to invest like research and development on treatments for neglected diseases (McCoy and McGoey 2011: 143–44). The foundation has historically not invested in health systems strengthening because it considers that a core responsibility of governments (Hafner and Shiffman 2013: 46), but it has signaled in recent years that it is more willing to get involved in this area (BMGF 2017). BMGF portrays itself as a partner to, rather than a replacement for, national governments. BMGF's operations in India illustrate how the foundation approaches its work and how it relates to governments (Mahajan 2018). When BMGF first started working in India in 2002, its energies were focused almost entirely on HIV/AIDS. It provided two hundred million dollars—its largest HIV/AIDS investment in a single country—to start an HIV/AIDS initiative, Avahan. Avahan stood out not just for the amount of money it had, but also for its disinterest in working with the national government or existing funding systems. Over time, though, BMGF began to engage more with the national government as part of a strategy to transition Avahan's programs to the government and to a broader mandate that focused on broader structural determinants of health. The organization's financial largesse may give it outsized attention and force others to pay attention to it, but it has gradually come to recognize the central role of national and local governments in implementing long-lasting health programs.

As BMGF's prominence in global health has grown, it has attracted increasing scrutiny from critics for at least four reasons. First, critics charge that BMGF focuses too much on technical interventions and pays too little attention to social determinants of health. Not only will these technical innovations be unworkable if they do not address these underlying factors, but a failure to consider the underlying social conditions means that the true drivers of ill health go unaddressed (Packard 2016: 269–70). Second, critics allege BMGF's money allows it to crowd out other voices and gives disproportionate influence to its priorities—regardless of whether those align with governments' health priorities (Youde 2013b: 151). Third, critics argue that BMGF has tended to focus on disease-specific programs, which can distort the global health landscape. Broad-based health programs make states more resilient and able to respond to emergencies, but they receive too little attention or funding (Clinton and Sridhar 2017: 77–81). As a result, we get a bunch of individual programs that do not speak to one another or share resources, and it creates a more complicated system for people to navigate. Finally, critics worry BMGF operates outside of traditional lines of authority and legitimacy. The foundation is accorded a degree of deference and flexibility to operate based on Gates's charismatic authority and wealth. This is a significant departure from our general understanding of why certain actors should have policy influence within the international system, such as receiving a popular mandate (Harman 2016). If we do not like the policy priorities of the WHO, we theoretically have the ability to work through our government to influence those policies. If we have concerns about BMGF's priorities, we have no recourse.

The mere fact that a private philanthropic organization like BMGF can play such a prominent and determinative role in global health reflects how globalization has altered the economic, social, and political dynamics. BMGF can elevate and intensify global health precisely because its founders were able to grow wealthy through the exchange of goods and services in a globalized marketplace.

THE INTERNATIONAL HEALTH REGULATIONS

The IHR are binding international agreements among all WHO member-states that address governments' obligations to address infectious disease outbreaks. They provide for "the management of the global regime for the control of the international spread of disease" (WHO 2016b: 1). They also underpin much of the framework for disease surveillance systems.

The IHR play a central role in trying to strike a balance between health and globalization. On the one hand, they reflect and respond to the ways in which the increased movement of goods and people across borders heightens the potential for diseases to spread. Indeed, the whole movement to create what we know today as the IHR came out of nineteenth-century fears about the relationship between commerce and the spread of disease. On the other hand, the IHR explicitly state that disease protection measures should not interrupt or unduly burden international commerce. The very thing that drives the fears about disease is privileged over public health, human rights, or any other consideration.

Increased trade ties during the first half of the nineteenth century made countries with strong export economies wealthy. These same trade ties also increased the threat of diseases like cholera. Today, we know that cholera spreads via bacteria in infected food, water, and bodily waste. In the nineteenth century, people only knew that cholera had a high mortality rate, could kill in as little as eighteen hours, and seemed to follow trade routes.

To stop the spread of cholera, many states instinctively fell back on quarantines at border crossings and ports (Harrison 2012: 66–67).

Quarantine is a system of separating and restricting the movement of people and goods who *may* be carrying an infectious disease to see whether they become sick. This is distinct from isolation, which separates sick people from the general population. The idea is that this separation period would allow an illness to run its course without putting the larger community at risk. The term "quarantine" comes from the Italian word "quaranta," which means forty—the number of days that goods and people had to be held in isolation. Quarantine was introduced in the late fourteenth century, and its efficacy was questionable. It was applied haphazardly, and governments often targeted disfavored groups (particularly foreigners and Jews) because they assumed that they were inherently diseased (Edelson 2003). Economically, holding people and goods offshore or in isolation for more than a month severely interrupted trade flows as international trade was becoming increasingly important. Governments would engage in tit-for-tat responses to quarantine policies, making quarantine's application even more inconsistent. This encouraged governments to start negotiations for international standards about the use of isolation and quarantine—a process that eventually gave rise to today's IHR.

In 1851, delegates from twelve European governments met in Paris at the first International Sanitary Conference to create a convention to address diseases "reputed to be importable" (Goodman 1971: 46). The attendees created an agreement, but only three governments ratified it—and two of those withdrew from the convention shortly thereafter. It took six more conferences over the next four decades to finally reach any sort of agreement. The first agreement successfully negotiated, the International Sanitary Convention of 1892, focused solely on quarantine and inspection measures for ships passing through the Suez Canal for the annual *hajj* to Mecca, but it established a basis for cooperation on cross-border health issues related to the movement of people and goods (Howard-Jones 1975: 45). Over the years, later International Sanitary Conferences negotiated additional agreements among the participants. In 1951, the WHA combined twelve different international treaties into a single document—the International Sanitary Regulations (ISR) (Youde 2012b: 118).

The ISR set out a series of requirements for governments about identifying, notifying, and preventing the spread of infectious disease. Specifically, the regulations identified six "notifiable" diseases whose spread was directly linked with the movement of people and goods: cholera, plague, relapsing fever, smallpox, typhus, and yellow fever. States were obligated to screen for these diseases at ports of entry, and they had to inform the WHO of any human cases of these diseases. In 1969, the ISR removed typhus and relapsing fever from the list of notifiable diseases after they were deemed to no longer pose an international threat, and the ISR were renamed the IHR (Taylor 1997). After smallpox's eradication, the IHR only applied to three diseases, and critics described the IHR as out of touch with the changing infectious disease threats. The IHR said nothing about newly discovered diseases like HIV/AIDS, and globalization was making it easier for diseases to spread across borders with increasing speed (Brower and Chalk 2003: 14–16). Furthermore, because the WHO had no power to take action against states that failed to live up to their IHR obligations, states could avoid compliance without facing any sanctions (Gostin 2014: 181). Globalization's economic, political, and social changes heightened human infectious disease threats, but the only international legal treaty addressing the spread of infectious diseases was irrelevant to these new challenges.

The push to update the IHR began in the 1990s. In 1992, the US Institute of Medicine issued a report, *Emerging Infections: Microbial Threats to Health in the United States*, that emphasized the need for robust, sustained, and internationally coordinated disease surveillance. Two years later, the WHO convened a meeting to create a proactive international disease surveillance system with the IHR as its foundation (Davies, Kamradt-Scott, and Rushton 2015: 22–23). The early negotiations crystallized around a new framework for empowering groups like the WHO in mediating the intersection of health and globalization: "the vision being promoted of a new global health security regime was not predicated on old-fashioned quarantine measures but on new networks of information sharing and capacity building to enable the containment of outbreaks *prior* to their international spread" (Davies, Kamradt-Scott, and Rushton 2015: 30; emphasis in the original). Over nearly a decade of negotiations, and after witnessing the WHO's highly effective response to SARS, a new IHR that could accommodate globalization came into focus. At the 2005 WHA, the delegates unanimously approved the new IHR (also referred to as IHR [2005]) with effect from 2007.

The new IHR balances a variety of different goals that address health and globalization. First, IHR (2005) employs an "all-risks" approach. Rather than naming specific diseases that must be reported, the new system focused on the likelihood of an outbreak spreading internationally and its potential economic, social, and political effects (Youde 2015: 62–63). Second, the new IHR explicitly allows nonstate actors to report outbreaks to the WHO, and it lets the WHO take action based on those reports. This makes it significantly harder for governments to cover up outbreaks and allows for an earlier response to potential epidemics (Davies 2015: 229–31). Third, the new IHR gives the WHO the power to name and shame countries that fail to cooperate (Kamradt-Scott and Rushton 2012). No government would want to lose face by being called out for ignoring an infectious disease outbreak. Fourth, the new IHR requires all states to develop and sustain a robust disease surveillance system that can report any discoveries to the WHO within 24 hours (Davies, Kamradt-Scott, and Rushton 2015: 58–60). Because outbreaks are inherently unpredictable, these surveillance systems must always be ready—and able to spot any potential problem, not just previously known diseases. Finally, IHR (2005) creates a new power for the WHO—the power to declare a Public Health Emergency of International Concern (PHEIC). A PHEIC is "an extraordinary event that could spread internationally or might require a coordinated international response" (Heymann and West 2015: 101). When the WHO declares a PHEIC, it elevates that issue on the global health agenda and focuses attention.

All of these changes reflect how globalization has altered how international society conceptualizes and responds to health challenges. The move to an "all-risks" approach recognizes that new pathogens are emerging and that previously known diseases are popping up in new areas. As globalization brings new threats to human health, the IHR must be adaptable enough to address them. By bringing nonstate actors into the reporting processes, the new IHR tacitly recognize that states no longer have a monopoly on power or information. Similarly, the power to name and shame recalcitrant states signals that information can flow around and outside of official channels. The WHO essentially employs a carrot-and-stick approach to disease reporting; it tells states that it will get this information one way or another, so it is in the state's best interest to make the reports directly itself. The surveillance requirements—and the fact that they are not limited solely to border crossings and ports of entry and exit—show how quickly diseases can spread in a globalized age. If and when the WHO declares a PHEIC, it concentrates international attention where state and nonstate actors should focus their resources and energies.

The changes to the IHR reflect shifting international norms about disease surveillance. They are the outgrowth of ideas that have been circulating over the previous twenty years (Davies, Kamradt-Scott, and Rushton 2015). None of this is to say that the new IHR are perfect. The treaty mandates that all states develop these robust disease surveillance systems that are always working, but it provides no funding for states to implement such systems. Countries that already face challenges in maintaining their health care systems may not have the resources for surveillance systems—or they may prefer to spend their limited health care resources on other, more directly relevant issues (Stevenson and Moran 2015: 329–33). Critics argue that this reality proves that the IHR actually prioritize the health anxieties of the Global North and its fear that diseases from the Global South will spread across borders (Weir 2015). Governments in the Global North recognize how globalization could increase their vulnerability to infectious disease outbreaks, but it has not led to a shared sense of health solidarity with the Global South.

DEVELOPMENT ASSISTANCE FOR HEALTH

The international community has undergone a radical shift in its views on its collective obligations to address health in low- and middle-income countries over the course of a single generation. This shift toward accepting the need to respond to global health concerns is rhetorical, behavioral, and financial—and has thus far sustained itself even in the face of austerity policies. This change is reflected in the increases for DAH that have occurred since 1990. The dramatic increase in global funding for cross-border health issues has enabled support for a wide array of programs that would not have otherwise happened, and it has improved the lives of many people around the world. The changes are by no means perfect, but the increased levels of DAH have undeniably improved health outcomes.

States still play the dominant role in funding their own health programs. Total spending on health worldwide in 2015 reached an estimated $9.7 trillion. Of that total, approximately 60 percent of it was financed through government sources, 22 percent came from out-of-pocket spending, 18 percent was from private insurance, and 0.5 percent was from donors (Institute for Health Metrics and Evaluation [IHME] 2018: 16). Donor support is particularly important for countries with lower per capita gross domestic products, but national governments still play the dominant role in financing health programs. This remains true even in the aftermath of Structural Adjustment Programs that forced governments in low- and middle-income states to cut their spending on social services like health and shift more of the payment burden on to individuals (Gros 2016: 100–01).

To assess the changes in DAH, we can draw on the IHME's accounting framework. As a side note, it is worth mentioning that IHME is connected to the University of Washington, but receives significant funding from BMGF. In 2017, BMGF pledged $279 million to the University of Washington for IHME, the largest private donation in the university's history (University of Washington 2017). Both BMGF and IHME share a keen focus on data-driven decision-making and developing measurable indicators (Reubi 2018: 103).

IHME's DAH data are unique because they include both public and private sources of funding since 1990. The institute also reports its figures in inflation-adjusted terms to allow for direct comparison between different years and different types of funders. In 1990, global DAH totaled $7.56 billion (in 2017 US dollars). In 1998, total DAH crossed the ten-billion-dollar threshold, reaching $10.4 billion (in 2017 US dollars). The following year was the first time that BMGF made a significant investment in DAH, contributing $120 million out of a worldwide total of $11.08 billion (in 2017 US dollars). In 2005, total DAH went above twenty billion dollars for the first time ($21.04 billion in 2017 US dollars). Three years later, the figure hit $30.68 billion (in 2017 US dollars), the first time it went higher than thirty billion dollars. In 2013, DAH went beyond forty billion dollars for the first and only time so far—$40.15 billion in 2017 US dollars. Between 2014 and 2017, DAH hovered around thirty-six billion to thirty-seven billion dollars. Throughout this period, the US government has been the largest funder of DAH, giving roughly one-third of the total. The United Kingdom is generally the second-largest DAH funder, and BMGF has ranked third or fourth every year since 2007 (IHME 2018: 112–13). In addition to the overall increase in DAH, health is becoming a larger portion of foreign aid overall. While overseas development aid fell overall between 1992 and 2000, DAH continued to increase in dollar terms and as a percentage of total aid (Grépin et al. 2012).

We can divide DAH funding into roughly three phases. During the first phase, from 1990 to 2000, DAH experienced moderate growth each year, increasing by an annualized average rate of 4.9 percent. In the second phase, between 2001 and 2010, DAH increased dramatically with an average annualized funding increase of 11.4 percent. During the third phase, which began in 2011 and continues to this day, DAH has remained relatively flat with an average annualized increase of less than 2 percent (IHME 2017: 20). When the global financial crisis hit, there was a strong fear among many global health observers that DAH would suffer irreparable harm because of austerity policies in donor states and reductions in foreign assistance. IHME even asked in its 2013 DAH report whether we were witnessing "the end of the golden age" (IHME 2013).

Instead, the most pessimistic predictions have largely failed to materialize. DAH growth is certainly down, but global health funding has not collapsed. Part of the reason for the robustness of funding is that the range of funders has expanded. Initially, DAH was almost entirely the realm of national governments. In 1990, more than 80 percent of all DAH came from national governments. Since 2000, though, private foundations and nongovernmental organizations have become increasingly important and have contributed at least 20 percent of the global total annually. While BMGF makes up a large portion of this increase, it is far from the only nonstate actor providing DAH. Consumer-facing campaigns like (RED) funnel money from the sales of specially branded consumer goods to the Global Fund to Fight AIDS, Tuberculosis, and Malaria to purchase ARVs for people living with HIV in low-income countries (Richey and Ponte 2011; Youde 2009a). These changes reflect the expanding range of actors prioritizing global health.

DAH faces its own limitations and criticisms. Maintaining DAH at a relatively constant level actually leads to decreases in the number of people who can access programs. For example, a good deal of DAH funding has gone toward providing ARVs in low-income countries. While the cost of these drugs has come down dramatically, they still remain too expensive for many people in poorer countries to obtain them on their own. Once a person starts taking ARVs to keep HIV in check, they must continue to take them for the rest of their lives. At the same time, WHO guidelines recommend that people start taking ARVs as soon as they are diagnosed with HIV, increasing the number of people who need access to them. If DAH funding for ARVs remains constant, that means there is little to no money for new people to access these drugs. Furthermore, because people need to stay on these drugs for the rest of their lives, the expense goes up every year just to cover those already receiving ARVs. As a result, constant funding effectively decreases the availability of these drugs.

Donor states' DAH priorities are also not in line with the global burden of disease. Between 1990 and 2017, HIV/AIDS received $141 billion in DAH funds—nearly one-quarter of all DAH. Malaria, other infectious diseases, and tuberculosis collectively received $69.3 billion, or 12 percent of DAH. Noncommunicable diseases come in even lower, with a total of $9.57 billion of DAH (IHME 2018: 45). These funding levels do not necessarily match the need. An estimated 36.9 million people were living with HIV at the end of 2017, which includes 1.8 million new HIV infections during 2016, and AIDS killed approximately one million people in 2017 (Joint United Nations Program on HIV/AIDS 2018). During the same year, there were 10.6 million new tuberculosis cases causing more than 1.7 million deaths. This makes tuberculosis one of the ten leading causes of death worldwide (WHO 2018f). Malaria caused even more illness, with more than 216 million cases of the disease and nearly half a million deaths (WHO 2017f). Noncommunicable diseases killed roughly forty million people in 2016. The mismatch between the number of cases of an illness and the amount of funding from donors shows that disease burden does not drive financing decisions. Instead, the global health agenda—and the funding decisions that result from it—are socially constructed and largely reflect the interests, priorities, and fears of donor states (Shiffman 2009). The dominance of HIV/AIDS funding may also crowd out funding for other health issues, though the effects may be somewhat mitigated by the overall increase in DAH (Shiffman 2008).

Relatedly, most DAH funding goes for disease-specific programs. Known as vertical interventions, these sorts of programs risk duplicating services and generally do not strengthen health care systems more broadly. They focus solely on a single issue. This is a problem, because a disease-specific program may be ill-equipped to respond or adapt to a different sort of disease outbreak. These vertical interventions often operate largely independently of each other, thus undermining more holistic efforts (Leon 2015: 14–17). They can also create a sort of therapeutic citizenship, whereby people get access to certain programs solely on the basis of their health status (Nguyen 2010). Benton (2015) recounts how some people in Sierra Leone would misrepresent their HIV status because HIV-positive people received access to food and nutrition programs that were not available to the general population. By contrast, horizontal interventions are more broadly focused and seek to strengthen health systems as a whole. If a vertical intervention may develop a set of programs specifically related to malaria, a horizontal intervention promotes the generalized ability of health care clinics to respond and adapt to a widening range of health issues that may present themselves. Vertical interventions, critics charge, operate largely outside and often hire away staff from existing health care structures. Horizontal interventions, by contrast, by their very nature work within a country's health care system and align with that country's priorities (England 2007; Garrett 2007). Despite these arguments, health systems strengthening is not a major emphasis area for DAH. Health systems strengthening received $4.24 billion (in 2017 US dollars) in 2017—only 11 percent of total DAH. Indeed, between 1990 and 2017, health systems strengthening has received a decreasing percentage of DAH (IHME 2018: 124–25). Donors may be less inclined toward horizontal interventions because they are longer-term processes that may be harder to monitor, evaluate, and quantify. They may also consider health systems strengthening to be the domain of national governments rather than the international community as a whole. Regardless, donors do not prioritize an issue area in global health that would make states broadly resilient to a wider range of health issues.

The changes in DAH reflect the broader dynamics of globalization. The economic, political, and social changes wrought by globalization mean that states see a compelling reason to take an active role in trying to prevent and mitigate health problems outside of their own borders. DAH is essentially a chance for donors to put their money where their mouth is; if they are going to *say* that global health is important, they can *show* how important they consider it by funding global health programs around the world. The fact that an increasing array of states and nonstate actors are putting their money into DAH also reflects how global health has moved up the international political agenda and become intertwined with other important issues.

CONCLUSION

The institutions of global health governance reflect the shifting relationship between health and globalization over time. The first movements toward harmonizing health policies among states were direct outgrowths of the emerging importance of cross-border trade and the recognition of how the spread of disease could impede commercial interests. This helped give rise to what we now know as the IHR, and it fostered the creation of intergovernmental organizations that eventually turned into today's WHO. More recently, DAH has come to play a growing role within the larger universe of foreign aid, and nonstate actors like the BMGF emerged to share power with the traditional state-based actors working in the global health realm.

These changes reflect the economic, political, and social changes brought about through globalization. Economically, globalization has encouraged the increased movement of goods and peoples across borders—but these border crossings come at the potential expense of bringing diseases into new environments. Politically, globalization has opened up spaces in which nonstate actors, which have generally not been accorded legitimacy and authority within a framework of Westphalian sovereignty, can play some role. Socially, there is a willingness to accept some of these trade-offs and to consider how to strike the appropriate balance.

If we consider the five key elements of globalization, we see clear evidence of how the global health governance system is an extension of the changes brought about through globalization. The movement of goods and peoples across borders has *intensified* the issue and forced international society to craft some way to regulate these systems. Health has become more *integrated* with other issues as the cross-border connections broaden and deepen. The expansion of actors involved in global health governance is a key reflection of the *deterritorialization* of health and globalization. The increased attention, money, and institutional gravitas associated with global health demonstrates how the issue has been *elevated* on the political agenda. Finally, as global health governance has continued to develop, it has *expanded* to include more actors and intersect with more issues.

The four institutions profiled in this chapter help illustrate the range of organizations at play in the globalization of health—and international relations more broadly. Some of the institutions are formal and concrete with rules and governmental processes, like the WHO. Informal organizations, on the other hand, are based more on some sort of shared understanding—like the idea that it is a good idea for wealthy states to provide money for health programs in low- and middle-income countries. National governments play an important role in how these global health governance institutions operate, but global health governance does not rely solely on states. There are international treaties to help shape our expectations of how governments should act when health emergencies arise, but the ability to enforce those rules varies widely. Institutions outside of the state also raise questions about sovereignty and what it means in the modern context when dealing with issues that transcend national borders.

The next chapter moves more toward the individual level to examine what happens when people come together to agitate for change. Transnational activism has played an important role in global health. Activists have often sought to use globalization to their advantage, building linkages among people scattered around the world to call attention to how globalization's impulses undermine people's ability to lead healthy lives.

CHAPTER 4

TRANSNATIONAL ACTIVISM FOR HEALTH

When someone gets off an airplane after a long international flight, they are usually interested in finding their luggage, freshening up, and grabbing some coffee. For one passenger getting off a flight from Thailand at Johannesburg's Oliver Tambo International Airport in October 2000, his first priority was to engage in transnational health activism. Zackie Achmat, the leader of South Africa's Treatment Action Campaign (TAC) and one of the world's most prominent activists on access to antiretroviral drugs (ARVs) for persons living with HIV, was smuggling drugs into the country by illegally importing five thousand doses of Biozole. Biozole is a bioequivalent version of fluconazole, a drug patented by Pfizer and marketed as Diflucan. Fluconazole is an antifungal drug to treat cryptococcal meningitis, an opportunistic infection common in people whose immune systems are weakened by HIV and is fatal unless treated quickly. At the time, a single dose of Diflucan in South Africa cost one hundred rand, or about fourteen dollars. In Thailand, the exact same dose of Biozole was roughly 1.65 rand, or less than twenty-five cents. Because Biozole and Diflucan are bioequivalent, they are for all intents and purposes the same drug. By entering the country with five thousand doses that he purchased over the counter in Thailand, Achmat violated Pfizer's intellectual property rights (IPRs), illegally imported the drug, and broke South African law (Mathiason 2001). For illegally importing Biozole, Achmat risked a ten-year prison sentence and a fine of forty thousand rand (just under fifty-eight hundred dollars) (Baleta 2000).

Why is the price for the same drug so wildly different between South Africa and Thailand? Thailand had issued a compulsory license for fluconazole, allowing generic pharmaceutical manufacturers in the country to make their own version of the drug without worrying about Pfizer's patent. The South African government, by contrast, only authorized Diflucan for sale in the country and did not allow for generic versions—even though it had the largest number of persons living with HIV of any country and an adult HIV prevalence rate of around 20 percent. Drawing on TAC's international network of supporters, Achmat purposefully broke the law to call attention to the lack of access to drugs for AIDS in South Africa and the international economic structures that allowed for such inequities.

International trade law may not seem like the most glamorous issue, but it has inspired transnational coalitions of activists to rally around Achmat and the larger cause of increasing access to pharmaceuticals. Activists have sought to embarrass pharmaceutical manufacturers in the court of public opinion and challenged them to enter into negotiations with African states. They have drawn inspiration from earlier success stories, like the Brazilian activists who pressured the World Bank to give their government a loan to make AIDS drugs free for all who needed them (Berkman et al. 2005). They have harnessed the power of globalization to keep activists in distant lands in constant connection with one another and put pressure on businesses and governments. They have made what could have been a local issue about medicines policy in one state into a global issue.

This chapter begins by analyzing the interplay between transnational activism and globalization. While globalization opens a number of opportunities for cross-border collaboration, there is also strong evidence that effective activist movements need to remain cognizant of local interests, needs, and perceptions. It then briefly looks at three case studies of transnational heath activism—the global HIV/AIDS movement, the push for increased access to pharmaceuticals in the Global South, and the ongoing efforts to implement a sugar tax to address the rise of noncommunicable diseases (NCDs).

TRANSNATIONAL ACTIVISM AND GLOBALIZATION

Globalization has changed activism. It is not simply the speed and ease of communication or the ability to deploy activists internationally at a moment's notice that changes transnational activism in the contemporary context. Globalization has altered the international institutional context in which activism occurs (Klotz 2002: 50–51). Activists have more potential venues for their activity, and they have an increasing array of tactics that they can deploy. While the proliferation of targets may mean it is more difficult to identify a single key target for any action, the expansion can allow activists to apply pressure against a wider range of targets. This gives even more groups an opportunity to get involved in a way that they hope will be productive. At the same time, the proliferation of groups can complicate efforts to build coordinated strategies.

Activist groups have harnessed globalization to further their causes and build alliances across borders. Hintjens stresses, "The core aims of many global social movements are remarkably similar, centered on those who feel excluded from the mainstream and from the solidarities and privileges reserved for the few" (Hintjens 2009: 370). Bennett (2003) emphasizes how the internet not only reduces communication costs for transnational activism, but also facilitates the creation of loosely structured networks. He cautions that these qualities could make movements vulnerable to capture by external forces, but they can also foment the transformation of individual organizations and entire networks into something even more powerful. Basu (2000) shows how transnational activism can benefit women's movements as complement to, rather than a replacement for, local activism. In this way, a globalized activist approach augments existing local interests rather than trying to create their own movements. Globalization may increase interdependence, but it does not erase the considerations of the local. Evans

shows how marginalized groups can use the systems created by globalization in order to counter their own marginalization and challenge
the dominant political, economic, and social systems. They can "shift
power by connecting disprivileged Third World groups and communities to political actors and arenas that can affect decisions in hegemonic
global networks" (Evans 2000: 231). Ahmed (2009) connects the rapid
increase in the number of nongovernmental organizations (NGOs) operating worldwide to the opportunities afforded by globalization. These
sorts of groups can find a variety of ways to engage in activism, from
educating the public and applying direct political pressure on government decision-makers to engaging in monitoring activities and calling
attention to policy failures or successes.

Globalization's deterritorializing impulses mixed with the continued presence of borders play a unique role in transnational activism.
Globalization can alter the balance between connections to people
in distant lands and those in our own community. Entrena worries,
"Ease of communication tends to make us forget what is going on
our doorstep and turns our attention to what is going on thousands
of kilometers away. We are becoming more and more linked to what
is distant and alien, and more and more detached from what is near
and familiar" (Entrena 2002: 221). Borders may, in some instances,
give governments some degree of license to ignore or minimize
transnational movements because political leaders might dismiss the
actions as being the work of outside agitators trying to advance their
own agendas. At the same time, though, the presence of "transla-
tors"—people who can bridge different movements or bring various
communities together around a common issue—can helpfully "clarify
what unites and separates the different movements and practices so as
to ascertain the possibilities and limits of articulation and aggregation
among them" (Santos 2004: 182).

Globalization does not necessarily make transnational activism
easier. Tarrow and Tilly, two leading scholars of social movements and
contentious politics, identify four factors that may limit globalization's
effect on transnational activism. First, they caution that economic interdependence is not necessarily the best predictor of whether activists
from different states connect. Instead, domestic political conditions and
engagement with international institutions seem to be better predictions of these sorts of cross-national ties. Second, while globalization

may lead to homogenization in some respects, there remain significant cultural gaps and differences in values among peoples in different states—to say nothing of the transaction costs that go along with organizing across borders. Third, they worry that transnational activism could morph into more destructive forms. There is no inherent reason why transnational activism will necessarily operate in productive ways. The same notions that propel globalization could provoke populist, nationalist backlashes. Finally, there remains the unsettled question of the role of states amid globalization. Globalization's effects on economic, social, and political capacity vary widely across the range of states. As a result, we need to consider how globalization affects the interplay between the domestic and the international—and not assume that this happens uniformly (Tarrow and Tilly 2007: 456).

One of the key roles that transnational activist movements can play is in framing issues in ways that resonate with governments and publics. A frame is "the decision-maker's conception of the acts, outcomes, and contingencies associated with a particular choice. The frame that a decision-maker adopts is controlled partly by the norms, habits, and personal characteristics of the decision-maker" (Tversky and Kahneman 1981: 453). Framing can have a big effect on the public and on policymakers because people often have different reactions to different descriptions of the exact same issue or problem (Frisch 1993).

To think about the effects of framing, consider the lowly Patagonian toothfish. When fishing boats first started to catch the fish commercially in the late 1970s, there was no market for it. The name did not inspire much interest among restaurants, chefs, or food manufacturers. In 1977, though, a fish wholesaler named Lee Lantz rechristened it as the Chilean sea bass. The name was far more appealing and gave the fish a new image—and it suddenly became a trendy item on restaurant menus and in grocery stores around the world (Knecht 2006). Absolutely nothing about the fish itself was different; Lantz simply reframed the fish's image to put it in a more attractive light—and that name change had a dramatic effect on chefs, the food industry, and the public. In the political realm, we can see similar effects. Governments and activist groups use frames to condition how policymakers and the public will respond to an issue. If an activist group is going to be successful, they need to get us to understand the issue in a way that they see as advantageous and useful. This is exactly why environmental groups are more likely to emphasize the loss of habitat for pandas—a cuddly, playful, and cute animal—than for a spider or a salamander.

In the political realm, frames serve four different functions. First, they define an issue as a problem. They try to make us think that something is wrong and should be fixed. Second, they highlight who or what is to blame for the problem. It is not just that something is wrong; there needs to be someone or something responsible for that situation being wrong. Third, they suggest a solution. Rather than sending us into despair, frames want us to think that we can remedy the identified problem. Finally, frames invoke a moral appeal. They try to connect to our underlying beliefs to motivate us to join with others to take action to right this wrong (Dardis 2007). Frames draw on facts, but they go further to encourage us to understand those facts in a particular way. They also simplify the world around us, making it easier for us to understand complex issues (Nelson 2011). Understanding the nuances of global trade regulation, agricultural subsidies, and advertising regulations around the world may make it hard to understand why smoking rates have increased in the Global South, but frames can make it easier for us to understand why that has happened.

A frame cannot in and of itself change public policy. That frame must resonate with people, so we need to pay attention to the audience for a frame. Frame alignment—"the linkage of individual and [social movement organization] interpretive orientations, such that some set of individual interests, values, and beliefs and [social movement organization] activities, goals, and ideology are congruent and complementary" (Snow et al. 1986: 464)—is a necessary precondition for social movement activism to occur. People may share a common grievance, but it will not motivate action unless those people also share an understanding or interpretation of that grievance and how to address it. The frame needs to resonate in order to encourage people to get out of their comfort zones and press for changes (Benford and Snow 2000: 619–22). Let's say that I think it is a travesty that all people do not have their own ponies, and let's say that the Union for More Ponies (UMP) is trying to get members to join its cause. How likely am I to join UMP? That will depend to a large degree on whether our frames of understanding why people lack ponies are aligned. If I think the problem is that there are not enough ponies to go around, but UMP blames the problem on the lack of pony-riding lessons in schools, those understandings lend themselves to very different policy solutions. This lack of alignment makes it highly unlikely that I will join UMP because the way it has framed the problem does not resonate with my understanding. Frames do not need to be perfectly aligned in order to prompt action, but there does need to be a significant degree of overlap (Ketelaars, Walgrave, and Wouters 2014).

The same dynamics operate in transnational health activism. The mere presence of an issue, regardless of its importance or potential positive effects, is not enough to get national governments and international organizations to respond. We know, for instance, that early childhood development is absolutely crucial for positive future health outcomes and cognitive development. We also know that early childhood development in low- and middle-income countries receives a comparatively small portion of national budgets and is not high on donor priorities. What explains this disjuncture? Shawar and Shiffman (2017) focus on the problem of framing. Groups that work on early childhood development have failed to coalesce around a shared frame. They disagree among themselves over which interventions should be prioritized, which problems are the most important, and even what age range constitutes early childhood. Without a shared frame, these groups are less effective because they cannot make plausible claims to governments or the public. They cannot get others on board with this issue when they do not even agree on what the issue is. On the other hand, pandemic influenza has been effectively reframed as an issue of national and international security rather than one of public health. That has made governments pay far more attention to it—and to devote their resources to it (Kamradt-Scott and McInnes 2012). The effect that framing can have on health issues is still relatively underappreciated, but it is increasingly important for understanding how decisions about the global health agenda are made (Koon, Hawkins, and Mayhew 2016).

HUMAN IMMUNODEFICIENCY VIRUS/ ACQUIRED IMMUNE DEFICIENCY SYNDROME

The Joint United Nations Program on HIV/AIDS (UNAIDS) estimates that 36.7 million people around the world were living with HIV/AIDS at the end of 2016, with 1.8 million new infections and one million deaths occurring. The number of deaths and new infections have declined significantly since 2005, and much of that improvement is the direct result of increased access to treatment in the Global South (UNAIDS 2017: 4–12). While we could ascribe a number of factors to the reason for these changes, one of the most important changes is the shift over time in the framing of HIV/AIDS—particularly HIV/AIDS treatment. Rather than premising these sorts of actions solely on public health or security grounds, the transnational HIV/AIDS activist community has successfully recast access to treatment and education services as a human rights issue. This is a change from some of the more traditional strategies upon which governments have relied in the face of infectious disease outbreaks, like "coercion, compulsion, and restrictions" (Tomasevski et al. 1992: 539). The move to a strategy based in human rights "represents a major and contentious shift in public health policy and human rights advocacy" (Youde 2009b: 69).

A human rights framing for HIV/AIDS education and treatment includes a few key hallmarks. First, there is an emphasis on avoiding isolation, stigmatization, and discrimination against those who are HIV-positive (or perceived to be infected or prone to infection). Reducing stigmatization and discrimination makes it more likely that people will seek out treatment and prevention, which in turn allows them to lead full and healthy lives. Second, there is a focus on providing equal access to education about how HIV is (and is not) transmitted and to treatment services. People have a right to education, and education allows people to make informed choices about their lives. Third, there is a recognition of how the social determinants of health, such as poverty and social inequality, can increase a person's risk for HIV infection and therefore must be addressed as part of any comprehensive HIV/AIDS strategy. We cannot adequately address the reasons that a person may be at greater risk of contracting HIV unless we understand the totality of their circumstances and recognize how larger structural forces play a significant role in understanding the sorts of options that are available to people. Though major international human rights treaties and declarations may not explicitly mention HIV/AIDS, this framing picks up on major themes contained within these treaties, like rights to education, information, and medical care (Tomasevski et al. 1992: 560). It also connects the spread of HIV/AIDS to the need to consider how structural economic, political, and social conditions give rise to the structural violence that increases a person's vulnerability to infection (Farmer 2003: 230).

When AIDS first emerged, the international community largely reacted with apathy. It was not even understood as an international issue. Since the first cases were in the United States and western Europe, an internal World Health Organization (WHO) memo in 1983 argued that the organization did not need to worry because the disease "is being very well taken care of by some of the richest countries in the world where there is the manpower and know-how, and where most of the patients are to be found" (Tomasevski et al. 1992: 567). As more cases were discovered outside of relatively affluent communities, there was an increased recognition of the need to address the disease on a global level. This led in 1987 to the creation of the Global Program on AIDS (GPA) within the WHO (Beigbeider 2000: 184).

In contrast to the early government policies that emphasized quarantine, isolation, and other discriminatory measures (Baldwin 2005), GPA and its leader, Jonathan Mann, embraced a human rights frame. Mann's commitment to human rights came from his own personal experiences working in Zaire on HIV/AIDS issues. He understood how stigma and discrimination stifled public health outreach efforts, particularly at a time when there were no effective AIDS treatments. Instead of promoting coercive policies, mandatory HIV testing, and criminal prosecution for HIV transmission, Mann and his colleagues offered a three-part framework for integrating health and human rights. First, they argued that quarantine policies and other coercive measures deprived individuals of their liberties and freedoms. Second, they posited that human rights violations themselves harmed health. Finally, they saw health and human rights as mutually reinforcing. Better access to information and education allowed people to be healthier, and that in turn allowed them to participate more fully in their communities (Gostin 2014: 245). This framework thus provided a foundation for GPA's work, encouraging governments to see strong human rights protections and respect for individuals as absolutely vital for stopping the spread of HIV. Mann took this framing directly to government leaders around the world, personally lobbying them to understand the value of the frame and to support GPA financially. While Mann's diplomatic outreach successfully increased international funding for HIV/AIDS programs, the human rights frame ran into fierce resistance within the WHO. The

WHO's leadership believed more traditional public health frames that emphasized a biomedical and individual-level approach would be better (Thomas and Magar 2018: 120–22). Hiroshi Nakajima, who became WHO's director-general in 1988, felt that GPA's programs went too far outside the appropriate bounds for WHO's operations, and he delayed or canceled GPA's initiatives with other UN agencies (Gibbons 1990: 1306). When Mann finally resigned in frustration in 1990, he sent Nakajima a blistering letter that chastised him for undercutting the international response to the disease. The repeated frame clashes eventually took their toll, and GPA was terminated in 1994 and replaced by UNAIDS. Not only would the new organization operate independently of the WHO, but it firmly placed human rights at the center of its mission (Heywood and Altman 2000).

Early transnational HIV/AIDS activist groups actively challenged discrimination as part of their human rights framing. In 1983, the US Centers for Disease Control and Prevention declared that there were four groups at increased risk for contracting AIDS: homosexuals, heroin users, hemophiliacs, and Haitians. This group became known as the 4-H Club (not to be confused with the international youth development organization with a four-leafed clover emblem), and members of these groups found themselves the target of discrimination, stigma, and suspicion (Siplon 2002: 6–9). On March 10, 1987, the playwright and activist Larry Kramer stood in front of nearly three hundred people at New York's Lesbian and Gay Community Center and exhorted, "You will be dead in five years. Two-thirds of you will die. What are you going to do to save yourself?" (cited in France 2016: 250). This inspired the creation of the AIDS Coalition to Unleash Power (ACT UP)— a direct action activist group that sought to bring attention to the lax responses to the AIDS crisis and the continued stigmatization and discrimination against people living with HIV/AIDS. ACT UP held actions on Wall Street in New York to protest the high prices of AIDS drugs and Washington to compel more federal funding for AIDS research. Beyond its direct interests in advancing AIDS awareness, promoting civil rights, and encouraging a global response to AIDS (Behrman 2004: 122), ACT UP also provided a space for challenging public and government perceptions of lesbian, gay, bisexual, and transgender (LGBT) people and to give people a space to grieve for loved ones who died of the disease (Gould 2009). From its origins in New York, ACT UP chapters spread across the United States and into Europe, and each chapter operated relatively autonomously and frequently eschewed hierarchical structures. The organization drew heavily on the intersectionality inherent within the movement; many of the early members came out of feminist, anti-apartheid, poverty reduction, and Black Liberation movements (Wyne 2015). At the same time, internal and external critics charged that the organization focused too much on the interests of middle-class white gay men (Brier 2009: 156–89).

This sort of transnational HIV/AIDS activism was not solely the domain of organizations based in the Global North. TAC has played an incredibly important role in getting international society to pay attention to the needs of those with HIV/AIDS in the Global South (Robins and Von Lieres 2004). It drew inspiration from previous activism against apartheid and for LGBT rights in sub-Saharan Africa. When Simon Nkoli, a prominent South African LGBT, anti-apartheid, and HIV/AIDS activist, died in November 1998, Achmat gave a eulogy at Nkoli's funeral that called for the creation of an organization dedicated to ensuring access to ARVs in South Africa. It was precisely because Nkoli could not get these drugs that he finally succumbed to AIDS. Those early members of TAC were experienced activists with connections throughout South Africa, and they could tap into international activist networks in order to further their cause (Grebe 2011: 851).

TAC activists explicitly connected their work on HIV/AIDS to human rights, employing a framework similar to the one that had successfully ended apartheid and made South Africa the first country in the world to explicitly recognize LGBT rights within its constitution. It was no coincidence that the organization's first action—distributing pamphlets calling for increased access to ARVs outside Cape Town's St. George's Cathedral—took place on December 10, 1998, International Human Rights Day. The group targeted the South African government, multinational pharmaceutical companies, and international organizations, aiming to spread its message as widely as possible with a goal of attracting supporters around the world (Heywood 2009).

TAC has used this human rights framing to bring suit against the South African government on a number of occasions, focusing on the government's failures to uphold the human rights guarantees within the South African Constitution and Bill of Rights and international human rights treaties. These documents place specific positive obligations on the government to uphold particular individual rights, including the rights to equality, dignity, and access to health care (Caron, Fitzpatrick, and Slye 2003: 675–77). In criticizing the government for failing to implement a comprehensive AIDS program including access to ARVs, TAC cited Article 25 of the Universal Declaration of Human Rights (on the right to an adequate standard of living for health and well-being), Article 16 of the African Charter of Human and Peoples' Rights (on the right to health and the government's responsibility to ensure it), the Rome Statute of the International Criminal Court (on crimes against humanity including the denial of medicine), and Section 27 of the South African Constitution (on the right to health care services and the government's responsibility to provide them) (Youde 2010: 110).

TAC has not limited its activities to South Africa. The organization has built alliances with AIDS service organizations and activist groups around the world, lending its credibility to these groups while presenting a united transnational front to the international community (Friedman and Mottiar 2005: 547). Achmat calls on fellow activists to cajole wealthy governments around the world to provide monies for treatment and to ensure that human rights are upheld for all people living with HIV/AIDS (Achmat 2004: 77–80).

While a transnational HIV/AIDS activism movement has developed over time, there remain important and unresolved internal tensions. HIV/AIDS cannot be fully understood without also addressing issues of sexual orientation, race, class, and gender, but HIV/AIDS organizations have shown a mixed willingness to engage with these issues of intersectionality. ACT UP's difficulties in addressing these dynamics contributed to the group's decline. While parts of ACT UP did engage in genuine anti-racism work, some felt that gay white middle-class men and their interests dominated the group—meaning that the organization paid too little attention to issues faced by women, people of color, and the poor (Gould 2012). Along similar lines, one lesbian activist in India remarked, "HIV/AIDS funding shifted the attention only to men, if you cannot link yourself with it, no one cares about your problems. Lesbians were already isolated and now they are even more isolated and ignored" (cited in Seckinelgin 2009: 115). Even the value of connecting the HIV/AIDS and LGBT rights movement created lines of division. Baldwin describes how, in North America and Europe, HIV/AIDS movements struggled with questions of whether to "degay" their strategies. Reframing the   more focus on heterosexuals and de-emphasizing the LGBT p   . could potentially bring greater public attention and suppoi   .ut it may also deflect attention from the communities most at risk and waste resources (Baldwin 2005: 197–201).

Local context plays a major role in understanding how context shapes framing and frame alignment. Some groups, for example, emphasized the idea of women and children as innocent and victims of HIV/AIDS, connecting to resonant norms around bodily integrity and protecting particularly vulnerable groups (Kapstein and Busby 2013). Some religious communities in Africa mobilized their HIV/AIDS responses around the idea of compassion rather than activism, which linked easily with Christian beliefs that may have otherwise sat uneasily with issues of sexuality (Patterson 2011). Harris (2017) shows how activists in Brazil, South Africa, and Thailand got their governments to prioritize HIV/AIDS care despite their national resource constraints by connecting their movements to the elites who may have otherwise opposed them. They collaborated with government officials, drafted legislation, and made HIV/AIDS care a political issue that could distinguish political parties. On the flip side, Anderson (2015) describes how taboos about the female body and the gendered structures of power prevent HIV/AIDS programs in Malawi from adequately addressing the underlying risk factors. In order for these frames to be compelling, they had to resonate within the local arenas in which the debates were occurring.

ACCESS TO MEDICINES

First published in 1977 with 212 medicines listed, the WHO's Model List of Essential Medicines is updated every two years to provide national health authorities with information about vital drugs "that satisfy the priority health care needs of the population" (Wirtz et al. 2017: 403). The existence of a drug to treat a medical condition does not mean that the people who need that drug can get it, though. Consider the case of Daraprim, known as pyrimethamine in its generic form. Daraprim is an anti-parasitic drug used to treat toxoplasmosis and pneumocystis pneumonia. These opportunistic infections can be fatal to HIV-positive persons, but Daraprim can treat them easily and effectively—and it is included on the WHO's Model List of Essential Medicines. Few people outside of AIDS specialists had probably even heard of the drug until Martin Shkreli came along. In addition to being the former owner of the most expensive single album ever produced (Wu-Tang Clan's "Once Upon a Time in Shaolin," for which Shkreli reportedly paid two million dollars for the only existing copy), Shkreli was the founder and chief executive officer of Turing Pharmaceuticals. In September 2015, Turing obtained the manufacturing rights for Daraprim. Once that happened, Turing promptly hiked the price from $13.50 per tablet to $750 per tablet—an increase of more than five thousand percent—simply because it could (Mullin 2015). Shkreli may have been called a "morally bankrupt sociopath," a "scumbag," a "pharma bro," and a "garbage monster" (Thomas and Swift 2017), but what he and his company did was entirely legal under international regulations. Inclusion on the WHO's Model List of Essential Medicines did nothing to make it easier for people to get the Daraprim they needed.

It is precisely this issue—the ability of pharmaceutical companies to restrict access to their drugs or charge exorbitant prices—that has motivated a transnational activist movement to challenge the IPRs regime. Rather than privileging the interests of pharmaceutical manufacturers and their pursuit of profit, these activists argued instead for prioritizing getting "drugs into bodies" (Smith and Siplon 2006: vii). They are essentially trying to compel both governments and pharmaceutical companies to change their policies in order to put the WHO's Model List of Essential Medicines into practice.

IPRs are complex, but we all deal with them every single day. At their core, IPRs give inventors and creators the exclusive right to control when, how, and under what conditions their creations can be used for a specified period of time. If you want to think about how this applies in your daily life, let's say that *Game of Thrones* is your favorite television show. You have a few different options for watching it. If you subscribe to HBO, you can watch the show when HBO airs it or record it on your DVR to watch later. You pay money to HBO each month for the right to watch its programming, and HBO pays the creators of the show for the right to air it, so this is entirely legal. You could also buy episodes on iTunes or Amazon. The makers of *Game of Thrones* have given their permission to Apple and Amazon to sell copies of their shows, so it would be entirely respectful of their IPRs to make the show available like this.

There are shadowy options, too. You could pirate the show from any number of websites, illegally downloading it to your computer for free. If you choose this option, you would not be alone; *Game of Thrones* was the world's most frequently pirated show every year between 2012 and 2017 (Hooton 2017). When you torrent *Game of Thrones*, though, you violate the IPRs of the show's creators and distributors because they have not consented to you obtaining the show this way. They lose control over the show's distribution, and they get no compensation for their work. These are violations of the IPRs of the show's creators.

IPRs are not limited to entertainment. When a company develops a new product or process for doing something, they can obtain a patent. The patent gives that company the right to exclude others from making, using, selling, or importing an invention for a specified period of time. If I receive a patent for inventing a new widget, I get a monopoly for that product for a certain number of years. I determine who can produce it, who can sell it, and what price to charge. Protecting IPRs is supposed to encourage creativity, allowing a creator to benefit from their creation and thus rewarding inventors for their creativity and hard work in developing the product or process (World Intellectual Property Organization n.d.: 3–5).

IPRs and patents play a huge role in understanding how and whether people around the world can obtain pharmaceuticals. When a drug company develops a new drug, it gets a patent that allows it to be the only company to manufacture it. Because it is the only source for this drug, though, the pharmaceutical company controls the market and determine the price at which it wants to sell the drug. Other drug companies may have the technical know-how to manufacture the drug, but they cannot produce their own version without the original manufacturer's explicit consent—even if this means that the drug is too expensive for many people who need it. From the perspective of pharmaceutical companies, this is entirely justified. Researching and developing new drugs takes a lot of time and money, and there is no guarantee that any particular research program will yield a new drug. As a result, they argue that they need patent protection in order to recoup their costs—which, they argue, spurs further innovation and encourages the development of new drugs.

At the same time, this system can create a series of perverse incentives for pharmaceutical companies. Let's say that you are the head of a pharmaceutical company, and you have two options for the next drug your company could research. You could create a new drug to treat malaria—a mosquito-borne disease that causes more than two hundred million cases annually and for which existing treatments are becoming less effective. You could also try to create your own version of Viagra. Which would you choose? From a strictly economic perspective, the second option probably makes more sense. Why? There might be a lot more people who could potentially benefit from a new malaria drug, but malaria cases are overwhelmingly concentrated in low- and middle-income countries. It is unlikely that they would be able to afford your new drug. On the other hand, no one is going to die from a lack of Viagra, but these sorts of lifestyle drugs will predominantly appeal to people in wealthy states with some amount of disposable income. People will also take the drug for a long time as opposed to just a short period while taking care of an infection. As a result, the patent system encourages pharmaceutical companies to focus on products that will improve the quality of life for people in wealthy states instead of focusing on the burden of disease (Goldberg 2009: 17).

Traditionally, states have had two options to try to get access to drugs that are covered by IPRs, but there are significant challenges to trying to implement either strategy. The first, parallel importing, involves a country buying a drug from a second country rather than directly from the manufacturer in order to take advantage of a lower price. Let's say that a pharmaceutical manufacturer will sell a drug to Thailand for five dollars, but charges ten dollars for that same drug in India. Under parallel importing, India would purchase that drug from Thailand rather than spending the extra money to buy it directly from the pharmaceutical manufacturer. The second, compulsory licensing, allows a country to declare a public health emergency so that they can manufacture generic versions of a drug even without the patent holder's consent. While international agreements technically allow for both parallel importing and compulsory licensing, they have also established a number of conditions that states had to satisfy in order to pursue them, and few governments have tried to exercise these rights because they feared potential retaliation if they tried to implement either strategy (Gostin 2014: 290–95).

Globalization has altered IPRs, which has had an effect on access to pharmaceuticals. The Agreement on Trade-Related Aspects of Intellectual Property Rights (TRIPS) was negotiated in 1994 as part of the creation of the World Trade Organization (WTO). This agreement, driven largely by the commercial interests of industrialized countries, required that all members of WTO establish minimum standards of intellectual property protections with patent rights of at least twenty years (Sell 2004: 371). This represented a major change for many countries, as a large number of states had previously specifically exempted medicines from patent protection because they believed it was not in the public interest to limit their availability ('t Hoen et al. 2011: 2–3). If states wanted the benefits of globalization that come from membership in the WTO, they had to strengthen patent protections for drugs at the very time when more people needed access to them. When the South African government amended its Medicines Act in December 1997 to allow parallel importing to improve access to ARVs, a coalition of thirty-nine pharmaceutical manufacturers sued it for violating TRIPS, and the United States placed it on a watchlist of countries violating international trade agreements (Fourie and Meyer 2016: 115).

The uncertainties of TRIPS and the aggressive actions being taken by pharmaceutical companies spurred the creation of a transnational coalition to improve access to AIDS drugs by reducing their price and altering the intellectual property regulations around pharmaceuticals. ARVs do not cure a person of AIDS, but they significantly extend a person's life by slowing down the speed with which HIV multiplies within the body. They also decrease a person's chance of infecting someone else with HIV. When they were first released in 1996, ARVs cost twenty-one thousand dollars per year—yet the countries with the highest number of people needing access to these drugs had an average annual total health expenditure of less than $250 per person (Reich and Bery 2005: 327). As such, there was simply no way for the vast majority of people who needed ARVs to afford them because the pharmaceutical companies controlled the patents and therefore held a monopoly on their manufacture and sale. A group of NGOs and AIDS activists held a conference on the compulsory licensing of HIV medicines at the United Nations in Geneva. This was one of the first times that activists directly engaged on questions of IPRs, and their emphasis on building flexibility into intellectual property law "caused a great deal of concern among patent holders" ('t Hoen et al. 2011: 3). Activists also sought to call attention to the optics of pharmaceutical companies suing Nelson

Mandela—a universally admired Nobel Peace Prize winner—and his government for trying to make it easier for AIDS patients in the country with the highest percentage of HIV-positive people in the world to get access to life-prolonging drugs. TAC joined the government's case defending itself against the pharmaceutical manufacturers as a friend of the court (Brier 2009: 194–98). Groups like the Consumer Project on Technology, founded by American consumer activist Ralph Nader, and Médecins Sans Frontières publicly argued that stringent patent protections caused illness and death in developing countries. They also challenged the idea that pharmaceutical companies needed to charge high prices to recoup their research and development costs, finding that most of the research that led to drug development was actually publicly funded (Sell 2004: 374–75). Countries with strong generic pharmaceutical manufacturing capabilities like India and Brazil demonstrated not only their ability to make bio-identical versions of patented ARVs, but also evinced their commitment to successfully providing low- or no-cost ARVs in resource-poor settings (Sell and Prakash 2004: 160–61).

By creating a movement with a coherent, unified message that crossed international borders and brought together unique constellations of actors, AIDS drug access campaigners managed to alter the supply-and-demand curves for ARVs (Kapstein and Busby 2013). The Clinton Foundation, for example, used its clout and ability to convene governments and drugmakers to help reduce costs. It convinced the pharmaceutical companies that they would have a guaranteed market if they agreed to reduce prices, thus making it financially feasible for more governments to buy these drugs (Youde 2011a).

This movement did not only target pharmaceutical companies, though. They also sought to convince governments to alter TRIPS to carve out more explicit guarantees for public health matters. When the WTO Ministerial Conference met in Doha, Qatar, in November 2001, the timing was fortuitous for reconsidering pharmaceutical IPRs. The conference came shortly after the anthrax-letter bioterrorist attacks in the United States, and American government officials were considering compulsory licensing of Cipro, an antibiotic effective at treating anthrax. Sell notes, "If the United States presumably was willing to engage in compulsory licensing to address a national emergency . . . how could it possibly deny the same prerogative to developing countries facing thousands of preventable deaths?" (Sell 2003: 160).

This dynamic helped bring together a number of developing countries' governments to push for an affirmative declaration that they could pursue affordable access to essential medicines policies with less fear of retribution. Though the United States and Switzerland, both home of large multinational pharmaceutical companies, initially opposed such a move, the developing countries won passage of the Declaration on the TRIPS Agreement and Public Health. Also known as the Doha Declaration, it proclaimed that TRIPS did not prevent members from taking action to protect public health, that countries had the right to grant compulsory licenses on grounds which they see fit, and that countries could declare national emergencies for public health crises. Significantly, though, the United States blocked the Doha Declaration from becoming binding international law; instead, it is more of a statement of beliefs. While this fell short of the initial goal, it did explicitly link intellectual property and public health in an unprecedented way (Sell 2003: 161–62).

These efforts had immediate effects. The Indian generic pharmaceutical manufacturer Cipla announced in 2001 that it had developed a course of ARVs for $350—less than one dollar per day, and a dramatic reduction in the price from name-brand manufacturers ('t Hoen et al. 2011: 4). Two years later, WHO and UNAIDS jointly declared that the lack of access to ARVs constituted a global public health emergency and launched the "3 by 5" campaign (seeking to provide ARV access to three million people by 2005) to generate political pressure to expand access (Youde 2008a). The US President's Emergency Plan for AIDS Relief (PEPFAR) also placed a high priority on expanding access to ARVs in developing countries, though it initially prioritized branded drugs rather than generics (Kapstein and Busby 2013: 183–91). As late as 2003, only four hundred thousand out of an estimated six million people in need had access to ARVs, and the overwhelming majority of those were in the Global North (Reich and Bery 2005: 325–26). By 2010, 7.5 million had access to ARVs. The number further increased to seventeen million in 2015, exceeding the goal that the United Nations had set in 2011 by two million (UNAIDS 2016: 1).

These successes do not mean that the problem has been solved. Nearly sixteen million people still lack ARV access, while nearly two million people become infected with HIV each year. Making matters even more urgent, the WHO's guidelines now recommend that people begin ARV treatment as soon as they are diagnosed. This improves health outcomes, but it also increases the number of people needing access to these drugs. Global health aid funding has plateaued since 2010, meaning that there is roughly the same amount of money available to cover an expanding population that needs ARV access (Clinton and Sridhar 2017: 84). This raises significant questions about the reliability of access for many in the Global South (Kavanagh 2014). Interruptions in ARV access increase the likelihood of viral mutations and of a person's ability to pass the virus to others. This means that activists need to continue their efforts, particularly in the face of decreased international funding and increased costs. Furthermore, limits on accessing ARVs are not solely due to IPRs. Significant limitations on procurement and distribution channels in a number of countries in the Global South also need to be addressed in order to expand access even more widely, but Moon and 't Hoen (forthcoming) argue that issues of price and IPRs have proven particularly salient for motivating political action.

As a result of these combined actions, the access to medicines movement has combined activists from developed and developing countries to work together toward a common goal and to address one issue from a variety of different sides—and succeeded in reducing costs and expanding access for more people. The question that emerges is whether activists working to expand drug access for other health conditions, like cancer, diabetes, and hepatitis C, can replicate the experience of HIV/AIDS activists. Kapstein and Busby (2013) sound a note of caution. They note that the United States and the European Union, along with multinational pharmaceutical companies, have become more diplomatically savvy in resisting activists' actions. Instead of working through the WTO, where TRIPS is in operation, they have instead turned toward bilateral free trade agreements. These bilateral arrangements operate under different rules, which can make it harder for activists to pressure pharmaceutical companies to change their practices. At the same time, globalization may provide greater opportunities for transnational health activists. Groups can try to name and shame multinational pharmaceutical companies for their practices to a worldwide audience, and these firms may not want to suffer the same reputation damage that they did when they actively opposed efforts to expand access to ARVs. While activists cannot simply replicate the strategies of one campaign and expect it to work for another health issue, the importance of frame alignment remains central.

SUGAR TAXES

NCDs have traditionally not attracted the same degree of popular mobilization as infectious diseases. Part of that may be due to their framing in the popular imagination; if NCDs are considered the result of individual decisions, then they may be less likely to inspire widespread activism. In recent years, though, there has been increased activism related to NCDs. The passage of the Framework Convention on Tobacco Control (FCTC) by the World Health Assembly in 2003, for example, demonstrated the ability and willingness of governments and activists around the world to collaborate on making global-level changes to seemingly individual-level decisions about health behaviors and the ability to confront powerful global tobacco companies (Collin, Lee, and Bissell 2002).

The success of the FCTC inspired activists to address other NCDs—and, in the process, challenge the power of multinational corporations. One target area for transnational activists is promoting sugar taxes as a way to decrease consumption. This movement draws inspiration from a number of sources. First, evidence suggests that increased taxes on tobacco products reduce cigarette consumption and provide governments with revenue that they can use to fund other health-promoting activities. Sugar tax activists want to apply the same logic in an effort to reduce sugary beverage consumption. Second, high rates of sugar consumption through sugary beverages and snack foods are a leading contributor to increasing rates of overweight, obesity, and type 2 diabetes (Murugesu 2018). Reducing sugar intake can thus play an important role in reducing NCD rates around the world. Third, the ill effects of excess sugar consumption disproportionately affect those with low socioeconomic status or live in low-income countries (STAX Group 2018: 2400). Higher costs can potentially change individual behaviors. Mexico implemented a one peso per liter tax on sugar-sweetened beverages in 2014. Over the next two years, the purchase of such beverages decreased by an average of 7.6 percent per year, and the effects were more pronounced in low-income households (Colchero et al. 2017). Finally, sugar taxes can send a message to both consumers and manufacturers. Levying a "sin tax" signals to the broader public that these are not healthy products and encourages them to reconsider their purchases (Sarlio-Lähteenkorva 2015: 1). It is also a far more obvious signal to consumers about a product's health effects than reading nutritional information (Bogenschneider 2017: 16–17). Taxes can also incentivize manufacturers to change their production processes to reduce the sugar content and avoid the higher tax rates. When the United Kingdom introduced a tax on sugary drinks, major soda producers announced plans to halve the sugar content of their products to reduce their tax liability (Roache and Gostin 2017: 489). Thus, a sugar tax can work to both change individual actions and compel broader changes that structure the social determinants of health.

Sugar taxes have become increasingly popular as part of the policy discussion around reducing the rates of NCDs, and there is a growing movement to encourage municipalities and countries to adopt them. Rather than a single NGO leading the charge, much of the work on sugar taxes has been spearheaded by smaller groups focused at the national and subnational policymakers, learning from the successes and failures of groups around the world. Philanthropic organizations like the Bloomberg Philanthropies and the Bill & Melinda Gates Foundation have provided financial support for the range of different local groups. In 2015, WHO advocated for the introduction of sugar taxes as part of its global action plan on reducing NCDs. As of May 2018, thirty-nine cities, states, and countries have adopted sugar taxes, and more than half of those have been adopted since WHO's recommendations came out. Interestingly, low- and middle-income countries have shown greater willingness to introduce sugar taxes than high-income states (Baker 2018). As with the case of the WHO's Model List of Essential Medicines, activist groups have sought to mobilize around these recommendations in an effort to put them into practice at the national and subnational level.

Competing frames have been central to the battles over sugar taxes. Proponents of sugar taxes position them as promoting public health and reducing health problems like obesity and diabetes. They also frame the issue as a means for funding healthy initiatives (Alvarez-Sanchez et al. 2016). In these ways, their arguments mirror many of the ones put forward by anti-tobacco groups (Fox 2005). Opponents of sugar taxes, including industry groups like the American Beverage Association, frame the issue as one of personal choice, individual responsibility, and regressive taxation (Elliott-Green et al. 2016). They have advocated for voluntary self-regulation by manufacturers to reduce sugar content as an alternative to taxes (Borges et al. 2017: 2), mirroring the tactics that tobacco companies took in the United States in the 1980s and 1990s and continue to promote in the Global South today (Nixon et al. 2015; Sebrie and Glantz 2007).

Sugar taxes can operate at different levels. Mexico's sugar tax, for instance, directly targets consumers to pay the higher cost, with the goal that the increased cost will dissuade people from buying these less-healthy products. When the United Kingdom adopted the Soft Drinks Industry Levy, it instead chose to tax manufacturers. The British system levies different tax rates based on the added sugar content. In this way, the government aims to convince manufacturers to reformulate their products to reduce the sugar level so that they can avoid paying the tax. If a producer chooses not to reduce the sugar content, then it either must pay the tax itself or pass the cost along to consumers. This sort of indirect taxation aims to change producer behavior as well as provide a price signal to shoppers (Thornton 2018).

The introduction of taxes on sugar-sweetened beverages has progressed internationally as groups in different countries have learned from other cases. Norway introduced the first such tax in 1981, but only five other countries or territories followed its example over the next thirty years. The momentum supporting sugar taxes really began in January 2014 when Mexico introduced its tax. The World Cancer Research Fund International identifies Mexico's decision as decisive because it both drew on WHO's recommendations to tax sugar-sweetened beverages to reduce NCD rates and it demonstrated to other countries and territories that they could take aggressive action in the face of fierce opposition by food and drink manufacturers. Since Mexico took its action, at least thirty-five countries, cities, and Native American nations have introduced their own sugar taxes (World Cancer Research Fund International 2018: 4–6).

The movement for introducing a tax on sugar-sweetened beverages is not led by a single organization. Medical and public health professional groups have frequently played a major role, and local groups have emerged in each country and municipality where the tax has been proposed. This is partly explained by the fact that the efforts to introduce a soda tax have varied widely; different organizational tactics are necessary if the effort is at the municipal rather than national level, or if it is a matter of winning a popular referendum as opposed to convincing legislators to adopt a piece of legislation. While there is not a single group leading the charge on this issue in all different locations, we can see evidence of a network—a "voluntary, reciprocal, and horizontal pattern of communication and exchange" (Keck and Sikkink 1998: 8)—developing. These transnational advocacy networks share principled discourse and try to affect political behavior by sharing strategies, learning from one another, and taking inspiration for the successes of others (Price 2003).

CONCLUSION

Public pressure can make governments more responsive or understand the connections between different elements of the larger global health agenda. Transnational activist movements have played significant roles in getting recalcitrant governments to adopt new policies, bring together a wide array of actors to collaborate on global health initiatives, and learn from the successes and failures of others. Globalization helps to foster the transnational element of this activism because it makes it easier for activists to collaborate and learn from one another. This does not mean that these movements always succeed, but it does make it easier for them to emerge.

What helps to explain the variation in the efficacy of transnational health activist networks? Researchers have pointed to a number of key factors. First, there need to be effective movement leaders to both bring together networks and make effective claims to government officials. Second, activists tend to be more successful when they effectively frame the issue as severe because of high mortality and morbidity and high socioeconomic costs. Third, transnational networks tend to be more effective when the affected groups are easily identifiable and viewed sympathetically. Fourth, external donor funding can increase the likelihood of success, as long as the groups do not become overly reliant on any single donor. Fifth, the ability to build alliances with groups focused on other issues can increase the chances of success. Sixth, the strength and public perception of the opposition to these health networks matter.

Stronger and/or more sympathetic opposition makes it harder for activists to promote their preferred polices. Finally, networks that can build and sustain a compelling frame are far more likely to achieve their goals (Gneiting 2016; Shiffman et al. 2016). The short case studies presented in this chapter help to reinforce these ideas, particularly around frame alignment and competition among frames.

Transnational activism for health clearly shows how the five key elements of globalization operate. Because this sort of political activity allows people who are physically distant from one another to work on issues of common interest, there is firm evidence of *intensification*. It also shows how issues are becoming increasingly *integrated*, as these movements directly challenge other political, economic, and social realms. The ease with which these sorts of movements can attempt to cross borders highlights the role of *deterritorialization*. The willingness of groups to take on entrenched political and economic issues—and their ability to get major international organizations on their side— shows how global health has been *elevated* in a globalized world. Finally, as transnational health activism addresses a wider range of issues related to both infectious diseases and NCDs, there is definite *expansion* of the range of issues that globalization brings to the forefront.

The sort of activism described in this chapter often seeks to extend the benefits of globalization to more people or to harness the social, political, and economic changes that globalization facilitates to improve lives. These same strategies and insights, though, can also be used to challenge globalization or to call attention to the ways in which globalization may disempower some groups. That is the issue we turn to in the next chapter by exploring the emergence of the idea of viral sovereignty.

CHAPTER 5

VIRAL SOVEREIGNTY

Prior to 2006, if you tried to talk to someone about viral sovereignty, you would probably receive a lot of confused looks. When Siti Fadilah Supari, the Indonesian minister of health, announced that her country would stop sharing H5N1 influenza virus samples with the World Health Organization (WHO) in December 2006—and did so by asserting Indonesia's right to viral sovereignty—she set off a debate about the nature of global health governance, in whose interests the system operated, and the intersection of economic interests and the operational requirements for functional disease surveillance systems.

Viral sovereignty directly implicates issues of globalization because it speaks to the debates about the international order and the relative power of states (and different types of states) relative to private companies. It is precisely because of the growing importance of globalization to understanding global health politics that viral sovereignty has become an issue. Furthermore, understanding why virus samples could be leveraged in a geopolitical dispute requires an appreciation of globalization. Globalization both made viral sovereignty an issue and provided the Indonesian government with a tool it could exercise to advance its interests within the global health governance system.

Indonesia's invocation of viral sovereignty was notable for two reasons. First, Supari explicitly spoke of her rejection of the virus-sharing system in terms of the system's outcomes. It was not about a lack of technical capacity; it was instead about an unwillingness to participate in a system whose benefits failed to accrue to states like Indonesia. Second, she connected her argument to the interplay between health and globalization. Viral sovereignty is thus a direct response and challenge to globalization's imperatives because it draws on and responds to the economic, social, and political pressures of globalization. It simultaneously fought back against globalization while using elements of globalization to bolster its case. The five key elements of globalization—intensification, integration, deterritorialization, elevation, and expansion—all come into play. This is not just a quirky case of a single state fighting back against globalization; instead, it illustrates how the intersection of health and globalization cannot be reduced to a simple question of good or bad. It provides a case of a state actively trying to resist globalization and using the ideas undergirding globalization to subvert globalization itself, and these ideas continue to reverberate to this day in the debates over virus samples and vaccine development for diseases like Ebola and Zika.

This chapter begins by describing the influenza virus–sharing arrangements that existed prior to Supari's declaration. It then highlights the questions over viral sharing in international law and whether viral sovereignty violates these standards. The third section puts the debates around viral sovereignty within the broader debates that were occurring at the time over the securitization of H5N1, and the fourth section looks at the relationships between sovereignty and globalization and how Supari's declaration fit into these debates. The fifth section then examines how the viral sovereignty debate altered the international systems for virus sharing. Finally, the last section discusses whether the viral sovereignty debate has had any lasting effects on global health politics and globalization.

VIRUS SHARING IN THE GLOBAL
INFLUENZA SURVEILLANCE NETWORK

To understand the controversy around viral sovereignty, we must first step back and examine the virus sample–sharing system that existed when human cases of H5N1 influenza first emerged. The WHO created the Global Influenza Surveillance Network (GISN) in 1952 to monitor the strains of the influenza virus circulating within human populations around the world at any given time. It relies on a network of WHO Collaborating Centers, National Influenza Centers, and laboratories to monitor influenza infection trends, track changes in influenza virus strains, update influenza vaccines, and identify new human influenza viruses. This last role is particularly important, as it allows GISN to note new potential pandemic strains early. To do its work, GISN relies on WHO member-states to collect and share samples of human influenza strains with its Collaborating Centers in the United States, China, the United Kingdom, Australia, and Japan. The idea is that GISN can provide the recommendations necessary for creating seasonal influenza vaccines and offer an early warning about potential pandemic influenza strains. In 2011, when the WHO adopted its new Pandemic Influenza Preparedness Framework (PIPF), GISN changed its name to the Global Influenza Surveillance and Response System (GISRS), but its operational and epidemiological mandates stayed the same.

GISN was not a legal treaty or international requirement, but the willingness of states to contribute to its operation was crucial to "global influenza governance" (Irwin 2010: 3). States shared samples and participated in the system because they understood that they would benefit from GISN's ability to stop future influenza pandemics before they got out of hand.

In many ways, GISN exemplified a global public goods framework. It positioned itself as something that would benefit all as long as everyone contributed. When the Indonesian government announced it would stop sharing H5N1 virus samples with GISN, it challenged the underlying assumptions of pandemic influenza preparedness as a global public good. If our people cannot actually get the vaccine being developed from the virus samples circulating within our borders, the Indonesian government essentially argued, then the system is not really based on public goods.

H5N1 influenza initially appeared in 1997. The first human cases were detected in Hong Kong, where eighteen people fell ill and six died. Sustained human-to-human transmission did not occur, meaning that infection was generally limited to those who were in close contact with chickens that harbored the virus. In response, the Hong Kong government ordered the culling of more than 1.5 million chickens (Chan 2002). Human cases of H5N1 re-emerged in 2003 in China and Vietnam. All four people with laboratory-confirmed cases of H5N1 in 2003 died, raising concern among officials. The following year, there were forty-six cases and thirty-two deaths from H5N1 in Thailand and Vietnam. By 2006, there had been roughly 250 cases and nearly 160 deaths in nine different countries (WHO 2017a).

Indonesia saw its first human cases of H5N1 in 2005 when twenty people fell ill and thirteen died. It recorded another fifty-five cases and forty-five deaths in 2006, and international officials were becoming concerned that the virus was undergoing a dangerous shift. In May 2006, the WHO identified a cluster of several members of the same family who all died of H5N1 within a short period of time. This raised fears that the virus might be mutating to allow for direct human-to-human transmission. If this occurred, it would heighten the chances of an H5N1 outbreak. Up to that point, infection required close contact with chickens, severely limiting how far the disease could spread. WHO officials could not confirm that these cases were the result of direct human-to-human transmission based solely on epidemiological data, but it could use virus samples from the victims to discover whether this was the case. This prompted the WHO to request human H5N1 virus samples from the Indonesian government—and set the stage for introducing the concept of viral sovereignty to the world.

SUPARI AND THE INVOCATION OF VIRAL SOVEREIGNTY

Using her authority as Indonesia's health minister, Supari rejected the WHO's suggestion that H5N1 in Indonesia was mutating into a more virulent strain that could be passed directly between people. She called the WHO's argument "a slanderous and inaccurate accusation that could damage Indonesia's economy" (Smith 2012: 74). Supari believed that genetic testing of these samples would ultimately vindicate her argument, and she criticized GISN for its lack of transparency. Access to GISN's genetic database was restricted, which led some to speculate that Supari feared that too few people would learn that she was correct for challenging the WHO if she was proven right (Smith 2012: 73–74). Supari may have worried that mutations in the H5N1 virus would reflect poorly on her and her leadership of the Ministry of Health. She may have been cognizant of the domestic political battles happening within Indonesia at the time and trying to better position herself and her ministry (Hameiri 2014). She may have worried about the economic, political, and reputational consequences for Indonesia if it became identified as the epicenter for a new influenza pandemic (Ali and Keil 2006). Whatever the case, Supari responded to the WHO's initial request for virus samples by calling the larger global influenza governance system into question.

The tensions between Supari and the WHO escalated throughout 2006 and reached their peak in January 2007. That month, Supari declared Indonesia would no longer share human H5N1 samples with GISN for either surveillance or vaccine development purposes (Fidler 2008: 88). In her subsequent book, Supari described the virus-sharing program as operating in "the shadow of imperialism" because it primarily benefited pharmaceutical manufacturers in the Global North. "Was this the neo-colonialism predicted by Soekarno, the first president of Indonesia, 50 years ago," she asked, "when the incapability or the powerlessness of a nation can be the source of prosperity for other nation [sic]?" (Supari 2007: 34). Though she saw the international system as stacked against countries like Indonesia and lamented that the country had historically evinced "no courage to stand against the establishment," Supari believed that the influenza situation in Indonesia was a divinely inspired opportunity to challenge the existing order: "God, You gave avian flu to the nation, but You are also opening our eyes to raise our awareness to be a nation with dignity and sovereignty, and I believe that I had to do something for the sake of humanity" (Supari 2007: 39).

Supari presented a number of reasons to justify her actions. First, she argued that the WHO and GISN had presented the results of laboratory analyses of the samples at various international meetings without the permission of the Indonesian government or the involvement of Indonesian scientists. These actions, she said, were both unethical and contravened the WHO's own stated guidelines (Sedyaningsih et al. 2008: 485). Second, she learned that the WHO was sharing the samples it had already received from Indonesia with an Australian pharmaceutical company, Commonwealth Serum Laboratories, that intended to create a patented H5N1 vaccine (Hinterberger and Porter 2015: 365). This action again violated WHO standards, she argued, and it was particularly unfair that a private Western company would profit from Indonesia's virus samples when Indonesians themselves would not receive and could not afford the resulting product. Fischer notes, "Indonesia attacked the WHO system as attuned to the protection of capital rather than to the needs of the populations most at risk" (Fischer 2013: 369). Third, she argued that GISN had essentially violated the trust of Indonesia—and all developing countries—by maintaining an inequitable system that only benefited wealthy states and denied the developing states the same access (Sedyaningsih et al. 2008: 486). Finally, she claimed that the WHO had sought patents on modified H5N1 samples that GISN had obtained from Indonesia, but had neither notified Indonesia nor sought its consent for such action. This, she noted, violated the WHO's own guidelines about intellectual property rights (IPRs) and eroded her ministry's trust in WHO's secretariat (Aldis and Soendoro 2015: 320–21).

Supari asserted Indonesia's viral sovereignty over the samples, claiming them as part of the country's biological heritage. She specifically cited the 1992 Convention on Biological Diversity (CBD) and the treaty's right for countries to determine access to genetic resources by others (Hinterberger and Porter 2015: 366). There had been previous controversies over the ability of private companies to patent viruses and other biological material (Tejera 1999), but Supari's announcement was the first time that a state claimed ownership over viruses circulating within its territory and asserted the right to control subsequent access to that biological material. Instead of sending virus samples through GISN, she would direct them to the Eijkman Institute and National Institute of Health Research and Development, both Indonesian institutions, to confirm H5N1 diagnoses (Supari 2007: 52). She also announced that Indonesia had entered into negotiations with Baxter Healthcare, a US-based pharmaceutical company. The government would share H5N1 virus samples with Baxter in exchange for its ability to retain the IPRs to those samples and guaranteed access to any vaccine that Baxter derived using them (Carter 2010: 719).

Supari's argument was groundbreaking. This was the first instance in which a government had extended the CBD to cover a virus (Hinterberger and Porter 2015: 366). More importantly, this was the first time in which a government had claimed viral sovereignty. By linking its refusal to share the virus samples to the notion of national sovereignty, Indonesia framed its argument in a way that it hoped would resonate with larger international norms and gain support from other developing countries. It sought to reassert its Westphalian sovereignty in the face of the deterritorializing and integrative imperatives of globalization.

Much of the international reaction to Indonesia's announcement was negative. One analysis characterized the dominant response as assuming Supari's decision was "arbitrary, inexplicable, or motivated by a desire for financial gain" (Aldis and Soendoro 2015: 320). Richard Holbrooke, the American diplomat and former ambassador to the United Nations, and Laurie Garrett, the prominent medical journalist and analyst, published an op-ed in the *Washington Post* calling viral sovereignty an "extremely dangerous idea" and "morally reprehensible" (Holbrooke and Garrett 2008). Most commentators assumed that the CBD did not apply to viruses because they were traditionally seen as being global in nature rather than connected to any specific place (Hinterberger and Porter 2015: 366). Fidler argued that Supari's argument twisted the CBD's intent. He wrote, "These viruses invaded Indonesia; their presence and spread owes nothing to the investment, nurturing, and utilization of the Indonesian government or people. Rather than seeking to conserve this virus, the strategy is to contain and ultimately eradicate it" (Fidler 2008: 90–91). The CBD, Fidler asserted, is about preserving diversity and managing it for sustainable development. Rather than being an element of that diversity, H5N1 threatens diversity in both Indonesia and internationally. H5N1 is not something to preserve, he posits; it is something that Indonesia and the rest of the international community should seek to eliminate (Fidler 2008). Others highlighted that the CBD explicitly states that countries cannot introduce overly burdensome requirements to prevent the sharing of biological materials, making Supari's argument incompatible with the goals of the CBD and "deliberatively retrogressive to the realization of the right to health" (Mullis 2009: 960). Mullis argued that Supari's actions would reduce both the quantity and quality of vaccines and negatively affect the right to health for people in other countries (Mullis 2009: 960–63).

These negative reactions, largely coming from the Global North, may have actually strengthened Supari's position. When commentators and policymakers from developed states harshly criticized Supari, it reinforced the perception that the system was rigged against Indonesia's interests and gave Supari greater leverage. "Public condemnation of such action," Stevenson and Cooper write, "without acknowledging the legitimacy of Indonesia's grievance will only exacerbate the crisis, and ultimately diminish the legitimacy of global health governance in the eyes of already suspicious states" (Stevenson and Cooper 2009: 1387). It showed a blindness to considering the rarely acknowledged power hierarchies inherent within the global health governance system (Shiffman 2014). It failed to address the tensions that exist between the emerging global health norms, which are often Western in origin, and the perception of those norms by states that had previously been colonized or victims of imperialism. Not only are these states frequently excluded from global health governance mechanisms, but their histories are replete with examples of public health rationales being employed to justify colonial rule (Bashford 2004). The result is a system that gives rise to the perception that "global health governance is merely a vehicle for imposing yet another set of exogenous norms that do not reflect the states' values or goals" (Stevenson and Cooper 2009: 1379).

Supari's decision did find support and understanding in a number of quarters. Thailand and India both expressed support for the idea of viral sovereignty and its use in international negotiations, as did the Non-Aligned Movement during its 2008 meeting (Elbe 2010a). An editorial in *The Lancet* called Indonesia's decision understandable and expressed some sympathy for Supari's action. The editorial highlighted how the existing limitations on global pharmaceutical manufacturing capacity and the inequities in access for developing countries called current pandemic influenza preparedness plans into question (*Lancet* 2007). Even *The Economist* praised her calls for increased transparency as a tool for fighting disease pandemics (*The Economist* 2006).

VIRUS SHARING, VIRAL SOVEREIGNTY, AND INTERNATIONAL LAW

It is unclear whether Supari's actions actually violated international law. Her argument linking viral sovereignty to the CBD had not previously been tested, and the CBD did not extend its understanding of sovereignty to include human biological and genetic resources. The H5N1 samples were human-isolated viruses, raising doubts over the applicability of the CBD (Vezzani 2010: 678–79). The International Health Regulations (IHR) would have not applied in this instance, either. When human cases of H5N1 first emerged, the 1983 version of the IHR, known as the IHR (1983), governed international obligations about reporting disease outbreaks to WHO—and it did not apply to influenza. Interestingly, Supari's announcement in late 2006 happened in the interim period after an updated, more extensive version of the IHR, known as IHR (2005), had been adopted but not yet gone into effect. Even if IHR (2005) were in effect, there is ambiguity over whether they would apply to virus sharing. On the one hand, Indonesia was still reporting the existence of human cases of H5N1 to WHO, even if it was not sharing the samples from those cases. The US government and others responded to this claim that Indonesia's refusal violated the spirit, if not the letter, of the law (Smith 2012). On the other hand, Article 46 of IHR (2005) says that member-states shall "facilitate the transport, entry, exit, processing, and disposal of biological substances and diagnostic specimens, reagents, and other diagnostic materials for verification and public health response purposes under these Regulations" (WHO 2016b: 31). Whether the Indonesian H5N1 samples fall under this obligation is uncertain, as Indonesia could claim that GISN wanted its samples for commercial, rather than verification, purposes. As a result of these questions, "international law was therefore equivocal and inconclusive, almost without exception" (Smith 2012: 72).

Regardless of its legal implications, Supari's announcement pointed out the weaknesses inherent within the intersection of international law and global health. The WHO may establish rules to require the adoption of pandemic preparedness plans that include various surveillance mechanisms, but it can neither guarantee that states follow these rules nor that it can offer any sort of meaningful guidance or treatment in the event that an outbreak event is discovered (Lisk, Sehovic, and Sekalala 2015: 33–34). The Council on Foreign Relations worried that Indonesia's embrace of viral sovereignty essentially flouted shortcomings in an already-weakened system. While a number of states may lack the technical capacity to meaningfully interact with global disease surveillance systems, it singled out Indonesia for criticism because it was *voluntarily choosing* not to participate in the system and thereby weakening it for everyone (Council on Foreign Relations 2013).

The practical effects of Supari's decisions are more nuanced than her public comments might suggest. Even while Supari was questioning whether Indonesia would share viruses with the WHO, the country continued to make regular reports to the WHO about human infections (Davies 2012a: 598). The government allowed other WHO virus-sharing collaborations to continue and expand even at the height of Supari's comments, and there was never any interruption in Indonesia's relationship to share H5N1 virus samples among chickens with the United Nations' Food and Agriculture Organization (Hameiri 2014: 341–42).

That may lead us to question whether Supari's announcement actually mattered. In actual effect, her actions played an important role in changing the international conversation around the contours of the globalization of health. Her rhetoric called into question the existing norms within the global health governance system. Norms are particularly important in the global health realm because there is relatively little formal international law to govern behavior (Gostin 2014: 66). Because of Indonesia's centrality to the H5N1 outbreak and its potential leadership role among developing countries, Supari possessed a unique ability to leverage her concerns about the globalization and equity in health to force the global community to address these issues in a way that it would not have otherwise done. Many of the practices upon which the global health system rests are normative rather than legal (Davies, Kamradt-Scott, and Rushton 2015). As a result, Supari could draw on Indonesia's unique position to challenge existing international norms around virus sharing or promote new norms. By reframing the issue as one of exploitation and a violation of the CBD rather than as a global public good, the Indonesian government offered a counter-frame to challenge the norm (Payne 2001). In this particular case, Indonesia pushed back against the globalization-supported obligations embedded within global health governance to defend a more traditional vision of Westphalian sovereignty. This is not to say that the Indonesian government's response was right or wrong; rather, it is to highlight the ways in which it is trying to leverage its opportunities to contest globalization.

THE SECURITIZATION OF H5N1
AND VIRAL SOVEREIGNTY

Supari's reaction to GISN did not exist in a vacuum; rather, GISN's practices and expectations operated within a context in which H5N1 influenza was increasingly securitized within the international community. Turning influenza into a matter for national and global security altered the ways in which governments conceptualized a potential outbreak, and it had an effect on why the Global North reacted as strongly as it did.

The prospect of a human H5N1 influenza pandemic inspired high levels of fear internationally. A 2005 op-ed in *The New York Times* written by two members of the US Senate—one the respected chair of the Foreign Relations Committee, the other three years away from being elected president—argued that an H5N1 pandemic would kill millions, destabilize Southeast Asia, and undermine governments (Lugar and Obama 2005). The British Civil Contingency Secretariat called H5N1 "as serious a threat as terrorism" for the United Kingdom, while the World Bank suggested that it was "a substantial threat to global public health security" (cited in Elbe 2010b: 47). At a 2004 meeting, WHO officials estimated that two to 7.4 million people could die in an H5N1 outbreak. Michael Osterholm, the director of the Center for Infectious Disease Research and Policy at the University of Minnesota, challenged the WHO's prediction for being too low and said that the death toll for an H5N1 outbreak on the scale of the 1918–1919 influenza pandemic could reach 180 to 360 million. In response, the WHO revised its estimates to suggest a death toll of two to fifty million, with seven million deaths as the "best-case scenario" (Brender 2014: 131–32). The Bush administration announced a $7.1 billion initiative to prepare for pandemic influenza in November 2005—in part because of the government's fears that H5N1 was "spreading west from Asia [and] could acquire the ability to be transmitted from human to human" (Kaiser 2005: 952). In 2007, the Association of Southeast Asian Nations (ASEAN) described H5N1 as one of the three most significant challenges to the region's security, stability, and peace (Hameiri and Jones 2015: 454). Interestingly, this declaration came out shortly after Supari's announcement—and Indonesia is one of ASEAN's original members.

These concerns from the highest levels of national governments and international organizations interpret the threat of a human H5N1 influenza outbreak as a national and international security issue. They are securitizing a global health matter—engaging in a political process to turn something into a security issue (Buzan, Waever, and de Wilde 1998). Making something a security issue moves it out of the realm of "normal" politics and changes the nature of political debate about it. It also allows it to receive additional attention and resources. By calling something a security issue, policymakers aim to convince their audiences that it *is* a security issue (Elbe 2010b: 11). If those audiences accept the security framing, then they are likely to accept taking extraordinary measures in order to respond to the threat. If we frame terrorism, for instance, as a security issue as opposed to a law enforcement issue, our governments will take different actions to combat it—and we as the public are likely to support those measures as necessary to protect us from an existential threat. By the same token, framing environmental issues or disease as security threats leads, for better or worse, to different types of responses (Deudney 1990). Securitization is one of the clearest elements of how elevation and intensification operate within the definition of globalization, because it can turn a disease on the other side of the world into a security threat for faraway countries—or for the world as a whole.

The securitization of H5N1 influenza had a number of key effects on the global political dimensions of health. For one thing, framing H5N1 as a security concern changes the political and preparatory calculus for a number of states. It encouraged states to hoard vaccines and treatments to ensure that they would be ready when and if a pandemic emerged. Given the limits on pharmaceutical manufacturing capacity and the inequities in the resources available to pay for these limited supplies, this sort of response to securitization hurt developing states (Elbe 2010a: 477).

Second, securitization makes an issue more prominent on the global political agenda. This means that governments are paying more attention to that issue and investing more energy toward addressing it. It also means that they are more willing to address the issue outside of the realm of normal politics (Elbe 2010a: 479–80). In this case, more countries are paying more attention to GISN and how it operates. GISN had been operating for nearly fifty years when Supari claimed viral sovereignty, yet it is highly doubtful that political leaders in the vast majority of countries knew much (if anything) about the system. Once the securitization of H5N1 called attention to GISN, though, these states paid the network a great deal of attention and opted to exercise advance purchase agreements for influenza vaccines and treatments—actions that were not part of their regular health strategies. Securitization encouraged governments in the Global North to pursue strategies that may have been individually rational, but they placed the global community as a whole at risk by making it harder to acquire the vaccines and treatments necessary to address an outbreak (Aldis and Soendoro 2015: 318).

Third, securitization alters the array of actors involved in planning and responding to an issue. In an October 2005 press conference in the White House Rose Garden, US President George W. Bush talked about how an avian influenza outbreak in the United States could potentially require widespread quarantine enforced by the military (Youde 2008b: 158). This sort of response would place the US military at the center of a response to a public health emergency—at the same time that there were allegations that the United States wanted to use human H5N1 virus samples to create a biological weapon at its laboratories in Los Alamos, New Mexico (Sipress 2009). Indeed, Supari herself wrote, "Whether they [the scientists at Los Alamos] used [the H5N1 virus samples] to make vaccine or develop biological weapon [sic], would depend on the need and the interest of the US government" (Supari 2007: 45).

Supari used the Global North's fears around the security implications of pandemic influenza and the need for H5N1 virus samples to create effective vaccines as leverage to change the conversation around equity in the globalized health space. The fear that states expressed about the possibility of an H5N1 pandemic made these samples "valuable." Because the H5N1 strain circulating in Indonesia at that time seemed to be more virulent than what was circulating in other countries and therefore of more interest for research and pharmaceutical development purposes, Supari had something that the rest of the world wanted—and she could use that to bring other states and the WHO to negotiate these issues of access and equity (Elbe 2010a: 477). Securitization raised the stakes for the international community, and the Indonesian Ministry of Health could use that heightened interest (Hameiri 2014: 335–36).

WHY SOVEREIGNTY?

At first glance, sovereignty and globalization are in direct conflict with one another. Globalization makes borders seem irrelevant, compresses time and space, and encourages a sense of interrelationship. Sovereignty, on the other hand, prioritizes independence and autonomy.

Instead of simplifying the narrative, the invocation of sovereignty itself adds a unique dimension to the debates over access to the human H5N1 virus samples. Sovereignty is "one of the constituent ideas of the post-medieval world" and "a distinctive configuration of politics and law that sets the modern era apart from previous eras" (Jackson 2007: 1). At the same time, globalization fundamentally alters our notions of sovereignty because it changes the power and authority structures operating within and outside states. Sassen writes of "sovereignty [having] been decentered and territory partly denationalized" (Sassen 1996: 29–30). This transformation of sovereignty is frequently understood as one of the hallmarks of globalization, and it is no different in global health.

In many ways, Supari's argument harkened back to an earlier understanding of sovereignty. Rather than embracing some globalized notion of the decreasing importance of borders, she instead used globalization against itself. She rejected the cliché that viruses do not respect borders to argue instead that a virus found within Indonesia's borders *belonged to* Indonesia. She drew on a territorialized vision of sovereignty to specifically tether the virus to a particular geographic space and governmental jurisdiction (Hinterberger and Porter 2015: 361–62). A concept like viral sovereignty may "appear anachronistic in contemporary biopolitical orders often characterized by a reconfiguration of the sovereign in diffuse, deterritorialized operations of power" (Hinterberger and Porter 2015: 363), but it instead highlighted just how wedded much of the international order remains to sovereignty. She could use the heightened concern about H5N1 and how globalization raised those fears to respond by drawing on a concept that challenged the very notion (or at least the perceived ubiquity) of globalization itself. She could argue that there was something different and unique about the particular strain of H5N1 in Indonesia and that this uniqueness is precisely what made it so important and valuable to the rest of the world.

Supari's sovereignty argument also raised questions about who gets to exercise sovereign power within the global community. The global health governance system had reconfigured the exercise of sovereign power by empowering new types of actors. A growing array of nonstate actors work—and potentially compete—with state-based actors to exercise power within the global health realm (Hinterberger and Porter 2015: 372). Private companies like pharmaceutical manufacturers are becoming more central to pandemic preparation strategies, and private philanthropic organizations are providing an increasing amount of development assistance for health—and, with that increased financial presence, playing a bigger role in setting the global health agenda (Harman 2016; Youde 2018). This diversification of global health actors has happened within a context that draws on histories of "physical conquest, resource extraction, violence, and economic exploitation—often under the auspices of scientific progress" (Hinterberger and Porter 2015: 372). Again, we see globalization being used against itself. In this case, the expansion of the range of actors involved in global health to include pharmaceutical companies becomes evidence for why Indonesia needs to reassert its sovereignty and challenge globalization's emphases.

The use of viral sovereignty in global health also demonstrates that globalization has not made nationalism disappear, but instead changed how it is deployed. Supari made an essentially nationalist appeal as part of a strategy to limit a seemingly emergent transnational ethos (Stephenson 2011: 622). It helped resolve crises of state power by creating new ways to regulate cross-cutting institutional pressures. It may have appeared internally inconsistent—why prevent access to a virus sample in the name of promoting health if such a denial will prevent other people from avoiding illness?—but it was this very combination of seemingly contradictory impulses that give it some degree of power and purchase in an uncertain and unsettled environment (Stephenson 2011: 628–29).

Indonesia's response to the securitization of H5N1 varied depending on its audience; the domestic response differed significantly from the international one. At the domestic level, the Indonesian government largely sought to thwart globalization's securitizing imperative by denying the disease's presence. Prior to Supari's announcement, the Indonesian government claimed that Newcastle disease, not H5N1, was infecting its chickens. Newcastle disease is highly contagious and can be fatal to chickens and other birds, but does not infect humans. The domestic poultry industry also sought to deny that H5N1 was circulating among Indonesian chickens because its presence could require the widespread culling of birds to stop the disease's spread. When the Indonesian Agriculture Department finally acknowledged that H5N1 was in fact circulating among chickens, it denied that the particular H5N1 strain could make the leap from animals to humans, and the government spent less than 2 percent of its budget on avian influenza control during the years in which the disease was most prevalent (Curley and Herington 2011: 156–57).

At the international level, though, Supari engaged with H5N1's securitization through her resistance. She did not refuse to share human H5N1 samples with GISN because she did not think that the disease was present in Indonesia or because she doubted the outbreak's severity; rather, it was precisely *because* she recognized the potential security implications of the globalization of this particular issue that she sought to leverage it to challenge the inequities within the system. During the 2007 World Health Assembly (WHA), she told the delegates that her actions were part of "the battle we have to wage against pandemic threat" and that the unfairness in the current system "could threaten global health security" (cited in Curley and Herington 2011: 158). Indeed, she framed viral sovereignty within a broader frame that spoke to Western fears about disease emerging from the Global South. This is something we have seen in previous conversations about the spread of disease. Wald singles out Laurie Garrett's (1994) *The Coming Plague* and Richard Preston's (1994) *The Hot Zone* for popularizing the narrative of "this 'microbial traffic' as [moving] one-way: *from* the primordial rainforests of the impoverished developing world *to* the metropolitan centers of commerce and capital" (Wald 2008: 34; emphasis in the original). Supari drew upon this same sort of thinking to highlight the inequalities in the current system. If international society does not provide necessary resources like influenza vaccines to the Global South, then the threat of disease coming to the Global North increases because of the compression and intensification brought about by globalization.

This seemingly contradictory approach to securitization and globalization is the concrete manifestation of regulating cross-cutting institutional pressures. It responds to the competing domestic and international imperatives and attempts to harness the impulses of globalization to improve Indonesia's position. Instead of seeing the globalization of health as an all-powerful force, Supari's deployment of viral sovereignty demonstrates how a developing country could challenge globalization's dictates. Her actions highlight how globalization in its various manifestations is a negotiated process, not an unstoppable force. In the same way that Indonesia's response to H5N1 helps illustrate securitization theory's biases toward Western and democratic states (Collins 2002; Grzymala-Busse and Luong 2002; Wilkinson 2007), it also demonstrates how securitization can provide a site of resistance to globalization.

THE EFFECTS OF VIRAL SOVEREIGNTY

Indonesia's decision to stop sharing human H5N1 virus samples forced the WHO and the larger global health governance system to engage in a serious discussion about the effects of globalization on larger questions of equity and benefit sharing. Shortly after Supari's declaration, the WHO announced that it would create a pandemic influenza vaccine stockpile that would specifically be available to low-income countries on the basis of demonstrated need. It also inaugurated a series of meetings between itself and the Indonesian government throughout 2007 as part of the lead-up to more wide-ranging formal international negotiations around virus sharing and benefit distribution (Kamradt-Scott and Lee 2011: 834). These international negotiations were of critical importance because Indonesia essentially forced the WHO and the international community to engage in widespread revisions to the WHO's pandemic plans that went beyond simple technical fixes (Gostin 2014: 373).

Over the next four years, the discussions around virus and benefit sharing covered a wide range of issues. Kamradt-Scott and Lee (2011) note that the negotiations gradually had to scale back their ambitions. The initial 2007 WHA resolution that authorized the negotiations talked about mobilizing financial support to increase access to vaccines, building technical capacity for vaccine manufacturing in developing countries, and addressing the range of human influenza viruses. Within a year, though, the scope of the negotiations narrowed to only cover H5N1 and other pandemic influenza viruses, did not address serious challenges to existing IPRs systems, and limited the scale of financial and resource transfer mechanisms. Supari also reportedly told her staff that it would be better for the negotiations to end in a deadlock than require significant compromises on Indonesia's part (Kamradt-Scott and Lee 2011: 835–36).

When the new PIPF was unveiled in April 2011, it presented the global community with some genuine changes to the virus- and benefit-sharing system. Gostin called it the first that time that the international community had established a before-the-fact agreement for a global health issue that addressed questions of multijurisdictional surveillance and benefit sharing (Gostin 2014: 374). McInnes and Lee highlighted that the agreement went beyond solely addressing the pandemic influenza security fears of wealthy states to recognize the inequities around access to needed vaccines (McInnes and Lee 2012: 161–62).

PIPF introduced four changes into the existing global influenza systems. First, it changed the name of GISN to the Global Influenza Surveillance and Response System (GISRS). This change helped to convey the message that a change had actually occurred as part of the negotiations. It also made clear that the system had to do more than just passively collect data; GISRS would act on the basis of the surveillance data it collected.

Second, it introduced new virus-sharing responsibilities. Member-states agreed to supply human influenza virus samples to GISRS labs and consent to the onward transfer of those samples in line with new standard material transfer agreements (SMTAs). In exchange, GISRS pledged to share its data and analyses with other laboratories and the originating state for its samples. The WHO pledged to develop traceability mechanisms for biological materials being shared with GISRS so that states could know where their samples had travelled (Gostin 2014: 374–75).

Third, it created new responsibilities around benefit sharing. GISRS would have to provide candidate vaccine viruses to manufacturers and member-states that requested them. It would also work to help increase technical capabilities in developing states and encourage technology transfers between the Global North and the Global South. PIPF directed the WHO's director-general to work to develop a stockpile of vaccines and treatments, and it urged vaccine manufacturers to set aside a quantity of vaccines for developing states (Gostin 2014: 375-376).

Finally, it created two SMTAs. SMTA-1 governed the sharing of virus samples from member-states to GISRS laboratories. The second, SMTA-2, focused on entities that were not technically part of GISRS, such as

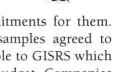

vaccine manufacturers, and created binding commitments for them. Under SMTA-2, private companies that received samples agreed to make financial contributions and/or vaccines available to GISRS which would total half of the system's annual operational budget. Companies also pledged make certain benefit-sharing commitments. These could include pledges to give a percentage of their pandemic vaccine production to WHO, grant licenses to generic pharmaceutical manufacturers on prearranged terms, or reserve a portion of their anti-viral output for sale to developing countries at affordable prices (Gostin 2014: 376–77).

Supari and the Indonesian government can rightly take credit for pushing the global community to negotiate the agreement which created PIPF. They leveraged the presence of the H5N1 virus within their territory, territorialized it by invoking notions of sovereignty, and forced the larger international community to address who benefited from the then-existent pandemic preparedness framework. They harnessed the fear and security concerns that H5N1 raised in a globalized world to change the terms of debate on pandemic influenza in humans. These would not have happened if it had not been for Supari's declaration, and Supari's declaration would not have been effective absent the challenges to global health posed by globalization.

At the same time, globalization is an incredibly powerful force to push back against, and certain actors had a vested interest in maintaining the existing system. While Indonesia may have compelled the global community to have the conversation about influenza virus and benefit sharing, it could not force a radical restructuring of political and economic structures. While the changes in PIPF are notable, the actual degree of change that they introduced to the system is rather small. Fidler and Gostin note the accomplishments and shortcomings in PIPF:

> The framework is a landmark in global governance for health, representing the first international agreement on influenza virus and benefit sharing. The framework, however, reflects compromises that could jeopardize more equitable allocation of benefits in a future pandemic. (Fidler and Gostin 2011: 201)

Overall, PIPF was celebrated less because of its content and more because it finally meant that contentious negotiations had come to an end. It did relatively little to change the status quo, imposed no specific and measurable requirements to take specific actions, and upheld the same IPRs regime that hampered the ability of pharmaceutical manu-facturers in developing countries to create vaccines themselves (Smith 2012: 79–81). It "secured the norm of virus sharing while providing only weak benefit sharing in return" (Gostin 2014: 377).

What makes PIPF so weak? First, it is nonbinding soft law. The WHO did not invoke its treaty-making powers when negotiating PIPF. Instead, it created a document that merely speaks of what states "should" do and "urges" parties to take particular actions without any significant punishments for states which violate PIPF. Second, wealthy states were ultimately unwilling to take actions or make bind-ing pledges that would pre-commit them to take actions in the face of a pandemic. They would not end their advance purchase agreements with pharmaceutical manufacturers, nor would they promise to make any specific quantity of vaccines or anti-viral treatments available to developing countries. Kamradt-Scott and Lee lament, "This lack of ob-ligation on member states is not unusual and reflects the long-standing inviolability of state sovereignty" (Kamradt-Scott and Lee 2011: 839). Developed states saw globalization as bringing a potential viral threat closer to them, but they responded by invoking their own selfish sov-ereign interests to protect themselves. Ultimately, PIPF made so few changes that "so little that triggered this controversy or transpired dur-ing it would violate the framework that supposedly resolves the virus and benefit sharing" (Smith 2012: 80).

PIPF's shortcomings challenge some existing ideas about how and under what circumstances global public goods for health will be provided. First, it suggests that cosmopolitan theories about health justice and the provision of global health may be overly optimis-tic—even in a globalized world. Rather than providing a universally protected public good around the world simply by virtue of being human (Brown and Paremoer 2014: 86–87), actors are unwilling to bind themselves in these ways or focus their energies on distant Oth-ers. Second, public goods face the free-rider problem. If it is impracti-cal to prevent someone to access the public good regardless of their contribution, then that discourages participation—and leads to the underprovision of the public good (Cornes and Sandler 1986). Third, the policy efforts necessary to undertake the provision of public goods on a transnational basis brings about a high degree of political, economic, and technical uncertainty (Kaul 2012: 730). Risk-averse policymakers are often unwilling to accept this degree of uncertainty even when they accept the need for the policy changes in the first place. Fourth, Smith suggests that a number of global public goods for health are better understood as luxury goods. Wealthy countries may consider something like a pandemic influenza vaccine a necessity, but poorer countries may prioritize other health-related interventions and would rather put their limited resources toward those programs that will benefit a higher number of people. In such a scenario, it would not be a surprise to see public goods being underprovided because there is not an agreement about how important those public goods actually are (Smith 2012). Finally, global public goods can be particularly difficult to provide because they necessarily involve political and economic decisions being made in a coordinated manner at both the domestic and international levels. This degree of cooperation, combined with the effects of global power imbalances, can be difficult to achieve in the best of circumstances (Kaul 2012: 738–39).

On a national level, Supari's rhetoric had additional effects that altered influenza surveillance systems. The United States created the Naval Medical Research Unit-2 (NAMRU-2) as the medical research arm of the US Navy to conduct influenza surveillance operations during World War II. It was initially hosted on Guam before moving to the Philippines and opening a satellite laboratory in Indonesia in 1970. In 1990, NAMRU-2 moved all of its operations to Jakarta. NAMRU-2 had a mission to "advance US diplomacy in the region by studying infectious diseases of critical public health importance to the United States, Indonesia, and other regional partners" (Lowe 2010: 154–55). It operated a regional reference lab for influenza testing and provided lab support to the Indonesian Ministry of Health. Its facilities included more than fifty thousand square feet of laboratory space spread among three buildings and 175 staff—including more than sixty Indonesian scientific staff (Ear 2012: 167). Indeed, NAMRU-2 operated the only in-country lab that could analyze both human and animal samples to confirm or deny the presence of H5N1 or other potential pandemic strains of influenza (Lowe 2010: 154). In this way, NAMRU-2 was a potent symbol of the globalization of health. It conducted surveillance operations to assess potential pandemic threats both near and far. The fact that the laboratory was supported by the military was not necessarily surprising, as the US military has funded a great deal of global health and surveillance research. That said, the presence of one country's military operation in another country is an overt display of one country's sovereignty and a challenge to another country's (Lowe 2010: 156).

In 2008, the memorandum of understanding (MOU) that allowed NAMRU-2 to operate in Indonesia was up for renewal. Supari led the efforts to terminate the agreement, arguing that NAMRU-2 should not send human H5N1 samples to the Centers for Disease Control and Prevention labs in Atlanta. Even more importantly, she argued that the Indonesian people themselves received few, if any, benefits from NAMRU-2. As with GISN, she said that NAMRU-2 used Indonesia for the raw materials, but that the benefits accumulated elsewhere. Supari "framed the presence of NAMRU-2 in Indonesia as a further violation of Indonesian sovereignty, employing a rationality that was both identitarian and anti-imperialist" (Lowe 2010: 160–61). Additionally, as H5N1 and other influenza strains became increasingly securitized, NAMRU-2's research priorities shifted more toward disease surveillance and focused less on addressing infectious disease concerns in the region. Ear also argues that the motivations of NAMRU-2's staffers were changing, moving away from applied treatment strategies and more toward clinical academic research. This created a further distance between the Indonesian population and the beneficiaries of NAMRU-2's research (Ear 2014: 73). This distance also helped to spawn conspiracy theories, suggesting that H5N1 was a biological agent specifically engineered to harm Indonesia and that NAMRU-2 was actually a spy agency (Lowe 2010: 160–61). This combination of concerns led the Indonesian government to terminate its MOU with NAMRU-2, and the lab moved to Cambodia in 2010. When Indonesia sought to create its own disease surveillance system—the Early Warning Outbreak Recognition System—the government lacked the financial resources to support it in an ongoing manner, and the system eventually stopped functioning (Ear 2012: 177).

Viral sovereignty continues to show up in Indonesia in interesting ways. In November 2009, the nationally owned vaccine production company PT BioFarma announced that it would provide the seasonal flu vaccine to all Indonesian pilgrims to Mecca and that all of the doses it supplied would be domestically produced. This announcement was notable for two reasons. First, seasonal flu vaccinations were generally a low priority in Indonesia. PT BioFarma's directors tried to address this seeming change of approach, telling people that "weather differences" between Saudi Arabia and Indonesia may increase the risk of infection. Second, by emphasizing that the influenza vaccine doses would be domestically produced, PT BioFarma was essentially asserting sovereignty within the scientific realm (Lowe 2010: 158–59). This connects with concerns about the potential for deliberate contamination of vaccines in other Muslim-majority areas (Yahya 2007). PT BioFarma was not only asserting its own capabilities, but emphasizing that it could be trusted because of its sovereign responsibilities to its fellow Indonesians.

DOES VIRAL SOVEREIGNTY MATTER?

Viral sovereignty's legacy is up for debate. On the one hand, it may seem like an aberration. Supari herself was out as Indonesia's health minister in October 2009 after Susilo Bambang Yudhoyono's re-election as president of Indonesia. Few, if any, states explicitly invoke viral sovereignty when discussing virus sample sharing. On the other hand, Supari's deployment of viral sovereignty galvanized the global community to consider the intersection of globalization and health. She forced the question, which in turn led to the creation of the WHO's new PIPF. It is true that PIPF does not go far in changing the underlying structures, and it is not clear how effective this new framework will be in the face of a human influenza pandemic, but the simple fact that the global community engaged in these debates is significant. Inequities within the globalization of health still exist, but the debates over viral sovereignty made this issue more prominent and part of the international agenda. That is unlikely to have happened without Supari's willingness to leverage Indonesia's human H5N1 virus samples to challenge the WHO's system. She provoked a debate that brought the Global North and pharmaceutical manufacturers to the negotiating table.

Viral sovereignty also illustrates the importance of framing global health issues. Human H5N1 became an important global issue because states in the Global North had framed it as a security issue. They cared about H5N1 because of their fears that the ease of travel, transport, and border crossing in our globalized age could put them and their citizens at risk. Global concern about H5N1 was not driven by concerns about the right to health or human rights or the potential detrimental effects an influenza outbreak could have on the development of poorer states. Globalization turned H5N1 into a reason that the Global North could or should fear the Global South. In this way, the securitization framing enabled Supari and her supporters to draw on sovereignty as a way to fight back against the excesses of globalization. Viral sovereignty territorialized an issue that had been conceptualized as floating freely and easily across borders.

We can envision how other states might try to harness Supari's arguments in the future by thinking about questions of medical technology development and access. Take, for instance, the efforts to develop an Ebola vaccine. The Ebola outbreak in West Africa has spurred a number of different companies to develop a vaccine, but these efforts "are not motivated primarily by humanitarian considerations—to save African lives—but rather by the desire to safeguard Western nations against emerging infectious diseases and weaponized infectious agents" (Hooker et al. 2014: 352). If pharmaceutical companies are successful in developing an effective Ebola vaccine that is largely unaffordable or inaccessible to people living in countries that have experienced Ebola outbreaks—and the countries where Ebola has occurred have among the lowest per capita health spending and weakest health care infrastructure (Rid and Emanuel 2014)—then it would not necessarily be a stretch to see the government of Liberia or the Democratic Republic of Congo assert some degree of ownership or control over the virus samples used to develop the vaccine and taken from their territory. A diplomatic and scientific row emerged in early 2019 over who had access to the Ebola virus samples taken from Guinea, Liberia, and Sierra Leone. West African scientists accused pharmaceutical companies and Western governments of "biological asset stripping" and denying them access to samples taken from their citizens and within their territory (Freudenthal 2019). The same dynamics could operate for governments in south and central America in response to the development of a Zika vaccine—another infectious disease that has recently captured the attention of pharmaceutical companies (Cohen 2016). Governments might be tempted to describe what pharmaceutical companies are doing as exploitation if their own citizens are unable to access the benefits derived from the viruses circulating within their territory.

CONCLUSION

Siti Fadilah Supari's refusal to share human H5N1 influenza virus samples with the global virus–sharing network and her invocation of the new concept of viral sovereignty presents one of the clearest demonstrations of how globalization has changed how different actors respond to the demands of globalization. H5N1 attracted a high degree of attention from the international community and was securitized by a number of actors, but Indonesia challenged these systems. Why should Indonesia share virus samples to facilitate the development of vaccines and treatments that it could not access and would instead enrich multinational pharmaceutical companies and protect people in the Global North?

In these ways, viral sovereignty sought to use the logics of globalization against the idea itself. It invoked nationalism as a challenge to the idea of globalization existing in a post-Westphalian space. It questioned the usefulness of virus sharing at a time when global health governance was placing an ever-increasing emphasis on surveillance. It conditioned its cooperation with the rest of the global community on the requirement of benefits flowing back to itself and the rest of the Global South, raising questions about how globally oriented global health governance truly was.

Viral sovereignty complicates our understanding of how globalization operates within the global health space because it calls attention to the inequities that persist. Globalization may have brought greater attention to a variety of global health issues, but it has not necessarily addressed the inequities or grievances. It also shows that the global health governance system retains at least some of the protective impulses that propelled international health governance—creating systems that protect wealthy states in the Global North from diseases originating in the Global South without regard for the problems those diseases may cause for people living in that region.

If we think back to the key attributes of globalization, we can see clear evidence of how they played a role in the viral sovereignty debate. Supari's argument against virus sharing addressed economic issues because she objected that Indonesians would not be able to afford the vaccines being manufactured from their samples. Her objections also embraced the social and political dimensions of globalization. She positioned viral sovereignty as a response to the political structures that prioritized the interests of the Global North over the Global South. She also framed her concerns within broader swaths of the historical experiences of colonialism and even invoked religion to support her arguments.

Her argument resonated domestically and internationally because of how it connected to or drew upon the key elements of globalization. The *intensification* of linkages among geographically distant states meant that international society needed to engage with Indonesia—even if the countries in the Global North had not yet seen cases of human H5N1 influenza. The existence of the GISN was premised on the *integration* among states brought about through globalization. By invoking elements of Westphalian sovereignty, Supari challenged the ideas that *deterritorialization* had become the new norm in international relations. The fact that influenza prompted intense international negotiations speaks to the *elevation* of global health to the ranks of key issues for international society. Finally, by connecting issues of IPRs, pharmaceutical manufacturing practices, neocolonialism, and global health, Supari's invocation of viral sovereignty relies on the *expansion* of issues under globalization.

The next chapter will go into some of these issues in greater detail by focusing on disease surveillance systems and their role in the globalization of health. Surveillance has become increasingly important and democratized, but its prominence has not necessarily come with the resources and support necessary to make these systems workable. Additionally, there remain questions about the relative priority of disease surveillance systems for countries whose public health budgets are already stretched thin responding to existing issues.

CHAPTER 6

SURVEILLANCE

Zombie movies are basically about disease surveillance, and nearly every one of them has this sort of scene. A brave band of survivors has established a remote campsite or taken up residence in a shopping mall to protect themselves. This ragtag bunch is vigilantly keeping watch for the undead to enter their protected zone, and they are doing their best to think about how they will beat back the zombie horde if (or when) it attacks. The group knows how important it is that no one gets bitten by a zombie because that will inevitably turn that person into a zombie—and thus the group will have to kill that person. Suddenly, one of the loveable moppets does something that inadvertently calls the zombies' attention to the presence of the humans, and a battle between the living and the undead breaks out. The humans prevail, and there is a celebration. Amid the celebration, though, one member of the group (probably a grandfather-type figure who has some special skill like making the best pancakes or being able to whistle two notes at once) approaches the leader. He shows the leader an open gash and sheepishly admits that a zombie bit him. The leader knows what this means and what the group must do. The bitten group member pleads for his life. The leader feels conflicted, but knows what the group must do—and that it has to be done *now*. Through tears, the leader shoots the bitten group member in the head in order to destroy his brain—and the group moves on to a different forested area or better protected part of the mall, saddened but determined to set up an even more robust zombie surveillance system. If humanity is to have any hope to survive, we need to know where the zombies are, how they can be identified, and how zombieism spreads (Drezner 2015; Payne 2017; Youde 2012a).

The same applies to infectious disease outbreaks in the real world. While we have not been confronted with an outbreak of zombieism (yet), we have seen numerous cases of new and re-emergent infectious diseases spreading across borders. We have seen examples of how effective surveillance has worked to stop outbreaks early—and examples of how states have refused to share information out of fears that others will retaliate against them and damage their economies, political systems, and reputation within the international community. We have seen how the range of actors and organizations engaged in surveillance has changed and expanded over time, and how this change has raised questions of human rights, authority, and privacy.

This chapter considers the role of surveillance in the intersection between health and globalization. It begins by looking at historical examples of how infectious disease surveillance has worked and the factors that have promoted or hindered cooperation with surveillance systems. It then looks at the international legal requirements relating to infectious disease surveillance systems and how those systems have changed over time. The next section digs into some of the concerns that have emerged about the role of surveillance, who conducts it, the techniques they use, and what opportunity people might have to respond to it. Even though surveillance is increasingly important to global health, there is a long history of people and governments reacting strongly and negatively to surveillance systems being applied without nuance or too rashly. Surveillance both has an effect on the intersection of health and globalization and is affected by it. Understanding this reciprocal process brings the importance of infectious disease surveillance systems in contemporary global health programs to the forefront.

DEFINING SURVEILLANCE

Public health surveillance—and the ability and capacity to carry it out promptly, accurately, and on an ongoing basis—has become one of the most significant issues within global health politics (Weir and Mykhalovskiy 2010). Alexander Langmuir, a professor of epidemiology at the Johns Hopkins University and creator of the Epidemiological Intelligence Service for the Centers for Disease Control and Prevention (CDC) in 1951, established the modern understanding of public health surveillance. He defined it as "the continued watchfulness over the distribution and trends of incidence through the systematic collection, consolidation, and evaluation of morbidity and mortality reports and other relevant data." This requires "the regular dissemination of the basic data and interpretations to all who have contributed and all others who need to know" (Langmuir 1963: 182–83). It emphasizes identifying the links between outbreaks and local conditions, and it recognizes the importance of maintaining ongoing operations to identify outbreaks and limit their spread.

The International Health Regulations (2005) (IHR [2005]) build upon Langmuir's vision. They define surveillance as "the systematic ongoing collection, collation, and analysis of data for public health purposes and the timely dissemination of public health information for assessment and public health response as necessary" (World Health Organization [WHO] 2016b: 14). One of the most important elements of this definition is on its emphasis on collecting information as a guide for action and interventions (Davies and Youde 2015). It also shifts the international understanding of surveillance away from a passive process occurring at a few discrete locations to one that is more active and widespread.

The IHR (2005)'s definition operationalizes surveillance in four key ways. First, with the all-risks approach discussed in chapter 3, the IHR (2005) places surveillance at the heart of the global system to prevent disease outbreaks. This information is vital for determining whether an outbreak constitutes a Public Health Emergency of International

Concern (PHEIC) and gathering the information necessary to make an informed decision. The surveillance data are then applied to a decision-making matrix to guide the international response. Any human cases of smallpox, polio, SARS, and new subtypes of influenza must be reported to the WHO. For other diseases, government officials need to consider four questions to determine whether they must be reported to the WHO for their potential to pose an international concern:

- Does the event have a serious public health impact?
- Is the event unusual or unexpected?
- Is there a significant risk of international spread?
- Is there a significant risk that the event could trigger trade and travel restrictions?

If the authorities answer at least two of the four questions affirmatively, then the event must be reported to the WHO for consideration about whether it constitutes a PHEIC.

Second, because the IHR (2005) applies to a wide range of potential public health events, it requires that states create and maintain permanent surveillance and reporting structures. The system needs to be ready at all times to identify potential threats and share that information with the WHO. The IHR (2005) mandates that all states establish a National Focal Point "which is accessible at all times (7/24/365) for communications with WHO IHR Contact Points" (WHO n.d.).

Third, the IHR (2005) allows the WHO to receive reports about public health events from nonstate sources. Timely reporting allows for a quicker response and decreases the chances of an outbreak causing widespread devastation. Governments may have reasons to avoid reporting disease outbreaks; they could fear that other states will impose sanctions against them, or they could worry about the political, economic, and social consequences of a disease outbreak. In the past, if a state did not want to report, there was nothing the WHO could do. Under the IHR (2005), nonstate sources like nongovernmental organizations or local health clinics could make reports to the WHO, which would then allow the WHO to follow up with the relevant authorities in that state. In addition to giving the WHO more access to a wider array of sources, this strategy also seeks to increase compliance. In essence, the WHO is telling states that it is going to find out about any outbreaks one way or another, so it is in the government's interest to report it itself.

Finally, the IHR (2005)'s surveillance requirements respect human rights. States cannot use these surveillance requirements to violate their citizens' fundamental rights without reason. Based on the data collected through surveillance, a government may decide to restrict certain rights (for example, closing public gathering spaces)—but only if it can provide a firm justification for doing so, make its application as minimal as possible, and limit the duration of any such policies to as short a period as possible. In this way, the treaty puts its surveillance requirements in line with 1985's Siracusa Principles (United Nations 1985), which explicitly lay out the narrow conditions under which governments can temporarily abrogate human rights (Davies and Youde 2015: 12).

There is one important caveat to emphasize about the IHR (2005)'s surveillance requirements. While the treaty mandates new surveillance standards that all member-states must meet, it provides no financial or technical assistance to governments to implement the requirements (Bakari and Frumence 2013; Wilson, Brownstein, and Fidler 2010). Under the initial terms of the treaty, states needed to demonstrate that their surveillance systems were operational by 2012 (with a possible two-year deadline extension if needed). Unfortunately, many states found it difficult to meet these requirements—though generally not due to a lack of trying (Youde 2011b). Most health authorities in most countries were genuinely interested in achieving the deadline, but they were often stymied by their government's lack of resources. Many of the surveillance requirements, for example, require a well-trained workforce, but most of the seemingly noncompliant states lack the personnel or resources to train, hire, and maintain such staff (Fischer, Kornblet, and Katz 2011: 13). By the initial 2012 deadline, only forty-two states reported that they were in full compliance. Two years later, the total number had increased to sixty-four. The remaining states either asked for an extension or failed to report to the WHO about their compliance efforts (Katz and Dowell 2015: e352). At the 2015 World Health Assembly, the body agreed to extend the compliance deadline to 2016 for all eighty-one countries that had requested it and gave another sixty countries until 2019 to meet the standards. Though globalization helped prompt the rewriting of the IHR and the attendant new surveillance requirements, that has not yet translated into a shared sense of responsibility for ensuring that the surveillance requirements are being achieved consistently. The WHO and its members believe in surveillance and its importance, but have not created funding mechanisms to support states trying to meet the standards (Gostin and Katz 2016: 269–70).

SURVEILLANCE, BIOPOLITICS, AND GLOBALIZATION

Surveillance can both protect and threaten us. It implies a combination of government powers and capabilities that "are as vital to the maintenance of our welfare and freedom . . . just as they might undergird a policy of rounding up undesirable minorities" (Scott 1998: 4). This is why Fairchild, Bayer, and Colgrove (2007: xvii) describe public health surveillance as "Janus-faced." They also note that both supporters and skeptics of public health surveillance liken these practices to Jeremy Bentham's panopticon.

Bentham was a British philosopher and social reformer in the late eighteenth and early nineteenth centuries. He is best known today for two things: for being one of the first advocates for the ethical theory of utilitarianism (Bentham 2004) and for his body being preserved in a glass case known as the Auto-Icon at University College London (UCL) (UCL n.d.). Bentham described utilitarianism's "fundamental axiom" as "it is the greatest happiness of the greatest number that is the measure of right and wrong" (cited in Burns 2005: 46). Under this framework, the interests of all in society should be considered, and government actions need to consider their consequences on human welfare.

It is this set of beliefs that led Bentham to champion the panopticon, which puts surveillance into practice. The panopticon is a prison—but one which Bentham believed would be more humane. Prisons in the late 1700s and early 1800s were nasty places. They were fetid, dark, and disease-ridden, and they required a lot of staff. Bentham proposed a new model that would rely on surveillance to make for a safer and better environment. The panopticon envisioned a circular building with a guard tower in the middle. The guard tower's windows would be coated so that the guards could see out, but the prisoners could not see in. For this reason, a prisoner could never know that they were being observed at any given moment—and would therefore believe that guards were watching them at *any* time. The result, Bentham believed, would be self-regulation; prisoners act better because they never knew if a guard might be watching them. This prison would be cheaper for the state to run, encourage better behavior among the prisoners, and lead to a better experience for all. Surveillance was thus a tool for moral and societal improvement because it helps to mold human behavior (Lyon 1991).

While Bentham saw the panopticon's surveillance as improving human behavior, Michel Foucault saw surveillance as more malevolent. He viewed the modern state as increasingly preoccupied with the intersection of power and human biological existence, and he identified surveillance as central to the extension of government power. Surveillance allows governments to exercise "disciplinary neoliberalism" over their subjects by convincing people to act in certain ways without even realizing how they are being molded and controlled (Gill 1995). In this way, it exerts control over the political agenda by regulating how people see their relationship to themselves, each other, and the government (Lukes 2005: 29).

For Foucault, the surveillance of human health is an exercise of power itself. "The body becomes a useful force only if it is both a productive body and a subjected body," he wrote (Foucault 1977: 26). As a result, the state has taken a growing interest in regulating, moderating, and overseeing the health of its citizens. It adopts policies, procedures, and regulations that allow the state to regulate and optimize life in accordance with its own interests (Youde 2010: 17). One observer cynically described the resulting policies and attitudes as "the reign of the monogamous jogger" because these sorts of behaviors both reinforce the state's power and are in line with its interests (Baldwin 2005: 16). These shifts allow the state to exercise its power through standardizing human existence and without needing to resort to more overt forms of compliance.

Let's use an example to illustrate the controversy over surveillance in the health realm. Many companies have employee wellness programs. If you take a certain number of steps each day or exercise for a certain length of time, you get a reward. It might be as simple as a T-shirt, but it might also be a reduction in your monthly health insurance premium. These programs have a few different motivations. For individuals, they may be tools for encouraging regular physical activity and perhaps creating new healthy habits. They may help a person drop some weight or get their blood pressure under control. For the business sponsoring the program, they want to see their costs go down, and healthier people are less likely to make health insurance claims. Supporters of these wellness programs promote them as an opportunity for people to take control of their health, encourage healthy habits, and stop potential health problems before they start (Baicker, Cutler, and Song 2010). Critics counter that they "treat wellness as a lifestyle that employees must be cajoled into adopting, extending the workplace not just into the home but into the bodies of workers" (Hull and Pasquale 2018: 180). They also argue that these sorts of programs place the focus on the individual rather than the larger social, economic, and political structures that change a person's risk of ill health (Glasgow and Schrecker 2015). Critics further worry that these data may be used inappropriately, and they charge that data abstracted from any context are insufficient for policymaking. For instance, could an insurance company refuse to cover your blood pressure medicine because you did not spend enough time on the treadmill or got too many pizza deliveries from Uber Eats? Others go even further, calling these efforts (and evidence-based medicine more broadly) "a good example of microfascism at play in the contemporary scientific arena" (Holmes et al. 2006: 181). This tension illustrates the debates over surveillance's purposes—is it being done for the collective good, or is it a tool of discipline (or both)?

The dynamics of globalization expand these debates about surveillance for both supporters and critics in important ways. First, globalization dramatically widens the space that needs to be under watch. If the US government wants to keep its citizens safe from infectious disease, it is not enough to only know what is happening within its own borders. It must keep an eye on what is happening all over the world. Second, it connects health surveillance to other national and international issues. Biopolitical surveillance is no longer simply about public health, but it gets connected with issues like security and constructs an image of health as a potential threat (Bell 2006; Horner, Wood, and Kelly 2013). Third, the globalization of surveillance expands the range of actors who might engage in such actions or use the data collected to promote some sort of action. Nongovernmental organizations, for example, could engage in panoptic surveillance to call attention to both abuses carried out by governments or to single out states for praise (Steele and Amoureux 2006). Disease surveillance systems supported by national governments and intergovernmental organizations are increasingly augmented by independent internet-based surveillance systems that can empower organizations like the WHO to take action (Collier 2015; Davies 2012b). Fourth, the expansion of public health surveillance introduces additional opportunities for abuses to occur. More surveillance activities mean more opportunities for a person's rights to be violated, for data to be use inappropriately, and for policies that run roughshod over local concerns. At the same time, the expansion of surveillance beyond the domestic level and beyond state actors complicates lines of accountability. If a person believes that their rights have been violated through public health surveillance measures, to whom would they complain? Who could provide them with some redress? These questions are far more difficult to answer in a more globalized context (Youde 2012a).

Bentham may have originated panopticism more than two hundred years ago, but he contributes to its ongoing operation to this day. Bentham's preserved body is kept in the Auto-Icon at UCL and is generally on public display at the end of the South Cloisters in the university's main building; those who cannot make it to London to see it in person can see it in a rotatable, 360-degree view on the university's website. When the UCL Council, the university's management and oversight accountability body, meets, Bentham's Auto-Icon is wheeled out so that he can attend, allowing him to provide oversight of the university's operations two centuries after his death. Bentham is generally listed as "present but not voting" in the Council's minutes, but he reportedly votes in favor of any motion where the Council is split "due to his mischievous personality" (Booth 2013).

SURVEILLANCE IN ACTION

With the changes in surveillance requirements in the IHR (2005), we see more mandates on national governments, the potential for conflict between state and nonstate sources of surveillance information, and a widening scope for where and how surveillance operations need to occur. This section takes three examples—H1N1 influenza, Ebola, and Zika—to examine how surveillance occurred, how the surveillance operations had an effect on policy choices, and whether the system functioned effectively. The WHO declared a PHEIC in all three of these cases, but those declarations generated their own controversies and were not necessarily universally embraced. The most striking takeaway from these experiences is that infectious disease surveillance continues to be a work in progress.

H1N1 INFLUENZA

A ten-year-old boy in San Diego County, California, came down with a fever, cough, and vomiting on March 30, 2009. His parents took him to an outpatient clinic, and doctors took a throat swab in an effort to identify what was making him sick. The lab confirmed that the boy had come down with influenza A, but not with any of the subtypes believed to be circulating that year. The county health department was notified, and it conducted a more extensive investigation. Two weeks after the boy fell ill, the CDC determined that he had influenza A (H1N1), better known as swine flu. Three days later, it received another anomalous influenza specimen. This one came from a nine-year-old girl in Imperial County, California, just east of San Diego. The CDC found that she had contracted the same flu strain (CDC 2009). These two kids from southern California were the first confirmed cases of an international H1N1 influenza outbreak that caused more than eighteen thousand deaths and saw cases appear in more than two hundred countries and overseas territories within a year (WHO 2010).

Influenza regularly circulates, causing seasonal epidemics nearly every winter. When we get the flu vaccine, we are trying to prevent seasonal influenza. This is a tricky process because the influenza strains that circulate change every single year. To understand why, we need to understand how strains differ from one another. Influenza A viruses are divided into subtypes based on two proteins—hemagglutinin (H) and neuraminidase (N)—found on the surface of the virus. Hemagglutinin has eighteen different subtypes (H1 through H18), and neuraminidase has eleven (N1 through N11). The combination of those subtypes are how we distinguish among different strains of influenza, and scientists base the seasonal flu vaccine on the strains they think will circulate that winter. This is important because a vaccine effective against one strain will not necessarily work for other strains. The other important element in the equation is that it takes a long time to make flu vaccines. The most common technique grows the vaccine in eggs, and it takes five to six months to produce the vaccine.

When the scientists are right, the flu vaccine is highly effective and the flu season is relatively mild. When they are wrong or an unexpected strain starts makes rounds, the potential for a widespread outbreak increases. It takes a long time to produce the flu vaccine, so manufacturers cannot just whip up a new version if an unexpected strain begins to circulate. When that outbreak starts spreading across borders, it can morph into an international epidemic that can strain health services. Since influenza spreads relatively easily, it can easily take advantage of the movement of people across borders that globalization facilitates.

H1N1's appearance in 2009 caused worries for two reasons. First, it was not part of that year's flu vaccine. While two cases are not proof of an international outbreak, H1N1's unexpected appearance raised alarms about the possibility of something happening on a wider scale. Second, H1N1 is a particularly infamous influenza strain. In January 1976, soldiers at Fort Dix, New Jersey, reported respiratory ailments, and one soldier died. Initial efforts to identify the virus were unsuccessful, so public health officials sent a virus culture from the dead soldier and some of the ill soldiers to the CDC's labs in Atlanta. On February 12, 1976, officials confirmed the presence of four cases of H1N1 among the soldiers (Neustadt and Fineberg 1982: 17–18). This set off a massive campaign to vaccinate all Americans against swine flu, including a live television event where doctors vaccinated President Gerald Ford (Neustadt and Fineberg 1982: 92–93). Today, this campaign is largely remembered as a fiasco. Not only was the spread of H1N1 incredibly limited, but the rush to manufacture so many vaccine doses in such a short period of time led to serious production problems. More people fell ill and died of complications and side effects associated with the vaccination program than cases of H1N1 itself (Evans, Cauchemez, and Hayden 2009). These problems bred a mistrust of vaccination programs that continues to bedevil public health campaigns to this day (Osterholm and Olshaker 2017: 260). More worryingly, H1N1 was responsible for the 1918 worldwide influenza pandemic that infected more than five hundred million people and killed fifty to one hundred million people (Barry 2009: 397). An outbreak on that same scale in the twenty-first century could potentially devastate political and economic systems around the world.

Those first two swine flu cases in California in 2009 were not the origin of the outbreak. Subsequent research has traced the virus to a small village called La Gloria in Veracruz, Mexico, in March 2009, but how exactly it made the leap to humans or traveled internationally is unclear. The Mexican Department of Health identified an unusually high number of influenza-like cases at a time when seasonal flu outbreaks were generally ending—though it was not known then whether this was due to a unique flu strain or just a statistical aberration (Davies, Kamradt-Scott, and Rushton 2015: 93–95). Shortly after H1N1 was discovered in California more cases appeared across the United States and internationally. This led the CDC to contact the WHO to report "laboratory confirmation [of] a new influenza virus with pandemic potential" in accordance with the IHR (2005)'s requirements (Davies, Kamradt-Scott, and Rushton 2015: 95). In addition to information from the Mexican and American governments, nonstate surveillance systems like the Global Public Health Intelligence Network, ProMED Mail, and Health Map provided crucial information that allowed public health agencies to "connect the dots" and recognize how the virus was spreading (Stoto 2014: 226). Toward the end of April 2009, the US government declared a public health emergency after it had confirmed twenty cases in five states. By this point, Mexico had experienced sixteen hundred cases of swine flu and at least twenty-two deaths.

Though the WHO did not recommend travel or trade bans, and the IHR (2005) mandates that governments are not supposed to implement policies more restrictive than the WHO's recommendations, some states took matters into their own hands. Various governments advised their citizens against travel to Mexico and banned the import of Mexican pork products, even though there was no evidence that swine flu spread through meat. China, Hong Kong, and Japan all introduced quarantine procedures for anyone suspected of swine flu (McNeil 2009). Egyptian authorities culled all pigs in the country, despite the fact that there was no reported outbreak of H1N1 among pigs anywhere in the world at the time and no human cases of H1N1 in Egypt. Gostin suggests that the Egyptian government's actions may have been motivated by prejudice against the country's Coptic Christian minority—the primary domestic consumers of pork (Gostin 2014: 2020). A zoo in Iraq even killed three wild boars to allay public fears that they could transmit influenza to

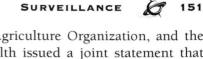

visitors. The WHO, the Food and Agriculture Organization, and the World Organization for Animal Health issued a joint statement that stressed that pork and pork products posed no risk of transmitting H1N1, and there were even complaints lodged with the World Trade Organization over the restrictions placed on the pork trade (Rushton and Kamradt-Scott 2015: 33–34).

The WHO took its own actions to prevent a worldwide influenza epidemic. Using the powers granted it by the IHR (2005), WHO officials declared H1N1 to be a PHEIC on April 25, 2009. This was the first time that the WHO had made such a declaration, and it came just forty-one days after the first case of H1N1 was detected (Hoffman and Silverberg 2018: 330). At that time, the WHO called on member-states to increase their surveillance activities. Two days later, WHO officials elevated H1N1's pandemic alert level from Phase 3 (limited human-to-human transmission) to Phase 4 (community-level outbreaks). After two more days, it again raised the pandemic alert level, reaching Phase 5 (sustained community transmission) (Davies, Kamradt-Scott, and Rushton 2015: 96–97). H1N1 reached the highest pandemic alert level, Phase 6 (pandemic with widespread geographic distribution) on June 11, 2009 (Gostin 2014: 366). These steps contributed to a sense of emergency and firmly placed H1N1 on the international agenda.

The speed with which the WHO elevated the H1N1 outbreak raised questions. On the one hand, this was the first major international outbreak to occur since the IHR (2005) had gone into effect. Just a few years earlier, SARS had shown the world had seen what could happen when political concerns delayed a public health response to an outbreak. The WHO went through all of the proper legal channels to ensure that its declaration was compliant with the treaty's requirements. It argued that, if it was going to implement an effective response to a potential outbreak, it needed to implement responses early enough to stop the outbreak before it got out of hand. This was a moment when the WHO needed to be able to speak authoritatively and act as a hub for information and communications (Gostin 2014: 202). Speaking about the H1N1 outbreak, WHO Director-General Margaret Chan declared, "This is the first pandemic to occur since the revolution in communications and information technologies. For the first time in history, the international community could watch a pandemic unfold, and chart its evolution, in real time" (Chan 2010).

On the other hand, the H1N1 outbreak turned out to be nowhere near as widespread or devastating as anticipated. Fewer people died of influenza in 2009 during the pandemic than die of it during nonpandemic years (Yin and Tambyah 2015: 336). Some of the WHO's actions during the outbreak even raised suspicions. It changed the definition of influenza pandemic, removing language about "enormous numbers of deaths and illness." This led the Council of Europe to allege that the WHO changed the definition so it could declare a pandemic without having to consider the virus' intensity. Similarly, the different pandemic phases refer to the *likelihood* of disease occurrence rather than the clinical *severity* of an outbreak (Doshi 2011: 532–33). Experts consulted by the WHO as part of its deliberations had financial and professional ties to pharmaceutical companies that make influenza vaccines and antiviral medicines, and the WHO insisted on keeping the composition of the Emergency Committee private (Cohen and Carter 2010). Based on the WHO's declarations, governments spent millions on vaccines and anti-virals which were of marginal effectiveness and did not arrive until after the outbreak had largely passed (Osterholm and Olshaker 2017: 90). Others criticized the WHO for devoting so much time and attention to a relatively mild outbreak and ignoring more serious events like cholera and extensively drug-resistant tuberculosis (Sparke and Anguelov 2012; Wilson, Brownstein, and Fidler 2010). Though an independent review of the WHO's handling of H1N1 largely cleared the organization of accusations of wrongdoing or conflicts of interest (Davies, Kamradt-Scott, and Rushton 2015: 100), the opacity of the process and the potential appearance of conflicts of interest undermined confidence in how the IHR (2005) would work in practice.

H1N1 was the international community's first test of the new surveillance powers and responsibilities contained within the IHR (2005), and it was an auspicious start. While the WHO took rapid action, that very speed became a basis for criticizing the organization. This experience highlighted the fact that surveillance is not apolitical; instead, its use and interpretation is invariably interconnected with larger economic, political, and social issues. Further, it raised questions about the role of domestic and Westphalian sovereignty and how those imperatives may come into conflict with broader interests. H1N1 surveillance efforts necessarily challenge a state's domestic sovereignty. At the same time, this sort of shared sovereignty incorporates both state and nonstate actors, which complicates our narratives about power and authority in international relations even further.

EBOLA

The Ebola outbreak in West Africa garnered a huge amount of international attention for a variety of reasons—its size, its scope, and its unexpected location. These factors contributed to a great deal of attention being focused on surveillance systems and how they intersected with questions of globalization. While there were certainly efforts to bulk up surveillance systems within the affected states (and some great success stories), globalization helped to prioritize surveillance to ensure that the disease would not enter the Global North. Rather than epitomizing international solidarity, the surveillance response to the Ebola outbreak ended up reinforcing divisions.

WHO officials confirmed the presence of human cases of Ebola in Guinea on March 23, 2014. Within six weeks, it announced that the disease had spread to neighboring Liberia and Sierra Leone. These announcements were remarkable for a number of reasons. First, while Ebola outbreaks are relatively rare, the disease's high case fatality rate makes its appearance anywhere particularly worrisome. Second, Ebola had not previously appeared in West Africa. Nearly every previous outbreak had occurred in Central Africa, but now the disease has emerged thousands of miles away, and there was no obvious answer to how or why it had made such a dramatic move. Third, there had never been a multicountry Ebola outbreak before. It can be difficult enough to coordinate between the WHO and a single national government. Trying to achieve cooperation among at least three national governments added additional complications. Fourth, the national borders between Guinea, Liberia, and Sierra Leone are quite porous, with people living in the region crossing them regularly. This could complicate efforts to conduct contact tracing or make it easier for people to avoid surveillance systems. Contact tracing, a key concept in epidemiology, is "the process of identifying, assessing, and monitoring people who may have been exposed to a disease to prevent onward transmission" (Wolfe et al. 2017). Once a person is diagnosed with Ebola, officials try to identify all of the people who may have come in contact with the patient. They closely monitor those contacts twice daily for twenty-one days to see if they develop the disease in order to get them care early if they do fall ill and decrease the chance that they spread the disease even further. Contact tracing is very resource-intensive (Armbruster and Brandeau 2007), "includes extended periods of personal interactions during times of high stress and fear" (Wolfe et al. 2017), and has historically raised questions about the right to privacy (Fairchild, Bayer, and Colgrove 2207: 74–79). These processes become significantly more complicated when it is hard to maintain contact with people. Finally, the scope and scale of the outbreak led some other states to call for travel bans, trade restrictions, and mandatory quarantine regimes. Such actions reflected both the fears about an international Ebola outbreak and a test of respect for the WHO's powers to determine trade and travel restrictions in the IHR (2005).

Ebola is a zoonotic viral hemorrhagic fever. Scientists are not entirely sure what Ebola's animal reservoir is, but current research suggests that fruit bats are the host (WHO 2018c). Once it gets into the human population, the virus spreads through intimate contact with blood and other bodily fluids of someone who is exhibiting symptoms of the disease. The disease starts off as a headache and fever two to twenty-one days after initial exposure to the virus. Vomiting, diarrhea, and nausea follow. While the popular image of Ebola is of people bleeding profusely, this does not happen in all cases. The combination of vomiting, diarrhea, and bleeding causes dehydration and low blood pressure, and this is what ultimately causes death. As the virus replicates and a person gets increasingly sick, they are more likely to transmit the infection to others. Roughly half of all Ebola patients die of the disease. There is no treatment for Ebola; health care workers try to provide supportive care to keep people from becoming too dehydrated. If a person recovers from Ebola, they may develop lifelong immunity to the virus. This may provide some clues that scientists can use in their efforts to develop a treatment or vaccine for the disease (Hayden 2017). Ebola survivors may also serve as a reservoir for the disease for months after the illness goes away and may develop additional medical problems. The virus has been found in semen as long as two years after recovering from the disease (Fischer et al. 2017), and survivors have reported long-term health effects like glaucoma, headaches, memory loss, depression, and muscle pain (Fox 2016). There are now experimental vaccines and treatments that have been used in the 2018–2019 outbreak in the Democratic Republic of Congo (Cohen 2018), but these did not exist when the West Africa outbreak occurred.

Ebola has loomed large in the popular consciousness since it was first identified in 1976 in the town of Yambuku in what was then Zaire. When patients started showing up at a health clinic run by Belgian Catholic missionaries that August, it seemed like they had malaria—a common problem in the area—until they started experiencing chest pains, sunken eyes, dehydration, fever, confusion, and hemorrhaging. Even more significantly, almost everyone who fell ill died (Garrett 1994: 100–06). Through the work of the WHO, the CDC, and local partners, they were able to stop the disease's spread and identify its characteristics, but they did not know where it came from or have a treatment available. When it came time to name the new disease, the scientists decided to call it Ebola after a nearby river. The Ebola River is about forty miles from Yambuku and was not in the area where the disease first appeared, but scientists opted against naming the disease after Yambuku because they did not want to stigmatize the local community (Breman et al. 2016: S97).

Ebola remains a rare disease. Between 1976 and 2013, there had only been twenty-four documented outbreaks of the disease. Ironically, given how globalization inspired such fears about the spread of the West African outbreak, the lack of globalization may have helped to keep the virus in check previously. Many of the areas where earlier outbreaks occurred were relatively remote and isolated. That made it difficult to get supplies and personnel into those regions, but it also made it hard for Ebola to spread very far. The lack of transportation infrastructure may have helped keep the world safe from widespread epidemics (Coltart et al. 2017). The West African outbreak occurred within a region that was far more mobile, had more cross-border connections, and more urbanized (Osterholm and Olshaker 2017: 146).

Though the WHO made its first announcement about the Ebola outbreak in West Africa on March 23, 2014, we now know that the outbreak began three months earlier. A child named Emile died on December 26, 2013, in Meliandou, Guinea, and subsequent analysis shows that he was the first victim of this outbreak. As more of Emile's family members fell ill and died, public health officials in Guinea initially suspected cholera or Lassa fever. Because they lacked the laboratory facilities to conduct viral testing, they had to send the blood samples they collected to the Pasteur Institute in France (Youde 2018: 119). This reflects one of the region's major problems—weak public health infrastructure with limited surveillance capacities. Guinea, Liberia, and Sierra Leone are among the poorest countries in the world, and none had invested heavily in their public health systems. Though they were at peace in 2014, these countries were still struggling to recover from civil wars and strife that had devastated them during the 1990s. As a result, their health systems remained underdeveloped, and nongovernmental organizations provided health care in significant portions of all three countries (Gros 2016: 246–47).

Modeling exercises provoked even greater fears about the scale and scope of the Ebola outbreak. In September 2014, roughly six months after the WHO made its initial announcement about the outbreak, the CDC released its estimates about how far the outbreak could spread. Without any sort of intervention, the model estimated that Liberia and Sierra Leone alone would see 550,000 confirmed cases of Ebola. Researchers cautioned, though, that there would be significant undercounting because not every case of the disease can be confirmed by a laboratory. Taking the potential for undercounting into consideration, the CDC estimated that these two countries would see 1.4 million cases in the absence of effective interventions to stop the outbreak (Meltzer et al. 2014). Prior to this outbreak, there had only been about two thousand known human cases of Ebola. When the modelers presented their estimates, West Africa had already seen approximately thirty-seven thousand laboratory-confirmed cases with no evidence that the epidemic was slowing down. It is also important to note that this estimate did not even include Guinea, the country where the outbreak began.

The appearance of human cases of Ebola should have put the WHO into overdrive. Ebola is one of the few diseases specifically identified in the IHR (2005), meaning that any cases must be reported to the WHO and that the WHO should consider declaring a PHEIC. Here was a case where a known highly infectious disease that can travel with people was appearing in a new part of the world and spreading across international borders. On its face, it would seem an obvious PHEIC. Instead, the WHO waited. It was not until August 8, 2014—eight months after the outbreak began and more than four months after the WHO made its first announcement—that it declared a PHEIC. By that time, more than one thousand people had died.

What explains the WHO's delay in declaring a PHEIC? The organization initially downplayed the severity of the outbreak, and it may have been reluctant to declare a PHEIC too quickly after the criticism it received for being too quick to declare one for H1N1 (Packard 2016: 329). In subsequent interviews, WHO officials stated that they worried that declaring a PHEIC would negatively affect their relationships with Guinea, Liberia, and Sierra Leone. They thought the declaration would stigmatize the region, reducing trade, tourism, and foreign investment. At the same time, WHO's funding and personnel structures meant that it had little that it could concretely offer in terms of an immediate response (Patterson 2018: 86–88). Nongovernmental organizations like Médecins Sans Frontières (MSF) that had an on-the-ground presence in the region urged the WHO to declare a PHEIC, noting that its own resources were already overstretched and that it lacked the sort of coordinated response and surveillance capabilities that the WHO possessed (Kamradt-Scott 2015: 175). It was not until the disease appeared in Nigeria and sparked fears that it could spread through Lagos, a city of twenty-one million and the most populous city in Africa, that the WHO relented and declared a PHEIC (Oduwole and Akintayo 2017). Along with the declaration, the WHO requested that other member-states not introduce any travel or trade restrictions against the afflicted states while also ramping up their own surveillance activities (Kamradt-Scott 2015: 175).

The reactions to the Ebola outbreak also led to some moments of inadvertent comedy borne of ignorance. In August 2014, a group of Brazilian business executives was scheduled to fly to Namibia to meet with economic development officials there to discuss foreign direct investment opportunities. After the WHO declared a PHEIC, the Brazilian executives canceled their travel plans (Dearden 2014)—even though Namibia is about three thousand miles from the center of the Ebola outbreak in West Africa. To put this in perspective, New York and Los Angeles are 2,451 miles apart. Not only is Namibia far from the outbreak, it has never had a case of Ebola within its borders. While globalization may have contributed to the interest and ability to develop trade ties between South American and African states, it has not necessarily helped people to understand that Africa is not a single country.

By the fall of 2014, the intersections among Ebola, surveillance, and globalization were becoming more pronounced. A Liberian American lawyer, Patrick Sawyer, flew from Monrovia to Lagos on July 20, 2014. When he arrived in Lagos, he collapsed and subsequently died of Ebola. Sawyer's case raised fears that the outbreak would spread globally via air travel (Cohen et al. 2016). Instead, Nigeria managed to avoid a widespread Ebola outbreak thanks to the robustness of its local surveillance systems. When Sawyer fell ill with Ebola in Lagos, it raised fears that the disease would take advantage of the lack of infrastructure and crowded conditions to explode. Further complicating the problem, public health clinics were closed due to a nationwide strike when Sawyer arrived in Nigeria, further reducing the country's response capacity. Despite all of this, Nigeria recorded only nineteen cases of Ebola, and WHO declared Nigeria officially free of Ebola six months after its first case appeared.

How did Nigeria do it? First, Nigerian officials had the advantage of seeing the outbreak's devastation in Guinea, Liberia, and Sierra Leone. They knew that there was a decent chance that Ebola could appear in Nigeria, so they prepared for the possibility. Second, rather than creating brand-new structures in the midst of an emergency, they drew on existing surveillance networks for polio and measles and adapted them to look for Ebola cases. Third, officials aggressively traced all of Sawyer's contacts and monitored them for possible Ebola symptoms. This included twice-daily check-ins in person or by text message with each person who had come into contact with Sawyer, and relying on a network of health professionals and volunteers to conduct face-to-face assessments (Zirulnick 2014). The government also set up handwashing and disinfection stations throughout Lagos, and they proactively engaged the media and community leaders to get accurate information to the public and to challenge rumors about the disease (Ogunsola 2015). The WHO praised Nigeria's efforts as "a piece of world-class epidemiological detective work" (WHO 2014a).

Some of the actions governments undertook to stop the spread of Ebola violated international human rights standards. Guinea, Liberia, and Sierra Leone announced a joint quarantine in their common border areas on August 1, 2004, even though evidence showed that the virus had already left that area. Liberian officials imposed a quarantine for ten days in the West Point neighborhood of Monrovia, preventing seventy-five thousand people from leaving the area and spurring protests and food shortages (Eba 2014). Not only did these

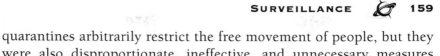

quarantines arbitrarily restrict the free movement of people, but they were also disproportionate, ineffective, and unnecessary measures that did not meet the basic justifications for violating human rights in favor of public health (Hills 2016: 221–23).

The United States' response to Ebola also elicited concern. Shortly before the WHO declared the PHEIC, two health care workers with Samaritan's Purse, a Christian medical charity, were evacuated to the United States from Liberia after contracting Ebola. Transporting them to Emory University's hospital in Atlanta for treatment led some to worry that they could cause an Ebola outbreak in the United States. Donald Trump, who had not yet announced his presidential bid, tweeted that "THE UNITED STATES HAS ENOUGH PROBLEMS!" and that "The U.S. cannot allow EBOLA infected people back. People that go to far away places to help out are great-but must suffer the consequences!" (Wilson 2018; capitalization and punctuation in the original). When Thomas Eric Duncan, a Liberian American businessman, flew to the United States in the middle of October 2014 and subsequently developed Ebola, it seemingly reaffirmed these fears. Adding to the problem, the Dallas hospital where Duncan initially sought treatment misdiagnosed him, and two of the nurses treating him contracted Ebola. This suggested that the United States' infectious disease surveillance systems were not robust enough to identify the disease (Deonandan 2014). The ease and speed with which people could cross international borders, and the chance that they might introduce the Ebola virus into new regions, heightened fears internationally. In fact, shortly after Duncan died of Ebola, the United States introduced new travel restrictions on passengers coming from countries with active Ebola infections. While there were no direct flights from Guinea, Liberia, or Sierra Leone to the United States, the US government decreed that all passengers coming from the region could only enter the country through specially designated airports that had heightened infectious disease screening procedures in place (Roberts 2014).

Kaci Hickox and Craig Spencer's experiences are emblematic of the larger fears and confusion about appropriate Ebola surveillance policies at varying levels of the American government. Hickox and Spencer are both health care workers who spent time providing services at Ebola treatment centers in West Africa with MSF; Spencer worked in Guinea, and Hickox in Sierra Leone. In October 2014, both made international headlines when they returned to the United States. On October 23, Spencer entered New York's Bellevue Hospital as the first Ebola patient in the city's history. He then came in for widespread criticism for the fact that he had taken the subway and gone bowling the day before he fell ill—even though he was not exhibiting any symptoms and therefore could not have transmitted Ebola to anyone else. His fiancée was placed in isolation while he was in the hospital (Spencer, C. 2015: 1089–90). The following day, Hickox arrived at the Newark International Airport, where officials forced her to stay in an isolation tent set up in the parking lot of University Hospital in Newark. Despite showing no signs of illness and having a normal temperature, New Jersey Governor Chris Christie ordered her isolated because he determined her to be "obviously sick." Christie is not a medical doctor, and he made his determination without meeting with Hickox or any medical professional who had examined her. When Christie allowed her to return to her hometown in Maine, Governor Paul LePage ordered her into a twenty-one-day isolation under the threat of court order. Maine filed a petition with District Court to isolate Hickox under the terms of the state's quarantine law, but the court rejected it because Hickox was asymptomatic and therefore posed no threat to the community (Miles 2015: 17).

Government responses to returning health care workers show how fears have perverted the quarantine processes. Spencer and Hickox provoked the governors of New York and New Jersey to impose twenty-one-day quarantines for all health care workers returning to the state after treating Ebola patients, ostensibly "out of an abundance of caution" (Gatter 2015: 376). The CDC even issued its own guidance on establishing voluntary self-isolation for twenty-one days for returning health care workers, but these lacked the force of law (Wulfhorst and Morgan 2014). Many public health officials responded by decrying these actions. While a mandatory quarantine may seem effective, it tends to be counterproductive. It strongly disincentivizes health professionals from traveling to infected regions to provide services. Epidemics like Ebola need to be stopped at the source, but telling volunteers that they will automatically be isolated for three weeks when they return—regardless of whether they show any signs of infection—is highly demotivating (Drazen et al. 2014). Such a reaction also reinforces the notion that Ebola is a disease "over there" rather than something that needs to be addressed collaboratively. It serves to increase the levels of fear and stigma, which end up actually making people *less* likely to seek out services (Whiteside and Zebryk 2015: 414). Instead of protecting people, these measures were more political in design, seeking to insulate government departments and agencies from allegations of a "perceived failure to protect Americans adequately" (Gatter 2015: 389). Spencer and Hickox showed the value in health care workers from around the world working together to try and stop an outbreak where it began. They modeled an appropriate response to a cross-border disease outbreak, but political and media forces sought to capitalize on fear instead. CNN ran a report that called Ebola "the ISIS of biological agents" (Hooton 2014). Texas Senator Ted Cruz, readying for a 2016 presidential run, called for a ban of all travelers from West African states dealing with Ebola (Gillman 2014). As a result of this sort of fear-mongering, nearly half of all Americans in a poll in October 2014 thought that they or their family members were likely to contract Ebola (Hamel, Firth, and Mollyann Brodie 2014).

In the aftermath of the outbreak, there have been a variety of efforts to improve surveillance efforts. The CDC reports that Guinea, Liberia, and Sierra Leone have all strengthened and integrated their surveillance systems, and public health staff have received extensive training on best practices in surveillance. They have also made sure that community-level health facilities have the ability to report into the surveillance systems easily (Marston et al. 2017). These responses to Ebola also raised questions about whether the efforts were sustainable in the longer term. Many of these efforts, while important, responded to the immediate situation rather than building up long-term surveillance and response capacities. The US government, for example, built eleven Ebola treatment units in Liberia in 2014. In April 2015, reports found that these units had only treated twenty-eight Ebola patients and that nine of the eleven had not seen a single Ebola patient (Belluz 2015). In countries that already lack trained health care workers, information technology resources, and frontline public health clinic capacities, vertical surveillance interventions that are unconnected to the rest of the public health system not only exacerbate existing limitations, but also fail to strengthen these systems over the longer term (McNamara et al. 2016). Furthermore, it is vitally important that any new programs resonate with the local contexts in which they are being implemented. External interventions to address Ebola were most effective in communities where these programs supported and reinforced existing community initiatives. By contrast, external programs that ignored or denigrated local knowledge were least effective and most resisted (Richards 2016). The surveillance efforts for Ebola have not translated into strengthening the wider health care systems in the effected states or built up their resilience to respond to the next infectious disease outbreak.

ZIKA

In February 2016, CDC Director Thomas Frieden tweeted out a picture of a small stack of papers that would not even fill a shoebox. This was the accumulated research that existed to that point on Zika—a disease that had recently reached the Americas right before Brazil was due to host the Summer Olympics (Plumer 2016). Surveillance systems had picked up this new outbreak and helped it to race up the global agenda, but awareness alone could not make up for the lack of information. Not only was there little research on the virus, but it was now appearing in a new part of the world and presenting new symptoms. With the large number of tourists and athletes from all around the world heading to Brazil during the Olympics, there was a real fear that the outbreak could spread farther if millions of tourists inadvertently took a viral souvenir home with them.

For most of its known history, Zika has posed relatively few problems for humans. Zika is a viral infectious disease usually spread by mosquitoes, but there is also evidence of sexual transmission. In most instances, the virus passes through the body harmlessly. When symptoms do occur, they are generally light and include a mild fever, rash, muscle ache, and headache. Scientists inadvertently discovered Zika in 1947 while conducting yellow fever surveillance among monkeys in Uganda's Zika forest. It took another five years before scientists discovered their first human case of Zika. From the 1960s through the 1980s, Zika expanded its geographic footprint, spreading across equatorial Africa and into Asia. Still, the number of human cases remained low, and the disease caused few complications beyond a few days of discomfort.

The first widespread Zika outbreak occurred in 2007 on the island of Yap in the Federated States of Micronesia. That year, scientists identified 185 suspected cases of Zika—a massive upsurge on an island that had only ever seen fourteen cases of the disease (Duffy et al. 2009). The large number of cases was perplexing, since there was no evidence of viral mutation. Why would so many people contract the virus on Yap as opposed to people in regions where it was more prevalent? It may suggest that the residents of Yap were a virgin population and thus did not have pre-existing antibodies to Zika. It could also mean that Zika in other regions had been dramatically underreported because of its mild effects. The appearance of a mosquito-borne disease so far from regions with known infections and in the middle of the ocean supports the idea that its appearance in Yap was due to the processes of globalization that accelerate trade and travel (Kindhauser et al. 2016).

Zika's spread from central Africa to Asia and the Pacific connects directly with globalization. On their own, mosquitoes cannot fly the thousands of miles necessary to bring Zika to new parts of the world. Fortunately for the mosquitoes, they do not need to. Instead, they can hitch a ride on massive container ships. The virus' global spread nicely mirrors global shipping routes, and it is easy for insects to find a comfortable home on the large ships that carry all sorts of goods as part of the contemporary global trading system. Once these ships arrived in Central and South America, their mosquito passengers adapted to the new geography quickly and found a hospitable environment in which they could thrive and spread (Imperato 2016). One analyst described Zika's spread as "the price we pay for globalization" (Koch 2016). This was not the result of deliberate actions; rather, it was merely an unintended consequence of the easy movement of goods and peoples across long distances. This is not unique to Zika or mosquitoes; scientists believe that the El Tor cholera epidemic in South America between 1991 and 2003 began when a freighter ship discharged infected bilge water in a Peruvian harbor (Price-Smith 2002: 41).

When Zika moved throughout the Pacific in 2013 and 2014, the disease displayed new symptoms. Amid thousands of suspected cases of Zika in French Polynesia, Easter Island, the Cook Islands, and New Caledonia, doctors raised the possibility of a link between the increasing rates of Zika infection and the upswing in congenital malformations among newborns and autoimmune complications in adults. In particular, the number of cases of Guillain-Barré syndrome—a rare autoimmune disease—increased twenty-fold. Identifying a direct link between Zika and these other complications was complicated, though, because the islands were also experiencing widespread dengue fever infections, and many patients were infected with both (Kindhauser et al. 2016: 686C). It did provide the first evidence, though, that Zika may pose a greater threat to human health than previously assumed. It was also during this outbreak that scientists first confirmed that pregnant woman can transmit the virus to their unborn children in utero (Besnard et al. 2014).

Zika reached Brazil—and, in many respects, international public consciousness—in 2015. That March, Brazilian officials informed the WHO of a widespread but mild illness in the northeastern part of the country causing rashes. Authorities did not suspect Zika, since the virus had never before been present in Brazil. Laboratory analysis discovered that Zika was causing these rashes, and Brazilian officials announced this finding on May 7, 2015. Over the next two months, the disease spread throughout Brazil and to other Central and South American countries. As the disease spread, clinicians also noted an increase in congenital malformations among newborns. Noting the correlation between the rising rates of birth complications and the spread of Zika, the Pan American Health Organization (PAHO) and the WHO asked member-states on November 17, 2015 to report cases of microcephaly—a medical condition where a child's brain does not develop properly due to an undersized skull at birth. Two weeks later, the organizations issued a joint alert that specifically linked Zika infection with rates of microcephaly. PAHO also provided laboratory diagnosis guidance to facilitate better surveillance of the outbreak (PAHO 2015). By February 2016, Zika was circulating in at least twenty countries in the Americas, and governments were warning pregnant women to avoid traveling in the region if they could (Gallagher 2016).

As Zika continued to spread and the number of children born with microcephaly increased, the WHO declared a PHEIC on February 1, 2016. Here was a viral disease unusually and unexpectedly appearing in a new part of the world, whose spread was seemingly connected to international trade and travel, and about which other governments were issuing travel warnings. This made it ripe for a PHEIC declaration—only the fourth such declaration. The PHEIC was not for Zika itself, though. Instead, it was based on the clusters of microcephaly and Guillain-Barré syndrome potentially linked to the Zika virus (WHO 2016d). It was precisely because of the uncertainty about the relationship between Zika and these other effects that the WHO decided it needed to prioritize surveillance and a coordinated international response (Heymann et al. 2016).

Part of the reason that Zika in Brazil gained such international attention is that Rio de Janeiro was preparing to host the Summer Olympics and Paralympics in August and September 2016. The prospect of thousands of athletes and millions of tourists from around the world descending on an area with an active Zika outbreak—and the connections between the disease's geographic spread and the movement of people—raised substantial fears. Some athletes withdrew from the Games due to their fears (Gregory 2016), and more than one hundred public health scientists urged WHO Director-General Margaret Chan to move or cancel the Olympics in a public letter (Sun 2016). This was hardly a consensus position, though. August is a winter month in Brazil, which means that the mosquitoes that transmit Zika are not particularly active. Furthermore, experts pointed out that Brazil is already a popular tourist destination, but Zika had not spread to new areas on a large scale. That did not negate the potential complications for pregnant women, but it did suggest that the Olympics in and of themselves are unlikely to cause a worldwide Zika outbreak (Zhang 2016). Indeed, there were no confirmed cases of Zika among attendees or athletes at the Summer Olympics (Doucleff 2016).

The Zika PHEIC lasted until November 18, 2016, a little more than eight months after it was initially declared. WHO officials stated that addressing Zika and its related complications required a sustained, long-term approach. A PHEIC is more designed to activate a quick, immediate response, so the organization decided it would be best to transition out of an emergency framework and toward something that could provide guidance and support surveillance systems over a longer time period (Vogel 2016).

Zika's emergence in South and Central America and the guidelines emerging out of its surveillance activities intersected with prevailing social and cultural mores in fascinating ways. The disease's most extreme effects fell on pregnant women and their unborn children, so much of the advice about avoiding Zika was targeted specifically toward women who were pregnant or might become so. At the same time, evidence pointed to the possibility of sexual transmission of Zika, meaning that a woman could do everything in her power to avoid mosquito bites and yet still contract the disease from a sexual partner. Given the connections between Zika's effects and pregnancy, a number of governments in the region simply advised women not to get pregnant. In Brazil, public health officials described avoiding pregnancy as "the wisest course of action" (cited in Douglas 2015). Officials in Ecuador, Colombia, Jamaica, and El Salvador shared similar advice, with El Salvador advising avoiding pregnancy until 2018—at least eighteen months from the time it issued the advice. The WHO stressed that people of reproductive age "should be correctly informed and oriented to consider delaying pregnancy" (cited in McNeil 2016a). WHO officials, though, stressed that their advice should not be construed as telling women not to get pregnant (Byron and Howard 2017).

This advice may seem plausible, but it ignores the larger context in which choices about sexuality and reproduction operate. Many of these states severely restrict access to birth control, reproductive health services, and abortions due to the influence of the Roman Catholic Church (Johnson 2017). Some local Catholic officials objected to the advice to avoid pregnancy, though Pope Francis himself conceded that "avoiding pregnancy is not an absolute evil" (cited in Boorstein, Itzkowitz, and Bailey 2016). Reproductive rights groups called governments that called for women to delay pregnancy while also limiting access to birth control hypocritical. Governments and international organizations were giving advice that failed to consider the health care realities in the effected countries. In these ways, the policy recommendations were essentially "biological reflections of social fault lines" (Farmer 1999: 5), demonstrating how a disease that emerges due to globalization cannot necessarily be completely separated from the specific territories where it emerges. The Brazilian government confiscated shipments of medications for nonsurgical abortions sent from abroad and announced plans to increase criminal penalties for women who have abortions for fetal abnormalities (Harris, Silverman, and Marshall 2016: 1). As such, biopolitical surveillance to track the Zika outbreak and its effects ends up having a disciplinary effect that allows the government to further strengthen its political power over its subjects. At the same time, women appear to be resisting this encroachment, with requests for nonsurgical abortion medications increasing significantly after PAHO made its initial alert about the possible connections between Zika and congenital malformations (Aiken et al. 2016).

Local transmission of Zika largely stopped in the Americas in late 2016, and the WHO issued its last alert about Zika during the first half of 2017. Most governments and international organizations still encourage pregnant women or people of child-bearing age to take precautions to avoid infection, but the danger level has seemingly dropped dramatically (Sifferlin 2018). Scientists are not entirely sure why this is the case, but it may be that people develop immunity to the virus after they have contracted it once (Siedner, Ryan, and Bogoch 2018). This would explain why the Zika outbreak on Yap was so widespread in contrast to the disease's previous appearances in Africa and Asia.

In the case of Zika, surveillance efforts helped to map the geographic spread and changing symptoms of an infectious disease. At the same time, the policy responses from government officials interacted powerfully with prevailing social and cultural norms. They also illustrated the power differentials and inequities around health and health care within the globalized system.

CONCLUSION

As globalization has made it easier for diseases to spread across borders, surveillance is an increasingly important tool for identifying potential outbreaks and stopping them before they spread too far. The IHR were rewritten in the late 1990s and early 2000s to specifically mandate that states increase their surveillance procedures and maintain constant contact with WHO in case of any adverse events. The treaty also expanded to allow nonstate actors to play a role in conducting these surveillance activities. At the same time, the evidence demonstrates that understanding how and under which circumstances these surveillance activities can positively inform global health activities remains uncertain.

The emphasis on surveillance clearly reflects the five key elements of globalization. There is greater attention paid to surveillance because of the *intensification* of linkages between physically distant peoples. The *integration* of commercial, political, and social relations is particularly important for surveillance, as the discovery of an outbreak in one country may lead other states to seek to introduce trade or travel restrictions. The ease with which diseases can travel across borders in this *deterritorialized* setting makes it all the more important for surveillance systems to operate—though those same systems may then lead governments to reinforce their territoriality in a seeming effort to protect themselves. The willingness of member-states to bind themselves to certain standards of surveillance reflects how global health issues have become *elevated* in a globalized context. Finally, globalization means that health has *expanded* to intersect with a wider range of issues, thus making governments even more interested in knowing where outbreaks are occurring.

Chapter 7

The Future(s) of Globalization and Health

Global health and globalization are inextricably linked. Globalization and the recognition of the importance of health as a global political issue emerged almost simultaneously, and they have continually evolved. New issues have come on to the agenda, new actors have mobilized, and widespread recognition of the importance of globalization and health has brought attention and resources to these issues. Formal institutions like the United Nations regularly hold meetings devoted to global health issues, and those summits necessarily incorporate elements of globalization. Development assistance for health (DAH)—demonstrating the willingness of donor states and other funding entities to commit financial resources to global health and the embodiment of an informal institution and norm—has regularly reached record or near-record levels nearly every year since 1990. The international community's outpouring of financial, logistical, and personnel support for the response to the Ebola outbreak in West Africa shows that governments acknowledge the importance of recognizing the links between globalization and health, sharing some degree of sovereignty and moving beyond a sole focus on domestic and Westphalian sovereignty. Efforts to frame global health variously as an issue of security, human rights, and development have spurred a massive increase in political, social, and economic attention for these issues. Everything in the global health world must be peachy because its agenda is so wide-reaching that it addresses most of the major issues, right?

Shockingly, the answer is no. The globalization and health agenda is indeed broad and covers a wide range of issues, but that does not mean that it has adequate coverage everywhere. This chapter will go into some of the biggest challenges on the horizon for globalization and health—issues that the current political agenda ignores, overlooks, or has avoided.

Pointing out omissions is not holding policymakers to an impossibly high standard. It is less an exercise in crying "gotcha" and more an effort to see where the future(s) of globalization and health may be going and trying to figure out how the structures, policymaking strategies, and actors involved may need to evolve or change in response. Rather than being an exercise in shaming policymakers and academics, it is an effort to provide a roadmap for issues that may be likely to appear in the near future. It is an exercise in anticipation—and an imperfect attempt at that. There is a danger inherent in any sort of prognostication exercise, but there is good reason to contemplate what the current globalization and health agenda holds. It is not just about identifying the absences, but also projecting into the future to consider the issues that are likely to pop up on the agenda or will need to be addressed in order to continue making progress on global health issues going forward.

This chapter focuses its attention on three issues that potentially challenge the ongoing efficacy of the globalization and health agenda or have received insufficient attention. The first issue is the relationship between globalization, health, and gender. For all of the talk about health equity and the need to address societal divisions within the provision of health services, gender remains underappreciated and overlooked. Gender conditions how both globalization and global health play out in policy in overt and covert ways, and the combination of globalization and global health raises a host of unique issues. Ignoring gender means ignoring the realities of social relations, which in turn undermines efforts to implement long-term global health programs or to proactively identify potential challenges.

The second issue pertains to the interplay between environmental, animal, and human health. The environment matters in a number of ways, such as how climate change has an effect on global health and the relationships between human, animal, and environmental health. This issue, commonly known as One Health, highlights the complexity of addressing health issues both in terms of how we intervene to improve health outcomes and who needs to collaborate in order to bring about significant meaningful changes. Addressing the roles of the environment and animal health necessarily complicates an already complicated global health agenda.

The third issue is more about the politics of globalization and global health separately and taken together. The international community has witnessed unmistakable signs of the rise of populist and nationalist movements, a questioning of multilateralism and the institutional structures that have given rise to globalization in the first place, and a decreased willingness to provide ongoing political and financial support for global health initiatives. If the period from roughly 1990 to 2015 was one of expanding global health and celebrating the role that international cooperation and collaboration could play in addressing cross-border health challenges, political leadership in the current era appears more skeptical and less willing to identify global health as a collective public good. These sorts of ambiguous attitudes not only threaten to stop the ongoing expansion of the global health agenda, but also to undermine the successes thus far.

GENDER, GLOBALIZATION, AND HEALTH

O'Manique describes the importance of taking gender seriously in unambiguous terms. She writes, "Social and political life is profoundly gendered and feminist scholarship has a crucial role to play in illuminating both the foundations of health insecurities and the effects of insecurities on differently gendered and located bodies" (O'Manique 2015: 48). Gender powerfully affects the ways in which a person experiences health and health care, and access to health and health care is mediated by the social, cultural, and power relationships that are inextricably linked to gender. These effects become even more important in the context of globalization.

Feminist approaches to international relations have played profound roles in understanding the positive and negative dimensions of the relationship between globalization, gender, and health. On the positive side, globalization has facilitated the emergence of a transnational women's health movement and encouraged the development of a rights-based orientation toward access to health and health care services (Chapman 2012; Petchesky 2003). This movement has encompassed a broad array of issues like freedom from forced sterilization and unwanted sexual interactions, access to safe abortions and birth control, freedom from sexual and domestic violence, and the prioritization of the social determinants of health such as clean water, proper nutrition, and adequate shelter (Hawkesworth 2006). While there remain tensions within these movements over which voices were being heard and whether organizations from the Global South received equal say in setting the international agenda (Petchesky 2003), and there is still a very long way to go before these rights are fully delivered, it is impossible to separate the emergence of a women's health movement from the changes brought on by globalization.

At the same time, globalization can have negative effects on gender and health. Global capitalism and macroeconomic restructuring have limited access to health care services, decreased the availability of healthy food and adequate nutrition, and allowed anti-feminist political forces to spread rapidly (O'Manique 2015: 51). Sen and Östlin highlight two additional avenues by which globalization can have adverse effects on gender relations and health. First, they note that globalization has transformed the composition of the workforce in ways that harm women's health. Globalization has brought more women into the workforce, but it has not provided most women with high wages, steady employment, or significant rights. Instead, women frequently work in precarious employment situations, giving them little ability to protest poor conditions or advocate for themselves. The working conditions these women experience frequently damage their health, and the lack of employment security can in turn undermine the health conditions of their family members. Second, they argue that globalization, with its dominant ideology of neoliberalism and an emphasis on reducing national expenditures and privatizing state services, has narrowed the range of acceptable national policy options available to governments. In particular, they see states as less able or willing to fund health and education programs, and the effects of these cuts fall disproportionately on women (Sen and Östlin 2008: 5–6). In all of these ways, women have less access, less control, and fewer options for taking control of their health and addressing the larger social determinants of health.

These negative health effects are not solely limited to women, though; men, nonbinary persons, and the transgender community similarly face serious challenges to their health and how they move through the world in relation to the changing policy and economic environment brought about by globalization (Sen and Östlin 2008: 5–7). Indeed, Bates et al. (2009) and Connell (2012) both argue that global health has generally taken too narrow a view of gender. As a result, the field is less able to appreciate the different ways that the social, economic, and political changes wrought by globalization affect various segments of the population. It is precisely because globalization can have such a wide range of effects that scholars, practitioners, and policymakers need to build and incorporate an understanding of gender that is "grounded in the inclusion of voices from the subaltern, and the recognition of their historical positioning, to construct knowledge for practice and praxis" (Anderson 2000: 221). Giving marginalized communities a voice is absolutely vital for improving health. When certain groups are excluded from the various processes that govern global health, they cannot bring their concerns to the table; indeed, the decision-makers may not even know what that group's concerns are. Social mobilization and empowerment have a reciprocal relationship with each other. Mobilization increases a group's ability to make its demands, and that in turn fosters further mobilization. It also facilitates providing access to the formal and informal institutions of global health governance. In these ways, empowering communities through listening to their interests and demands can work to reduce power inequities.

Paying attention to gender, health, and globalization also promotes security and stability. Previous research has convincingly demonstrated that states with lower levels of women's political, economic, and social equality are less stable and more prone to conflict (Caprioli 2005; Caprioli and Boyer 2001; Hudson et al. 2012). When women have less of a voice in political, economic, and social structures, they end up with fewer rights—and society as a whole is worse off. This link suggests that improving women's health would contribute to larger improvements in national and international stability because it would address the underlying social determinants of health.

We do see some efforts to better incorporate gender and women's health into the global health agenda. In 2000, the international community committed to improving maternal health by reducing maternal mortality and achieving universal access to reproductive health as part of the Millennium Development Goals (MDGs) developed by the United Nations (UN). The successor to the MDGs, the Sustainable Development Goals (SDGs), features an even more expansive dedication to women's health, pledging to reduce poverty through gender-sensitive strategies, double the agricultural productivity of women farmers to increase food security, reduce maternal mortality, ensure access to sexual and reproductive health care, improve access to quality health care services, end all forms of discrimination and violence against women and girls, expand educational and economic opportunities for women, and promote gender equality at all levels. Taken together, these strategies demonstrate at least a rhetorical interest in improving women's physical and mental health as part of an overall strategy to promote peace and prosperity.

There is some reason for optimism that this commitment to women's health is more than rhetoric and has led to actual concrete action. In 2000, the MDGs called for reducing maternal mortality ratio, or the number of maternal deaths of women while pregnant or within forty-two days of the end of pregnancy due to any cause related to or aggravated by pregnancy and its management per one hundred thousand live births, by 75 percent between 1990 and 2015 (United Nations 2000). This goal built upon earlier international efforts to reduce maternal mortality, such as the 1987 Safe Motherhood Conference in Nairobi, the World Summit for Children in 1990, 1994's International Conference on Population and Development, and the Fourth World Conference on Women in 1995 (Zurleck-Brown et al. 2013: 32). Data from the United Nations Children's Fund shows a maternal mortality ratio in 1990 of 385 deaths per one hundred thousand live births, meaning that more than five hundred thousand women and girls died from complications of pregnancy and childbirth. By 2000, the ratio had dropped to 341 deaths per one hundred thousand live births. Data from 2015 show a maternal mortality ratio of 216 per one hundred thousand live births

(United Nations Children's Fund 2018). While this outcome fell short of the stated MDGs target, it nonetheless represents a significant decrease in maternal mortality.

The biggest question is whether international society can harness this apparent momentum to do better going forward. The UN incorporated improved maternal health into the SDGs. Specifically, SDG 3, Good Health and Well-Being, calls for the global maternal mortality ratio to be reduced to less than seventy per one hundred thousand live births by 2030 (United Nations Development Programme 2018). That would require a substantial reduction—just over 66 percent—from the 2015 levels.

Achieving such an audacious goal would require both substantial funding and deep political commitment. Current efforts cast doubt on whether either is plentiful enough to push this goal forward. Funding for maternal and child health has not kept pace with the stated ambitions. While funding for maternal and child health has stayed above three billion dollars since 2009, development assistance for maternal and child health dropped 12 percent in constant 2017 US dollars between 2013 and 2017 (Institute for Health Metrics and Evaluation 2018). Similarly, policy efforts have been stymied by a lack of resources, an inability of government officials and advocates to cohere on a common understanding, and ongoing tensions between the national government and state and local officials in a highly federalized system (Shiffman and Okonfua 2007). Global strategies to prioritize safe motherhood have fallen victim to disagreements over the definition of key terms, advocates who have relatively little power within political systems, and issue framing that has not resonated with key policymakers and donor states (Shiffman and Smith 2007).

More broadly, we need to understand the complex ways in which health, gender, and globalization interact. Few global health programs take gender equality and equity seriously, women are over-represented in informal caretaking roles, and, despite some progress at the World Health Organization (WHO), women are consistently underrepresented in leadership and decision-making roles within global health institutions. Rectifying these imbalances requires that we "challenge structural and social power inequalities within patriarchal societies that produce inequalities that disadvantage women" (Davies et al. 2019: 601). Davies et al. (2019) offer four suggestions for how the global health community can undertake serious efforts to address to create a more equitable world. First, while gender quotas can help address underrepresentation, there need to be far-reaching efforts to target both formal and informal processes that prevent gender issues from being taken seriously. These efforts need to take proactive steps toward promoting institutional cultural change. Second, we must recognize that gender and gender discrimination do not exist in a vacuum. Gender intersects with ethnicity, class, race, religion, disability, and religion, so intersectional approaches that bring the wide range of voices to the table are vital to overcoming oppression and exclusion. Third, women perform the vast majority of caring and domestic labor roles both in the home and in the field. Global health institutions frequently rely heavily on this uncompensated labor, but the women themselves rarely benefit from this sort of care. Formal institutions need to ensure that they do not replicate patterns that undervalue women's involvement and appropriately compensate women. Finally, we need to recognize that mainstream research methods inadequately recognize the hidden and informal means that foment and reinforce gender inequality. As such, global health needs to employ a diversity of research methods in order to get a fuller understanding of the roots and causes of inequality and inequity (Davies et al. 2019: 601–02). Not only will these steps improve the delivery of health services, but they will also lead to a more comprehensive knowledge base for researchers.

THE ENVIRONMENT, HEALTH, AND GLOBALIZATION

Health and infectious disease have assumed a more prominent role on the global community's policy agenda in recent years. This has occurred for a number of reasons. First, the world has witnessed an increasing number of new and re-emergent infectious diseases. New diseases like SARS and AIDS have definitively demonstrated that medical science has not vanquished the microbial threat. Indeed, the Centers for Disease Control and Prevention (CDC) report that at least thirty-three new infectious diseases emerged among humans during the last quarter of the twentieth century (Price-Smith 2002). Significantly, most new infectious diseases in humans come from animal sources. At least 65 percent of major recent human infectious disease outbreaks have animal origins (Kuehn 2010).

Second, governments increasingly recognize the potential political and economic consequences of diseases crossing borders. On December 23, 2003, the US Department of Agriculture announced the discovery of the first cases of bovine spongiform encephalopathy (BSE) in the United States. BSE, colloquially known as "mad cow disease," causes cattle to progressively lose motor control before dying. The disease can infect people if they eat beef from BSE-infected cattle. Among humans, the illness manifests itself as variant Creutzfeld-Jacob disease, which causes catastrophic neurological damage and a severe decline in mental capacity and motor function. After the US Department of Agriculture made its announcement, seventy countries banned US beef imports. This caused US beef exports to drop 83 percent in 2004, leading to losses estimated at between $3.2 and $4.7 billion (Price-Smith 2009: 126–29). This incredible economic cost all resulted from a single infected cow.

Third, a number of governments and intergovernmental organizations have promoted the idea that health is a development issue. A country that wants to prosper economically needs a healthy populace. Health is not an isolated issue, but rather an integral element of a grander global effort to increase prosperity. The SDGs' expanded goals include issues like ensuring health and well-being at all ages, protecting and promoting sustainable use of the environment, combating climate change and its effects on the planet, and achieving food security and proper nutrition. Achieving these goals will allow for broad-scale prosperity and enable people from around the world to live lives of their choosing.

These three reasons clearly link human health to the wider environment and broaden the concept of health. The international community cannot adequately address human health without understanding the effects that the health of animals and ecosystems have on people. Infectious disease outbreaks in humans frequently arise initially in animal populations, and environmental and ecosystem changes may facilitate the ease of transmission of diseases from animal reservoirs to humans.

The interconnectedness of human, animal, and ecosystem health has come to be known as One Health. The One Health Initiative, a collaborative effort of scientists, physicians, veterinarians, researchers, and professional organizations, has defined One Health as "the collaborative efforts of multiple disciplines working locally, nationally, and globally, to obtain optimal health for people, animals, and our environment." To that end, One Health's advocates emphasize the importance of controlling infectious diseases that "have helped shape the course of human history"—be they human or animal illnesses (One Health Initiative Task Force 2008: 9).

Recognizing the links between human and animal health is simultaneously a very old and fairly new concept. Currier and Steele (2011) note that Hippocrates and Galen both drew on observations from animals and humans to formulate their ideas about health, and early physicians attended to both humans and animals. Rudolf Virchow, the German doctor often credited as the father of modern pathology, argued, "Between animal and human medicine, there are no dividing lines—nor should there be. The object is different, but the experience obtained constitutes the basis of all medicine" (cited in Kahn, Kaplan, and Steele 2007: 6). By the early twentieth century, though, human medicine, veterinary medicine, and public health largely saw each other as distinct fields of study and research, and practitioners in each field did not necessarily draw on the insights of others (Currier and Steele 2011). Over time, these divisions have been reinforced through a variety of different means. To take one example, veterinary medical schools in the United States tend to be located at land-grant universities, which are typically in more rural areas. Medical schools, on the other hand, tend to be located at flagship universities (Rabinowitz and Conti 2013: 197). This spatial separation could potentially work against collaboration. Another observer suggested that the decreased recognition of the connections between human and animal health in the early twentieth century resulted from increased urbanization and the decreased use of horses and oxen as a means of transportation. These changes meant that there was a less immediate connection between most people and animals (Cardiff, Ward, and Barthold 2008).

In the late twentieth century, new developments in human health forced scholars and practitioners to take stock of the connections between human, animal, and ecosystem health. No single agency or international organization collects health information on both human and animals, but "diseases pay no regard to the divisions among species or academic disciplines" (Karesh and Cook 2005: 42). The 1997 H5N1 influenza outbreak in Hong Kong arose from birds, and authorities culled 1.5 million birds in an attempt to stop the disease's spread. The outbreak of West Nile virus in New York in 1999 puzzled medical and public health authorities until veterinarians at the Bronx Zoo connected the outbreak in humans with a simultaneous outbreak among birds (General Accounting Office 2000). The emergence of SARS in 2002 and 2003 has been variously linked to civets, bats, and other small mammals (Doucleff 2012). These and other outbreaks of new and re-emergent infectious diseases spurred collaborative efforts among those concerned with human health, animal health, and environmental issues that eventually crystallized into One Health (Fisman and Laupland 2010).

One Health seeks to bring more systematic attention to understanding how human and animal health interact with each other within the larger international community. This relationship can be direct, like when animals act as reservoirs for human illnesses. They can also be more indirect, as animal diseases can have profound social and economic effects on human societies. Consider rinderpest. Before it was eradicated in 2011, an outbreak of rinderpest could devastate a community even though it only infected cattle. If a family lost its cattle to a rinderpest outbreak, it could lose its livelihood and sink into poverty. As a family's economic standing became more precarious, people may have less ability to obtain nutritious food or medical care, which in turn could have a negative effect on their health. Furthermore, colonial officials in southern Africa used the presence of rinderpest as an excuse to isolate local populations and introduce discriminatory policies that further reduced their access to political, economic, and social power (Youde 2013a). Rinderpest's eradication thus removed a potential economic and social stressor from the lives of millions.

To see how these interconnections play out in the real world, consider the Hendra virus. This virus was first discovered in 1994 when thirteen horses and their human trainer died of a new virus at a training center in suburban Brisbane, Australia. Since then, scientists have identified more than ninety horses—and seven people, including four who died—that have fallen ill with the virus (Queensland Government 2017). What explains the emergence of Hendra virus? At its most direct, people in close contact with horses are at risk of infection, but the causal linkages go much further. Flying foxes serve as the reservoir for Hendra virus, spreading it to horses. Evolutionary changes within the virus and increased contact opportunities between horses and flying foxes heighten the transmissibility of the virus, and those factors are affected by changes in equine ecology, the distribution of flying foxes, food availability and distribution, the availability of foraging and roosting habitats, the presence of exotic flowering and fruiting plants in urban areas, urban expansion into previously agricultural lands, and global climate change (Lapinski, Funk, and Moccia 2015: 55–56). In order to understand how four people die of a horse virus in Queensland, we have to incorporate human, animal, and environmental health together—and address them simultaneously. It gives us a more comprehensive and holistic and understanding of health, but also one that becomes infinitely more difficult to address.

Despite recognizing the relationships between human, animal, and environmental health, implementing policy programs that meaningfully embrace the One Health ethos has proven challenging. There have been no new international institutions dedicated to One Health created, nor do the current health surveillance systems integrate analysis across human, animal, and environmental health (Lee and Brumme 2013: 778–79).

The impediments to operationalizing One Health are two-fold. First, the One Health framework has fallen victim to the larger shortcomings within global health governance. Despite all of its advances over the past thirty years, global health governance often remains fragmented, uncoordinated, and misaligned with global priorities. It finds itself caught in the debates about the relative merits of disease-specific vertical interventions and broad-based horizontal interventions. As a result, trying to graft One Health on to existing global health governance structures risks exacerbating the existing flaws within the system's architecture. While Chien (2013) argues that groups like the WHO, the Food and Agriculture Organization, and the World Organization for Animal Health have sought to reduce tensions among themselves over One Health and that each organization has had key personnel who have championed the concept, she acknowledges that each group retains a degree of autonomy that can complicate efforts to remake existing institutional relationships. As a result, it is challenging to move beyond the rhetoric of One Health to change existing practices (Degeling et al. 2015).

Second, One Health's underlying meaning remains contested. Lee and Brumme note, "There is a lack of consensus regarding which (if any) specific diseases the approach should focus on, or whether systems-based approaches are preferable" (Lee and Brumme 2013: 782). This ongoing debate makes it difficult to describe One Health's agenda (Gibbs 2014: 90). For instance, Lerner and Berg (2015) say that the

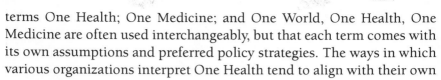

terms One Health; One Medicine; and One World, One Health, One Medicine are often used interchangeably, but that each term comes with its own assumptions and preferred policy strategies. The ways in which various organizations interpret One Health tend to align with their own pre-existing areas of technical expertise.

Regardless of the specifics of the One Health agenda, the links between the environment, globalization, and health are undeniable. The Intergovernmental Panel on Climate Change warned in 1998, "The direct and indirect impacts of climate change on human health do constitute a hazard to human population health" (Intergovernmental Panel on Climate Change 1998: 7). Environmental change threatens to shift conditions for various plant and animal species outside of this range, the effects of which we cannot entirely understand or predict ahead of time. As global temperatures change, habitats for animal and insect disease vectors will also change. This will mean that mosquitoes that carry diseases like malaria and yellow fever may be able to live—and thus spread disease—in more northerly settings. Cholera also becomes a greater risk, as the bacillus multiplies more rapidly in warmer water. As diseases begin circulating among immunologically virgin populations, the outbreaks of these diseases moving to new areas could be even more intense (Price-Smith 2002: 143–46).

These changes are not limited to infectious diseases. McMichael (2013) identifies a positive relationship between climate change and childhood stunting in Kenya since 1975. As temperatures rise and rainfall decreases, food yields decline. This in turn worsens nutrition and combines with demographic pressures and shifting land use patterns to increase rates of stunting and its attendant physical, educational, and social consequences. Extreme weather events brought on by climate change, like Hurricane Maria in 2017, can have long-term health consequences. When the storm hit Puerto Rico, it wiped out the island's power grid for months. Without power, hospitals were forced to run on generators, and those who needed dialysis treatments found themselves out of luck. It also left more than half of the island's residents without access to clean drinking water, increasing the chances of water-borne diseases. Furthermore, the storm and its destruction severely limited access to necessary pharmaceuticals (Sciubba and Youde 2017). These factors contributed to thousands of deaths in Puerto Rico alone. McMichael (2013) suggests that environmental changes could also lead to increases in mental health problems among marginalized groups within societies as the shifting weather patterns and the associated changes in health outcomes increase levels of stress and tension.

While we may understand intellectually the connections between human, animal, and planetary health, that does not necessarily translate into political action. The contestation over what One Health means makes it difficult—if not impossible—for its advocates to develop and deploy an effective issue frame that can mobilize public support and policymaker attention. There are no formal institutions that encompass all three issue areas, so there is no natural home for these issues and they can easily fall through the bureaucratic cracks. Philanthropies that fund human health tend not to provide monies for animal health or environmental mediation. The international community is also lacking in informal institutions that could take up the cause of One Health. Development assistance for animal health is minimal at best, and it is rarely (if ever) a key issue in foreign policy. The ongoing debates, which are notably political rather than scientific in nature, about whether climate change results from human activity make the situation even harder. If policymakers cannot even agree on the cause of climate change, they are ill-equipped to address its consequences. This makes it hard to recognize any need for a sense of shared sovereignty to tackle the interconnections between human, animal, and environmental health.

QUESTIONING MULTILATERALISM AND THE VALUE OF GLOBAL HEALTH

While the global health governance system has grown dramatically and come to play a bigger role in international politics since 1990, there have been signs throughout the 2010s that changes were afoot within the global health system. After years of rapid annual increases for global health, DAH has remained essentially flat since 2010 with an average annualized growth rate of only 1.0 percent (Institute for Health Metrics and Evaluation 2018: 15). Within this uncertain environment, some of the countries that have traditionally led international efforts to address cross-border health concerns are pulling back from their earlier commitments.

Much of this concern centers on Donald Trump and his policies because he has repeatedly questioned the value of global health programs. During the Ebola outbreak in West Africa, though he was not yet a presidential candidate, Trump repeatedly took to Twitter to call for travel restrictions for people from Ebola-infected countries (in contravention of the International Health Regulations and WHO's recommendations) and a ban on flights from the affected states to the United States (despite no such flights existing). He infamously tweeted that health care workers who provided care to Ebola patients "must suffer the consequences" if they fell ill. Trump tweeted about Ebola more than fifty times during the outbreak (Hatch 2017). Trump also campaigned on a platform that questioned both multilateralism and foreign aid (Boon 2017)—two central elements of contemporary global health governance.

As an example, look at the President's Emergency Plan for AIDS Relief (PEPFAR). Introduced in 2003 by President George W. Bush, the program provided fifteen billion dollars over five years for HIV/AIDS treatment and prevention efforts in low- and middle-income countries. In 2008, the program was reauthorized with a budget of forty-eight billion dollars (including thirty-nine billion dollars for HIV/AIDS programs alone) for the next five years—and was again reauthorized in 2013 for another five years. PEPFAR has been the largest global health program for any single disease, providing more than eighty billion dollars and giving nearly fifteen million people access to life-extending antiretroviral drugs as of September 2018 (Kaiser Family Foundation 2019). It has been one of the rare bright spots of bipartisan agreement in American politics (Fauci and Eisinger 2018) and helped to cement American leadership in global health. Shortly after Trump won office, though, Trump's aides circulated a questionnaire to the Departments of State and Defense that asked, "Is PEPFAR worth the massive investment when there are so many security concerns in Africa? Is PEPFAR becoming a massive, international entitlement program?" (Cooper 2017). The threats to PEPFAR even spurred George W. Bush to write an op-ed for the *Washington Post* to support the program, arguing, "When we confront suffering—when we save lives—we breathe hope into devastated populations, strengthen and stabilize society, and make our country and the world safer" (Bush 2017).

Upon taking office, Trump's actions raised more fears about the future of global health. His budget proposals gave observers little cause for optimism about the future of American leadership in global health.

In May 2017, the Trump administration released its first proposed budget. It proposed cutting funding for global health activities by $2.2 billion, or 26 percent, for fiscal year 2018. This would have included zeroing out birth control support for women in developing countries ($607.5 million), cutting international HIV/AIDS funding by 17 percent (eight hundred million dollars), and reducing funding for anti-malaria programs by 11 percent (eighty-one million dollars) (Aizenman 2017). With the US government contributing roughly one-third of DAH, these cuts would have had significant ripple effects and reduce the United States' global health spending to its lowest level in at least a decade (Schneider and West 2017). Though former Secretary of State Rex Tillerson spoke positively about PEPFAR and its usefulness in promoting American values abroad, the program was targeted for a funding cut of at least 18 percent. Cutting the international HIV/AIDS budget by $1.1 billion would cause the deaths of at least one million people due to reduced access to medicines and prevention programs. Administration spokespeople said that everyone currently receiving treatment would continue to receive it, but they never explained how that would have been possible (Harris, G. 2017). Subsequently, when Trump released his proposed 2019 budget, he sought to cut two-thirds of the funding for the Global Health Security Agenda (GHSA), dropping its budget to sixty million dollars. The GHSA, launched in 2014, "is a growing partnership of over 64 nations, international organizations, and non-governmental stakeholders to help build countries' capacity to help create a world safe and secure from infectious disease threats and elevate global health security as a national and global priority" (Global Health Security Agenda 2018). In three broad categories of action—surveillance, prevention, and response—the GHSA sets measurable objectives to bring international core capacities in line with the 2005 International Health Regulations. Such a cut would significantly hamper early disease detection capabilities and force the program to cease operating in thirty-nine of forty-nine countries (Doucleff 2018).

Trump's budget proposals went beyond reductions to specific health interventions to making far-reaching cuts to institutions and organizations that provide crucial support for global health. The National Institutes of Health (NIH) was targeted for a $5.8 billion cut, roughly 20 percent of its budget. Reducing the NIH budget would cut the number of grants available for developing treatments or vaccines for diseases like Ebola. More importantly, the NIH cuts would eliminate all funding for the Fogarty International Center, which supports global health training and research programs. There was a call for supporting a new Federal Emergency Response Fund to provide money during disease outbreaks, but the budget did not specify whether its funding would come from new money or the reallocation of existing budgetary outlays (Belluz 2017). Tom Frieden, the CDC's former director, warned that the proposed cuts to the NIH, CDC, and other global health institutions would make American and the world less safe (Belluz 2018b). Trump also proposed cutting the United States' contributions to UN organizations, including the WHO. Since the US government supplies nearly 19 percent of WHO's annual budget, any such cuts would have a noticeable effect (Shendruk 2017).

Such extensive cuts would have far-reaching effects on global health. In 2017, the United States was the highest DAH funder at $12.4 billion, but that was a decrease of $1.5 billion since 2016. If the Trump administration's budget requests for 2018 were implemented, global health aid would decrease another $2.5 billion (Institute for Health Metrics and Evaluation 2018: 33).

While Congress largely blocked the proposed cuts to global health, the effects of the Trump administration's proposals go far beyond the dollar amounts. Any president's budget is less of an operational document and more a statement of belief. The budget blueprint reflects Trump's values and the avenues by which he envisions the United States influencing the global community. The political science literature, particularly the new institutionalist strain, emphasizes that institutions—including budgets—are expressions of societal values (Lowndes and Roberts 2013: 186). By cutting funding for global health programs, the Trump administration presents the international community with a very clear signal about the value it places on global health. It is not just the withdrawal of funding from multilateral institutions that raises concerns; the Trump administration and its actions also call the underlying legitimacy and authority of the global governance architecture into question. By calling these institutions into question, there is also a concern about the possibility of a "multiplier effect" and an accompanying shift in the political priorities of great powers (Boon 2017: 1076–77).

There may yet be some hope that the United States is unwilling to cede its global health leadership. Trump has made public statements that suggest at least a modicum of recognition of the importance of global health within contemporary international politics. In his 2017 address to the UN General Assembly, Trump proclaimed:

> The United States continues to lead the world in humanitarian assistance. . . . We have invested in better health and opportunity all over the world, through programs like PEPFAR, which funds AIDS relief; the President's Malaria Initiative; the Global Health Security Agenda; the Global Fund to End Modern Slavery; and the Women's Entrepreneurs Finance Initiative, part of our commitment to empowering women all across the globe. (Trump 2017a)

During that same UN trip, Trump told a lunch of African leaders:

> But we cannot have prosperity if we're not healthy. We will continue our partnership on critical health initiatives. Uganda has made incredible strides in the battle against HIV/AIDS. In Guinea and Nigeria, you fought a horrifying Ebola outbreak. Namibia's health system is increasingly self-sufficient. My Secretary of Health and Human Services will be traveling to Africa to promote our Global Health Security Agenda. (Trump 2017b)

People can argue whether Trump genuinely believes these global health-related statements and whether his budget proposals belie his public rhetoric, but the rhetoric itself is worth acknowledging. At some level within the Trump administration, there is at least tacit recognition of the validity of the global health governance system and the United States' role within it. While it is impossible to know what is genuinely in any political leader's head, it is entirely appropriate to look at what a leader is saying in a particular context to a particular audience (Krebs and Jackson 2007). The fact that Trump is saying these words about US leadership on global health in multilateral settings suggests that there is some recognition of these values.

It is also important to recognize that the problems in global health governance go beyond Trump. Harman and Davies (2018) argue that blaming Trump for the problems in global health governance displaces a much-needed critical analysis of how the current global health governance system operates. Instead, they posit, Trump's global health policy preferences brings the shortcomings in the current system to light. In particular, they note that global health has ignored reproductive health, become too reliant on American leadership and financing, and paid too little attention to incorporating global health into a broader human security framework. Trump may magnify these problems, but the shortcomings in the system pre-date him and will need to be addressed by global health governance. No one can assume that global health will magically improve when Trump leaves office.

The populist challenge and the open questioning of the multilateral structures that form the basis for the global health governance system (to say nothing of global governance as a whole) is not unique to the United States. We can look to the Brexit referendum in the United Kingdom, the rise of far-right populist parties in Europe, the challenges to the European Union's authority and legitimacy in light of the ongoing refugee crisis, and the emergence of figures like Rodrigo Duterte in the Philippines, Viktor Orban in Hungary, Recep Tayyip Erdogan in Turkey, and Jair Bolsonaro in Brazil to see that these populist impulses and challenges to the existing international order go beyond a single nation. Indeed, it is not without a bit of irony that these intensely nationalist movements have often sought to build transnational alliances facilitated by globalization's compression of space and time (Ferguson 2016).

It is impossible to tell in the moment whether the rise of populism and its disdain for (if not hostility toward) multilateralism is emblematic of a long-term trend that threatens to bring down the post–World War II global order or merely a cyclical variation where multilateral institutions play a less prominent role. Bosco describes the current climate as more akin to Charles de Gaulle's attacks on the United Nations during the 1950s and 1960s—a "crusade against . . . the excesses of multilateralism [that] made plenty of waves, but . . . didn't amount to much in the long run" (Bosco 2017: 12). Even if there is generalized antipathy toward the current multilateral orders, the populist voices "are strikingly vague on what they want the world architecture to look like" (Bosco 2017: 14). While that position may ultimately prove to be correct, Linn counters that we "better act as if the threats are long-term and serious in nature, for if we are wrong in the assumption that they are cyclical and that they therefore can safely be ignored, the damage to the world could be catastrophic" (Linn 2018: 88).

Populism and nationalism can pose particular challenges for global health policy. If there is a political movement largely premised on the idea of foreigners as outsiders and that prioritizes protection of one's own country above all else, it can be a challenge to rally support for spending time, energy, and resources to improve the health of others. In the United Kingdom after Brexit, for example, there have been calls for changing the structure of the health care system to require overseas patients to pay for any and all services upfront. This move is fundamentally premised on the idea that "freeloading health tourists" come to the United Kingdom to take health care away from others—and it undermines the fundamental basis on which the National Health Service is premised (Speed and Mannion 2017: 250). This attitude flies in the face of the evidence that migrants pay into the system significantly more than they receive and at higher rates than native-born citizens (McKee and Galsworthy 2016: 3).

Global health is specifically premised on an outward-focused, interconnected framework, but it is challenged by the weakening of multilateralism and the strengthening of nationalist and populist parties. Regardless of whether these challenges are a momentary blip or a sign of long-term changes, the question is how this interregnum will affect the existing global health governance architecture—and how it changes those systems.

CONCLUSION

The intersection of globalization and health has brought new issues to public attention, but that hardly means that international society has addressed all of the emerging issues. This chapter showed how issues of gender, the environment, and changing attitudes toward multilateralism present serious challenges for understanding the relationship between globalization and health. What's more, the important points that these three issues raise are driven by exactly the same key elements that propel globalization itself. They represent *intensification* because they are further expanding the range of issues that are affecting and being affected by each other. They highlight the importance of *integration* because we witness the tying together of a diverse range of seemingly disparate concerns. They embody *deterritorialization* because their effects and the reasons that they are becoming important are almost wholly divorced from the specific territories. Some may even argue that globalization is narrowing the policy options available to governments to such a degree that individual governments play little role in charting their own courses. They foster the *elevation* of issues because they raise concerns that cannot be addressed by a single government. No individual state will be able to address climate change or shifting gender relations, and the effects of rising populism and mistrust of multilateral institutions necessarily spread far beyond individual borders. Finally, as the range of issues continues to broaden and incorporate an ever-diversifying spread of concerns, we witness globalization's ability to foster the *expansion* of the political realm.

There is no single relationship between globalization and health. Instead, they intersect with each other in a wide variety of ways—sometimes mutually reinforcing, sometimes antagonistic, and sometimes uncertain. After reading an entire book about globalization and health, it may be frustrating to have the sense that there is no clear answer to how these two concepts relate to each other. Rather than seeing this as a shortcoming, it is better to understand this ambiguous relationship as reflecting the tensions and contradictions within both of these concepts. Globalization and health are both such multifaceted and complex phenomena that it would be impossible to reduce them to simple slogans or pithy phrases.

If the international community is going to understand how to address global health, then it is absolutely vital that it acknowledge the unwieldiness of globalization and its manifestations. We know that there will be disease outbreaks in the future, but we do not know where they will occur, when they will happen, or what will cause them. We do know that without an understanding of the dynamics of globalization, though, we will be utterly ill-equipped to present an effective response. Globalization may seem frustrating at times, but it is absolutely vital to understand if we want to make any progress toward realizing the Universal Declaration of Human Rights' claim that all people—regardless of their gender, race, religion, class, or any other attribute—have a right to "a standard of living adequate for the health and well-being of himself and his family" (United Nations 1948).

REFERENCES

Aberth, John. 2011. *Plagues in World History*. Lanham, MD: Rowman & Littlefield.

Abimbola, Seye, Asmat Ullah Malik, and Ghulam Farooq Mansoor. 2013. "The final push for polio eradication: addressing the challenge of violence in Afghanistan, Pakistan, and Nigeria." *PLoS Medicine* 10(10): e1001529.

Achmat, Zackie. 2004. "The Treatment Action Campaign, HIV/AIDS, and the government." *Transformation* 54(1): 76–84.

Afshin, Ashkan, Renata Micha, Shahab Khatibzadeh, Laura A. Schmidt, and Dariush Mozaffarian. 2014. "Dietary policies to reduce noncommunicable diseases." In *The Handbook of Global Health Policy*, Garrett W. Brown, Gavin Yamey, and Sarah Wamala (eds.), 177–94. Malden, MA: Wiley Blackwell.

AFP. 2017. "Globalisation an 'irreversible historical trend': Xi Jinping." *The Straits Times*, November 10. https://www.straitstimes.com/asia/east-asia/globalisation-is-an-irreversible-historical-trend-xi-jinping (accessed February 19, 2019).

Ahmed, Shamima. 2009. "Nongovernmental organizations." In *Globalization and Security: An Encyclopedia, Volume 1: Economic and Political Aspects*, G. Honor Fagan and Ronaldo Munck (eds.), 293–311. Santa Barbara, CA: ABC-CLIO.

Aiken, Abigail A., James G. Scott, Rebecca Gomperts, James Trussell, Marc Worrell, and Catherine E. Aiken. 2016. "Requests for abortion in Latin America related to concern about Zika virus exposure." *New England Journal of Medicine* 375(4): 396–98.

Aizenman, Nurith. 2017. "Trump's proposed budget would cut $2.2 billion from global health spending." NPR, May 25. https://www.npr.org/sections/goatsand soda/2017/05/25/529873431/trumps-proposed-budget-would-cut-2-2-billion -from-global-health-spending (accessed February 19, 2019).

Albrow, Martin. 1997. *The Global Age*. Palo Alto: Stanford University Press.

Alderson, Kai, and Andrew Hurrell. 2000. *Hedley Bull on International Society*. New York: Palgrave Macmillan.

Aldis, William L., and Triono Soendoro. 2015. "Indonesia, power asymmetry, and pandemic risk: the paradox of global health security." In *Routledge Handbook of Global Health Security*, Simon Rushton and Jeremy Youde (eds.), 318–27. London: Routledge.

Ali, S. Harris, and Roger Keil. 2006. "Global cities and the spread of infectious disease: the case of severe acute respiratory syndrome (SARS) in Toronto, Canada." *Urban Studies* 43(3): 491–509.

Alirol, Emilie, Laurent Getaz, Beat Stoll, Francois Chappius, and Louis Loutan. 2011. "Urbanization and infectious diseases in a globalized world." *Lancet Infectious Diseases* 11(2): 131–41.

Alvarez-Sanchez, Cristina, Isobel Contento, Alejandra Jimenez-Aguilar, Pamela Koch, Heewon Lee Gray, Laura A. Guerra, Juan Rivera-Dommarco, Rebeca Uribe-Carvajal, and Teresa Shamah-Levy. 2016. "Does the Mexican sugar-sweetened beverage tax have a signaling effect? ENSANUT 2016." *PLoS One* 13(8): e0199337.

Anderson, Emma-Louise. 2015. *Gender, HIV, and Risk: Navigating Structural Violence*. New York: Palgrave Macmillan.

Anderson, Emma-Louise, and Amy S. Patterson. 2017. *Dependent Agency in the Global Health Regime: Local African Responses to Donor AIDS Efforts*. New York: Palgrave Macmillan.

Anderson, Joan M. 2000. "Gender, 'race,' poverty, health, and discourses of health reform in the context of globalization: a postcolonial feminist perspective in policy research." *Nursing Inquiry* 7(4): 220–29.

Andrade, Luis Jesuino de Oliveria, Argemiro D'Oliveira, Rosangela Carvalho Melo, Emmanuel Conrado de Souza, Carolina Alves Costa Silva, and Raymundo Parana. 2009. "Association between hepatitis C and hepatocellular carcinoma." *Journal of Global Infectious Diseases* 1(1): 33–37.

Armbruster, Benjamin, and Margaret L. Brandeau. 2007. "Contact tracing to control infectious disease: when enough is enough." *Health Care Management Science* 10(4): 341–55.

Armelagos, George J., Peter J. Brown, and Bethany Turner. 2005. "Evolutionary, historical, and political economic perspectives on health and disease." *Social Science and Medicine* 61(4): 755–65.

Baicker, Katherine, David Cutler, and Zirui Song. 2010. "Workplace wellness programs can generate savings." *Health Affairs* 29(2): 1–8.

Bakari, Edith, and Gasto Frumence. 2013. "Challenges to the implementation of International Health Regulations (2005) on Preventing Infectious Diseases: experience from Julius Nyerere International Airport, Tanzania." *Global Health Action* 6(1): 20942.

Baker, Tom. 2018. "The state of sugar and health taxes around the world." *Kerry-Digest*, June 18. https://kerry.com/uae-en/sitecore/content/kerrysite/pages/insights/kerrydigest/2018/the-state-of-sugar-and-health-taxes-around-the-world (accessed February 19, 2019).

Baldwin, Peter. 2005. *Disease and Democracy: The Industrialized World Faces AIDS.* Berkeley: University of California Press.

Baleta, Adele. 2000. "AIDS activists force attention to fluconazole in South Africa." *Lancet* 356(9241): 1584.

Bansal, Paritosh. 2018. "Indian PM Modi defends globalization at Davos summit." Reuters, January 23. https://www.reuters.com/article/us-davos-meeting-modi/indian-pm-modi-defends-globalization-at-davos-summit-idUSKBN1FC1AL (accessed February 19, 2019).

Barnes, Amy, and Justin Parkhurst. 2014. "Can global health policy be depoliticized? A critique of global calls for evidence-based policy." In *The Handbook of Global Health Policy*, Garrett W. Brown, Gavin Yamey, and Sarah Wamala (eds.), 157–73. Malden, MA: Wiley Blackwell.

Barquet, Nicolau, and Pere Domingo. 1997. "Smallpox: the triumph over the most terrible of the ministers of death." *Annals of Internal Medicine* 127(8): 635–42.

Barrett, Scott. 2007. *Why Cooperate? The Incentive to Supply Global Public Goods.* Oxford: Oxford University Press.

Barrett, Scott. 2013. "Economic considerations for the eradication endgame." *Philosophical Transactions of the Royal Society B* 368(1623): 20120149.

Barry, John M. 2009. *The Great Influenza: The Story of the Deadliest Pandemic in History.* New York: Penguin.

Bashford, Alison. 2004. *Imperial Hygiene: A Critical History of Colonialism, Nationalism, and Public Health.* New York: Palgrave Macmillan.

Basu, Amrita. 2000. "Globalization of the local/localization of the global: mapping transnational women's movements." *Meridians* 1(1): 68–84.

Bates, Lisa Michelle, Olena Hanvinsky, and Kristen W. Springer. 2009. "Gender and health inequities: a comment on the Final Report of the WHO Commission on the Social Determinants of Health." *Social Science and Medicine* 69(7): 1002–04.

Bazin, Herve. 2000. *The Eradication of Smallpox: Edward Jenner and the First and Only Eradication of a Human Infectious Disease.* San Diego: Academic Press.

Behbehani, Abbas M. 1983. "The smallpox story: the life and death of an old disease." *Microbiological Review* 47(4): 455–509.

Behrman, Greg. 2004. *The Invisible People: How the US Has Slept Through the Global AIDS Pandemic, the Greatest Humanitarian Catastrophe of Our Time.* New York: Free Press.

Beigbeider, Yves. 2000. "Challenges to the World Health Organization." In *The Politics of Emerging and Resurgent Infectious Diseases*, Jim Whitman (ed.), 178–99. New York: Palgrave.

Bell, Colleen. 2006. "Surveillance strategies and populations at risk: biopolitical governance in Canada's national security policy." *Security Dialogue* 37(2): 147–65.

Belluz, Julia. 2015. "9 of the 11 Ebola treatment centers built by Americans have never seen a single Ebola patient." *Vox*, April 13. https://www.vox.com/2015/4/13/8402613/Ebola-US-response (accessed February 19, 2019).

Belluz, Julia. 2017. "Trump's budget on health: 3 losers and 2 winners." *Vox*, March 16. https://www.vox.com/2017/3/16/14943816/trumps-budget-health-winners-losers (accessed February 19, 2019).

Belluz, Julia. 2018a. "Fox News says the migrant caravan will bring disease outbreaks. That's xenophobic nonsense." *Vox*, November 1. https://www.vox.com/science-and-health/2018/11/1/18048332/migrant-caravan-fox-news-disease-smallpox-outbreaks-vaccines-xenophobia (accessed February 19, 2019).

Belluz, Julia. 2018b. "Trump vs. 'disease X.'" *Vox*, February 26. https://www.vox.com/science-and-health/2018/2/23/16974012/trump-pandemic-disease-response (accessed February 19, 2019).

Benford, Robert D., and David A. Snow. 2000. "Framing processes and social movement: an overview and assessment." *Annual Review of Sociology* 26: 611–39.

Bennett, W. Lance. 2003. "Communicating global activism: strengths and vulnerabilities of networked politics." *Information, Communication, and Society* 6(2): 143–68.

Benson, Christopher, and Sara M. Glasgow. 2015. "Noncommunicable disease as a security issue." In *Routledge Handbook of Global Health Security*, Simon Rushton and Jeremy Youde (eds.), 175–86. New York: Routledge.

Bentham, Jeremy. 2004. *Utilitarianism and Other Essays*, Alan Ryan (ed.). New York: Penguin.

Benton, Adia. 2015. *HIV Exceptionalism: Development through Disease in Sierra Leone*. Minneapolis: University of Minnesota Press.

Berkman, Alan, Jonathan Garcia, Miguel Munoz-Laboy, Vera Paiva, and Richard Parker. 2005. "A critical analysis of the Brazilian response to HIV/AIDS: lessons learned for controlling and mitigating the epidemic in developing countries." *American Journal of Public Health* 95(7): 1162–72.

Besnard, M., S. Lastere, A. Teissier, V.M. Cao-Lormeau, and D. Musso. 2014. "Evidence of perinatal transmission of Zika virus, French Polynesia, December 2013 and February 2014." *Eurosurveillance* 19(13): pii: 20751.

Bhattacharya, Shaoni, and Debora MacKenzie. 2003. "Exotic market animals likely source of SARS." *New Scientist*, May 23. https://www.newscientist.com/article/dn3763-exotic-market-animals-likely-source-of-sars/ (accessed February 19, 2019).

Bill & Melinda Gates Foundation. N.d. "Who we are—foundation fact sheet." https://www.gatesfoundation.org/Who-We-Are/General-Information/Foundation-Factsheet (accessed February 19, 2019).

Bill & Melinda Gates Foundation. 2017. "Health systems strengthening: ensuring effective health supply chains (round 19)." https://gcgh.grandchallenges.org/challenge/health-systems-strengthening-ensuring-effective-health-supply-chains-round-19 (accessed February 19, 2019).

Bill & Melinda Gates Foundation. 2018. *Annual Report 2017.* https://www.gatesfoundation.org/Who-We-Are/Resources-and-Media/Annual-Reports/Annual-Report-2017 (accessed February 19, 2019).

Bloom, David E., David Canning, and Günther Fink. 2008. "Urbanization and the wealth of nations." *Science* 319(5864): 772–75.

Bogenschneider, Bret N. 2017. "'Sin tax' as a signpost in food labelling." *European Food and Feed Law Review* 14(1): 14–21.

Bollet, Alfred Jay. 2004. *Plagues and Poxes: The Impact of Human History on Epidemic Disease.* New York: Demos.

Bollyky, Thomas. 2018. "Health without wealth: the worrying paradox of modern medical practices." *Foreign Affairs* 97(6): 168–78.

Boon, Kristen. 2017. "President Trump and the future of multilateralism." *Emory International Law Review* 31: 1075–81.

Boorstein, Michelle, Colby Itzkowitz, and Sarah Pulliam Bailey. 2016. "Pope: contraceptives could be morally permissible in avoiding spread of Zika." *Washington Post*, February 18. https://www.washingtonpost.com/local/social-issues/pope-contraceptives-could-be-morally-permissable-in-avoiding-spread-of-zika/2016/02/18/64d029de-d673-11e5-be55-2cc3c1e4b76b_story.html?utm_term=.8a05ff377614 (accessed February 19, 2019).

Booth, Nicholas J. 2013. "Bentham 'present but not voting.'" UCL Museums and Collections Blog, 12 July. http://blogs.ucl.ac.uk/museums/2013/07/12/bentham-present-but-not-voting/ (accessed 19 February 2019).

Borges, Maria Carolina, Maria Laura Louzada, Thiago Hérick de Sá, Anthony A. Laverty, Diana C. Parra, Josefa Maria Fellegger Grazillo, Carlos Augusto Montiero, and Christopher Millett. 2017. "Artificially sweetened beverages and the response to the global obesity crisis." *PLoS Medicine* 14(1): e1002195.

Bosco, David. 2017. "We've been here before: the durability of multilateralism." *Journal of International Affairs* 70(2): 9–15.

Breman, Joel G., David L. Heymann, Graham Lloyd, Joseph B. McCormick, Malonga Miatudila, Frederick A. Murphy, Jean-Jacques Muyembe-Tamfun, Peter Piot, Jaen-Francois Ruppol, Pierre Sureau, Guido van der Groen, and Karl M.

Johnson. 2016. "Discovery and description of Ebola Zaire virus in 1976 and relevance to the West African epidemic during 2013-2016." *Journal of Infectious Diseases* 214(Supplement 3): S93–S101.

Brender, Nathalie. 2014. *Global Risk Governance in Health.* New York: Palgrave Macmillan.

Brier, Jennifer. 2009. *Infectious Ideas: US Political Responses to the AIDS Crisis.* Chapel Hill: University of North Carolina Press.

Brower, Jennifer, and Peter Chalk. 2003. *The Global Threat of New and Reemerging Infectious Diseases: Reconciling US National Security and Public Health Policy.* Santa Monica: RAND Corporation.

Brown, Garrett W., and Lauren Paremoer. 2014. "Global health justice and the right to health." In *Handbook of Global Health Policy*, Garrett W. Brown, Gavin Yamey, and Sara Wamala (eds.), 77–95. Malden, MA: John Wiley and Sons.

Bull, Hedley. 1995. *The Anarchical Society: A Study of World Order in Politics*, second edition. New York: Columbia University Press.

Burns, J. H. 2005. "Happiness and utility: Jeremy Bentham's equation." *Utilitas* 17(1): 46–61.

Buse, Kent, and Sarah Hawkes. 2016. "Sitting on the FENSA: WHO engagement with industry." *Lancet* 388(10043): 446–47.

Bush, George W. 2017. "PEPFAR saves millions of lives in Africa. Keep it fully funded." *Washington Post*, April 7. https://www.washingtonpost.com/opinions/george-w-bush-pepfar-saves-millions-of-lives-in-africa-keep-it-fully-funded/2017/04/07/2089fa46-1ba7-11e7-9887-1a5314b56a08_story.html?utm_term=.d938ee056dad (accessed February 19, 2019).

Buzan, Barry, Ole Waever, and Jaap de Wilde. 1998. *Security: A New Framework for Analysis.* Boulder: Lynne Rienner.

Byron, Katie, and Dana Howard. 2017. "'Hey everybody, don't get pregnant': Zika, WHO, and an ethical framework for advising." *Journal of Medical Ethics* 43(5): 334–38.

Caplan, Arthur. 2009. "Is disease eradication ethical?" *The Lancet* 373(9682): 2192–93.

Caprioli, Mary. 2005. "Primed for violence: the role of gender inequality in predicting internal conflict." *International Studies Quarterly* 49(2): 161–78.

Caprioli, Mary, and Mark A. Boyer. 2001. "Gender, violence, and international crisis." *Journal of Conflict Resolution* 45(4): 503–18.

Cardiff, Robert D., Jerrold M. Ward, and Stephen W. Barthold. 2008. "'One medicine—one pathology': are veterinary and human pathology prepared?" *Laboratory Investigation* 88(1): 18–26.

Carney, Matthew. 2016. "China's cancer rates exploding, more than 4 million people diagnosed in 2015, report says." *ABC News*, March 24. http://www.abc.net.au/news/2016-03-24/chinas-cancer-rates-exploding-study-says/7272266 (accessed February 19, 2019).

Carolina, Martinez S., and Leal F. Gustavo. 2003. "Epidemiological transition: model or illusion? A look at the problem of health in Mexico." *Social Science and Medicine* 57(3): 539–50.

Caron, David D., Joan Fitzpatrick, and Ron C. Slye. 2003. "Republic of South Africa v. Grootboom. Case No. CCT 11/00. 2000(11) BCLR 1169 and Minister of Health v. Treatment Action Campaign, Case No. CCT 8/02." *American Journal of International Law* 97(3): 669–80.

Carter, Jason. 2010. "WHO's virus is it anyway? How the World Health Organization can protect against claims of 'viral sovereignty.'" *Georgia Journal of Comparative and International Law* 38(3): 717–40.

Castells, Manuel. 1996. *The Rise of Network Society*. Cambridge: Polity.

Centers for Disease Control and Prevention. 2004. "SARS update—May 19, 2004." https://www.cdc.gov/sars/media/2004-05-19.html (accessed February 19, 2019).

Centers for Disease Control and Prevention. 2009. "Swine influenza A (H1N1) infection in two children—Southern California, March–April 2009." *Morbidity and Mortality Weekly Report* 58(15): 400–02.

Chan, Lai-Ha, Lucy Chen, and Jin Xu. 2010. "China's engagement with global health diplomacy: was SARS a watershed?" *PLoS Medicine* 7(4): e1000266.

Chan, Margaret. 2010. "Progress in public health during the previous decade and major challenges ahead." Speech to the World Health Organization Executive Board at its 126th Session. Geneva, January 18. http://www.who.int/dg/speeches/2010/executive_board_126_20100118/en/ (accessed February 19, 2019).

Chan, Paul K. S. 2002. "Outbreak of avian influenza A(H5N1) virus infection in Hong Kong in 1997." *Clinical Infectious Diseases* 34(Supplement 2): S58–S64.

Chapman, Audrey. 2012. "The contribution of a human rights approach to health." In *Ashgate Research Companion to the Globalization of Health*, Ted Schrecker (ed.), 261–76. Burlington: Ashgate.

Chen, Wanqing, Rongshou Zheng, Hongmei Zeng, and Siwei Zhang. 2015. "Epidemiology of lung cancer in China." *Thoracic Cancer* 6(2): 209–15.

Chien, Yu-Ju. 2013. "How did international agencies perceive the avian influenza problem? The adoption and manufacture of the 'One World, One Health' framework." *Sociology of Health and Illness* 35(2): 213–26.

Christensen, Tom, and Martin Painter. 2004. "The politics of SARS—rational responses or ambiguity, symbols, and chaos?" *Policy and Society* 23(2): 18–48.

Clark, Helen. 2013. "NCDs: a challenge to sustainable human development." *Lancet* 381(9866): 510–11.

Clark, Ian. 1997. *Globalization and Fragmentation: International Relations in the Twentieth Century*. Oxford: Oxford University Press.

Clift, Charles, and John-Arne Rottingen. 2018. "New approaches to WHO financing: the key to better health." *BMJ* 361: k2218.

Clinton, Chelsea, and Devi Sridhar. 2017. *Governing Global Health: Who Runs the World and Why?* New York: Oxford University Press.

Cohen, Deborah, and Philip Carter. 2010. "WHO and the pandemic flu 'conspiracies.'" *BMJ* 340: c2912.

Cohen, Jon. 2016. "The race for a Zika vaccine is on." *Science* 351(6273): 543–44.

Cohen, Jon. 2018. "Ebola vaccine is having 'major impact' but worries about Congo outbreak grow." *Science*, December 10. http://www.sciencemag.org/news/2018/12/ebola-vaccine-having-major-impact-outbreak-may-still-explode-west-africa (accessed February 19, 2019).

Cohen, Nicole J., Clive M. Brown, Francisco Alvarado-Ramy, Heather Bair-Brake Gabrielle A. Benenson, Tai-Ho Chen, Andrew J. Demma, N. Kelly Holton, Amanda W. Lee, David McAdam, Nicki Pasik, Shahrokh Roohi, C. Lee Smith, Stephen H. Waterman, and Martin S. Cetron. 2016. "Travel and border measures to prevent the international spread of Ebola." *Morbidity and Mortality Weekly Report* 65(3): 57–67.

Colchero, M. Arantxa, Juan Rivera-Donmarco, Barry M. Popkin, and Shu Wen Ng. 2017. "In Mexico, evidence of sustained consumer response two years after implementing a sugar-sweetened beverage tax." *Health Affairs* 36(3): 564–71.

Collier, Nigel H. 2015. "A review of web-based epidemic detection." In *The Politics of Surveillance and Response to Disease Outbreaks: The New Frontier for States and Non-State Actors*, Sara E. Davies and Jeremy R. Youde (eds.), 85–105. Burlington: Ashgate.

Collin, Jeff, Kelley Lee, and Karen Bissell. 2002. "The Framework Convention on Tobacco Control: the politics of global health governance." *Third World Quarterly* 23(2): 265–82.

Collins, Kathleen. 2002. "Clans, pacts, and politics in Central Asia." *Journal of Democracy* 13(3): 137–52.

Coltart, Cordelia E. M., Benjamin Lindsey, Isaac Ghinai, Anne M. Johnson, and David L. Heymann. 2017. "The Ebola outbreak, 2013–2016: old lessons for new epidemics." *Philosophical Transactions of the Royal Society of London B: Biological Sciences* 372(1721): 20160297.

Connell, Raewyn. 2012. "Gender, health, and theory: conceptualizing the issue, in local and world perspective." *Social Science and Medicine* 74(11): 1675–83.

Cooper, Helene. 2017. "Trump team's queries about Africa point to skepticism about aid." *New York Times*, January 13. https://www.nytimes.com/2017/01/13/world/africa/africa-donald-trump.html (accessed February 19, 2019).

Cornes, Richard, and Todd Sandler. 1986. *The Theory of Externalities, Public Goods, and Club Goods*. Cambridge: Cambridge University Press.

Cortell, Andrew P., and James W. Davis, Jr. 2000. "Understanding the domestic impact of international norms: a research agenda." *International Studies Review* 2(1): 65–87.

Council on Foreign Relations. 2013. *Global Governance Monitor: Public Health*. https://www.cfr.org/interactives/global-governance-monitor#!/public-health (accessed February 19, 2019).

Council on Foreign Relations. 2014. *The Emerging Global Health Crisis: Noncommunicable Diseases in Low- and Middle-Income Countries*. New York: Council on Foreign Relations.

Cox, Robert W. 1996. "A perspective on globalization." In *Globalization: Critical Reflections*, James Mittelman (ed.), 21–30. Boulder: Lynne Rienner.

Crosby, Alfred W. 2003. *America's Forgotten Pandemic: The Influenza of 1918, New Edition*. Cambridge: Cambridge University Press.

Curley, Melissa G., and Jonathan Herington. 2011. "The securitization of avian influenza: international discourses and domestic politics in Asia." *Review of International Studies* 37(1): 141–66.

Curley, Melissa, and Nicholas Thomas. 2004. "Human security and public health in southeast Asia: the SARS outbreak." *Australian Journal of International Affairs* 58(1): 17–32.

Currier, Russell W., and James H. Steele. 2011. "One Health—One Medicine: unifying human and animal medicine within an evolutionary paradigm." *Annals of the New York Academy of Sciences* 1230: 4–11.

Czaika, Mathias, and Hein de Haas. 2015. "The globalization of migration: has the world become more migratory?" *International Migration Review* 48(2): 283–323.

Dardis, Frank E. 2007. "The role of issue-framing functions in affecting beliefs and opinions about a sociopolitical issue." *Communication Quarterly* 55(2): 247–65.

Davies, Sara E. 2008. "Securitizing infectious disease." *International Affairs* 84(2): 295–313.

Davies, Sara E. 2012a. "The international politics of disease reporting: towards post-Westphalianism?" *International Politics* 49(5): 591–613.

Davies, Sara E. 2012b. "Nowhere to hide: informal disease surveillance networks tracing disease behavior." *Global Change, Peace, and Security* 24(2): 95–107.

Davies, Sara E. 2015. "Internet surveillance and disease outbreaks." In *The Routledge Handbook of Global Health Security*, Simon Rushton and Jeremy Youde (eds.), 226–38. New York: Routledge.

Davies, Sara E., and Jeremy Youde. 2015. "Surveillance, response, and responsibilities in the 2005 International Health Regulations." In *The Politics of Surveillance and Response to Disease Outbreaks: The New Frontier for States and Non-State Actors*, Sara E. Davies and Jeremy Youde (eds.), 9–22. Burlington: Ashgate.

Davies, Sara E., Sophie Harman, Rashida Manjoo, Maria Tanyag, and Clare Wenham. 2019. "Why it must be a feminist global health agenda." *Lancet* 393(10171): 601–03.

Davies, Sara E., Adam Kamradt-Scott, and Simon Rushton. 2015. *Disease Diplomacy: International Norms and Global Health Security*. Baltimore: The Johns Hopkins University Press.

Dearden, Lizzie. 2014. "Ebola outbreak: Brazilians cancel Namibia visit over Ebola fears, despite conference being 3000 miles from disease hotspot." *The Independent*, August 19. https://www.independent.co.uk/news/world/africa/ebola-out

break-brazilians-cancel-namibia-visit-over-ebola-fears-despite-conference-being
-3000-miles-9678108.html (accessed February 19, 2019).

Degeling, Chris, Jane Johnson, Ian Kerridge, Andrew Wilson, Michael Ward, Cameron Stewart, and Gwendolyn Gilbert. 2015. "Implementing a One Health approach to emerging infectious disease: reflections on the socio-political, ethical, and legal dimensions." *BMC Public Health* 15: 1307.

DeLaet, Debra L., and David E. DeLaet. 2012. *Global Health in the 21st Century: The Globalization of Disease and Wellness.* Boulder: Paradigm.

Deonandan, Raywat. 2014. "The Ebola outbreak proves the need for health surveillance." *Huffington Post,* October 9. https://www.huffingtonpost.ca/dr-raywat
-deonandan/ebola-outbreak_b_5949994.html (accessed February 19, 2019).

Desmond-Hellman, Sue. 2015. "Reflections on my first year as CEO of the Gates Foundation." *Medium,* May 15. https://medium.com/bill-melinda-gates-founda
tion/reflections-on-my-first-year-as-ceo-of-the-gates-foundation-3d43f437345f
(accessed February 19, 2019).

Deudney, Daniel. 1990. "The case against linking environmental degradation and national security." *Millennium* 19(3): 461–76.

Doshi, Peter. 2011. "The elusive definition of pandemic influenza." *Bulletin of the World Health Organization* 89(7): 532–38.

Doucleff, Michaeleen. 2012. "Holy bat virus! Genome hints at origin of SARS-like virus." NPR, September 28. https://www.npr.org/sections/health-shots/2012/09/
28/161944734/holy-bat-virus-genome-hints-at-origin-of-sars-like-virus (accessed February 19, 2019).

Doucleff, Michaeleen. 2016. "Guess how many Zika cases showed up at the Olympics?" NPR, August 26. https://www.npr.org/sections/goatsandsoda/2016/
08/26/491416709/guess-how-many-zika-cases-showed-up-at-the-olympics (accessed February 19, 2019).

Doucleff, Michaeleen. 2018. "Trump proposes deep cuts in detecting disease outbreaks worldwide." NPR, February 12. https://www.npr.org/sections/goatsand
soda/2018/02/12/585119417/trump-proposes-deep-cuts-in-detecting-disease
-outbreaks-worldwide (accessed February 19, 2019).

Douglas, Bruce. 2015. "Brazil warns women not to get pregnant as Zika virus is linked to rare birth defect." *The Guardian,* December 4. https://www.theguard
ian.com/global-development/2015/dec/04/brazil-zika-virus-pregnancy-micro
cephaly-mosquito-rare-birth-defect (accessed February 19, 2019).

Dowdle, Walter R. 1999. "The principles of disease elimination and eradication." *Morbidity and Mortality Weekly Report* 48(SU01): 23–27.

Drazen, Jeffrey M., Rupa Kanapathipillai, Edward W. Campion, Eric J. Rubin, Scott M. Hammer, Stephen Morrisey, and Lindsey R. Baden. 2014. "Ebola and quarantine." *New England Journal of Medicine* 371(21): 2029–30.

Drezner, Daniel W. 2015. *Theories of International Politics and Zombies, Revised Edition.* Princeton: Princeton University Press.

Duffy, Mark R., Tai-Ho Chen, W. Thane Hancock, Ann M. Powers, Jacob L. Kool, Robert S. Lanciotti, Moses Pretrick, Maria Marfel, Stacey Holzbauer, Christine Dubray, Laurent Guillamot, Anne Griggs, Martin Bel, Amy J. Lambert, Janeen Laven, Olga Kosoy, Amanda Panella, Brad J. Biggerstaff, Marc Fischer, and Edward B. Hayes. 2009. "Zika virus outbreak on Yap Island Federated States of Micronesia." *New England Journal of Medicine* 360(24): 2536–43.

Dutton, Michael. 2009. "911: the after-life of colonial governmentality." *Postcolonial Studies* 12(3): 303–14.

Ear, Sophal. 2012. "Emerging infectious disease surveillance in southeast Asia: Cambodia, Indonesia, and the US Naval Area Medical Research Unit 2." *Asian Security* 8(2): 164–87.

Ear, Sophal. 2014. "Towards effective emerging infectious disease surveillance: evidence from the politics of influenza in Cambodia, Indonesia, and Mexico." *Politics and the Life Sciences* 33(1): 69–78.

Eba, Patrick. 2014. "Ebola and human rights in West Africa." *Lancet* 384(9960): 2019–93.

The Economist. 2006. "A shot of transparency." August 10. http://www.economist .com/node/7270183 (accessed February 19, 2019).

The Economist. 2016. "What the world thinks about globalisation." November 18. https://www.economist.com/graphic-detail/2016/11/18/what-the-world-thinks -about-globalisation (accessed February 19, 2019).

Edelson, Paul J. 2003. "Quarantine and social inequity." *Journal of the American Medical Association* 290(21): 2874.

Edwards, Martin S. 2006. "Public opinion regarding economic and cultural globalization: evidence from a cross-national survey." *Review of International Political Economy* 13(4): 587–608.

Elbe, Stefan. 2010a. "Haggling over viruses: the downside risks of securitizing infectious disease." *Health Policy and Planning* 25(6): 476–85.

Elbe, Stefan. 2010b. *Security and Global Health*. Cambridge: Polity.

Elgot, Jessica. 2016. "Trump's election is a 'global wake-up call', Corbyn to say in speech." *The Guardian*, November 12. https://www.theguardian.com/politics/ 2016/nov/12/donald-trump-election-global-wake-up-call-jeremy-corbyn (accessed February 19, 2019).

Elliott-Green, Ale, Lirije Hyseni, Ffion Lloyd-Williams, Helen Bromley, and Simon Capewell. 2016. "Sugar-sweetened beverages coverage in the British media: an analysis of public health advocacy versus pro-industry messaging." *BMJ Open* 6(7): e011295.

Ellner, Steve. 2002. "The 'radical' thesis on globalization and the case of Venezuela's Hugo Chávez." *Latin American Perspectives* 29(6): 88–93.

Enemark, Christian. 2017. *Biosecurity Dilemmas: Dreaded Diseases, Ethical Responses, and the Health of Nations*. Washington: Georgetown University Press.

England, Roger. 2007. "The dangers of disease specific programs for developing countries." *British Medical Journal* 335(7619): 565.

Entrena, Francisco. 2002. "Socioeconomic restructurings of the local setting in the era of globalization." In *Borderlines in a Globalized World: New Perspectives in a Sociology of the World Systems*, Gerhard Preyer and Mathias Bös (eds.), 217–28. Norwell, MA: Kluwer Academic Publishers.

Evans, David, Simon Cauchemez, and Frederick G. Hayden. 2009. "'Prepandemic' immunization for novel influenza viruses, 'swine flu' vaccine, Guillain-Barre syndrome, and the detection of rare severe adverse events." *Journal of Infectious Diseases* 200(3): 321–28.

Evans, Peter. 2000. "Fighting marginalization with transnational networks: counter-hegemonic globalization." *Contemporary Globalization* 29(1): 230–41.

Fairchild, Amy L., Ronald Bayer, and James Colgrove. 2007. *Searching Eyes: Privacy, the State, and Disease Surveillance in America*. Berkeley: University of California Press and New York: Milbank Memorial Fund.

Farmer, Paul. 1999. *Infections and Inequalities: The Modern Plagues*. Berkeley: University of California Press.

Farmer, Paul. 2003. *Pathologies of Power: Health, Human Rights, and the New War on the Poor*. Berkeley: University of California Press.

Fauci, Anthony S., and Robert W. Eisinger. 2018. "PEPFAR—15 years and counting the lives saved." *New England Journal of Medicine* 378(4): 314–16.

Fenner, F., D.A. Henderson, I. Arita, Z. Jezek, and I.D. Lanyi. 1988. *Smallpox and Its Eradication*. Geneva: World Health Organization.

Ferguson, Niall. 2016. "Populism as a backlash against globalization—historical perspectives." *Horizons: Journal of International Relations and Sustainable Development*. https://www.cirsd.org/en/horizons/horizons-autumn-2016—issue-no-8/populism-as-a-backlash-against-globalization (accessed February 19, 2019).

Fidler, David P. 1997. "The globalization of public health: emerging infectious disease and international relations." *Indiana Journal of Global Legal Studies* 5(1): 11–51.

Fidler, David P. 2003. "SARS: political pathology of the first post-Westphalian pathogen." *Journal of Law, Medicine, and Ethics* 31(4): 485–505.

Fidler, David P. 2005. "From International Sanitary Conventions to global health security: the new International Health Regulations." *Chinese Journal of International Law* 4(2): 325–92.

Fidler, David P. 2008. "Influenza virus samples, international law, and global health diplomacy." *Emerging Infectious Diseases* 14(1): 88–94.

Fidler, David P. 2010. *The Challenges of Global Health Governance*. New York: Council on Foreign Relations.

Fidler, David P., and Lawrence O. Gostin. 2011. "The WHO Pandemic Influenza Preparedness Framework: a milestone in global governance for health." *Journal of the American Medical Association* 306(2): 200–01.

Finnemore, Martha, and Kathryn Sikkink. 1998. "International norm dynamics and political change." *International Organization* 52(4): 887–917.

Fischer, Julie E., Sarah Kornblet, and Rebecca Katz. 2011. *The International Health Regulations (2005): Surveillance and Response in an Era of Globalization.* Washington: Stimson Center. https://www.stimson.org/sites/default/files/file -attachments/The_International_Health_Regulations_White_Paper_Final_1.pdf (accessed February 19, 2019).

Fischer, Michael M. J. 2013. "The peopling of technologies." In *When People Come First: Critical Studies in Global Health,* Joao Biehl and Adriana Petryna (eds.), 347–73. Princeton: Princeton University Press.

Fischer, William A., Jerry Brown, David Alan Wohl, Amy James Loftis, Sam Tozay, Edwina Reeves, Korto Pewu, Galapaki Gorvego, Saturday Quellie, Coleen K. Cunningham, Carson Merenbloom, Sonia Napravnik, Karine Dube, David Adjasoo, Erin Jones, Korlia Bonarwolo, and David Hoover. 2017. "Ebola virus ribonucleic acid detection in semen more than two years after resolution of acute Ebola virus infection." *Open Forum Infectious Diseases* 4(3): ofx155.

Fisman, David N., and Kevin B. Laupland. 2010. "The 'One Health' paradigm: time for infectious disease clinicians to take note?" *Canadian Journal of Infectious Diseases and Medical Microbiology* 21(3): 111–14.

Fleck, Fiona. 2003. "How SARS changed the world in less than six months." *Bulletin of the World Health Organization* 81(8): 625–26.

Foucault, Michel. 1977. *Discipline and Punish: The Birth of the Prison.* New York: Vintage.

Fourie, Pieter, and Melissa Meyer. 2016. *The Politics of AIDS Denialism: South Africa's Failure to Respond.* New York: Routledge.

Fox, Brion J. 2005. "Framing tobacco control efforts within an ethical context." *Tobacco Control* 14(Supplement 2): ii38–ii44.

Fox, Maggie. 2016. "Ebola survivors suffer long-term consequences: studies." *NBC News,* February 25. https://www.nbcnews.com/storyline/ebola-virus-outbreak/ ebola-survivors-suffer-long-term-consequences-studies-n525146 (accessed February 19, 2019).

France, David. 2016. *How to Survive a Plague: The Story of How Activists and Scientists Tamed AIDS.* New York: Picador.

Freedman, Amy. 2005. "SARS and regime legitimacy in China." *Asian Affairs* 36(2): 169–80.

French, Maddy. 2011. "Why non-communicable diseases hit the developing world so hard." *The Guardian,* June 30. https://www.theguardian.com/journalismcom petition/why-non-communicable-diseases-hit-the-developing-world-so-hard (accessed February 19, 2019).

Freudenthal, Emmanuel. 2019. "Ebola's lost blood: row over samples flown out of Africa as 'big pharma' set to cash in." *Telegraph,* February 6. https://www.telegraph

.co.uk/news/0/ebolas-lost-blood-row-samples-flown-africa-big-pharma-set-cash/ (accessed February 19, 2019).

Friedman, Steven, and Shauna Mottiar. 2005. "A rewarding engagement? The Treatment Action Campaign and the politics of HIV/AIDS." *Politics and Society* 33(4): 511–65.

Frisch, Deborah. 1993. "Reasons for framing effects." *Organizational Behavior and Human Decision Processes* 54(3): 399–429.

Fudge, Judy, and Brenda Cossman. 2002. "Introduction: privatization, law, and the challenge to feminism." In *Privatization, Law, and the Challenge to Feminism*, Judy Fudge and Brenda Cossman (eds.), 3–38. Toronto: University of Toronto Press.

Gallagher, James. 2016. "Zika outbreak: travel advice." *BBC News*, February 5. https://www.bbc.com/news/health-35441675 (accessed February 19, 2019).

Galley, Andrew. 2009. "City of plagues? Toronto, SARS, and the anxieties of globalization." *Vis-à-vis: Explorations in Anthropology* 9(1): 133–42.

Garrett, Geoffrey. 2000. "The causes of globalization." *Comparative Political Studies* 33(6/7): 941–91.

Garrett, Laurie. 1994. *The Coming Plague: Newly Emerging Diseases in a World Out of Control*. New York: Penguin.

Garrett, Laurie. 2007. "The challenge of global health." *Foreign Affairs* 86(1): 14–38.

Garrett, Laurie. 2016. "WHO's fairy dust funding." *Foreign Policy*, May 27. http://foreignpolicy.com/2016/05/27/whos-fairy-dust-financing-world-health-organization-zika-budget/ (accessed February 19, 2019).

Gatter, Robert. 2015. "Ebola, quarantine, and flawed CDC policy." *University of Miami Business Law Review* 23(2): 375–99.

General Accounting Office. 2000. *West Nile Virus Outbreak: Lessons for Public Health Preparedness*. Washington: National Academies Press.

Gibbons, Ann. 1990. "New head for the WHO Global Program on AIDS." *Science* 248(4961): 1306–07.

Gibbs, E. Paul J. 2014. "The evolution of One Health: a decade of progress and challenges for the future." *Veterinary Record* 174: 85–91.

Giddens, Anthony. 1990. *The Consequences of Modernity*. Cambridge: Polity.

Gill, Stephen. 1995. "The global panopticon? The neoliberal state, economic life, and democratic surveillance." *Alternatives* 20(1): 1–49.

Gillman, Todd J. 2014. "Ted Cruz: ban travel from African nations battling Ebola." *Dallas Morning News*, October 14. https://www.dallasnews.com/news/news/2014/10/14/ted-cruz-ban-travel-from-african-nations-battling-ebola (accessed February 19, 2019).

Gilpin, Robert. 1987. *The Political Economy of International Relations*. Princeton: Princeton University Press.

Gilpin, Robert. 2001. *Global Political Economy: Understanding the International Economic Order*. Princeton: Princeton University Press.

Glasgow, Sara, and Ted Schrecker. 2015. "The double burden of neoliberalism? Noncommunicable disease policies and the global political economy of risk." *Health and Place* 34: 279–86.

Glenn, Brian J. 2004. "God and the red umbrella: the place of values in the creation of institutions of mutual assistance." *Connecticut Insurance Law Journal* 10(2): 277–307.

Global Fund to Fight AIDS, Tuberculosis, and Malaria. N.d. "Bill and Melinda Gates Foundation." https://www.theglobalfund.org/en/private-ngo-partners/partners/bill-melinda-gates-foundation/ (accessed February 19, 2019).

Global Health Security Agenda. 2018. "What is GHSA?" https://www.ghsagenda.org (accessed February 19, 2019).

Gneiting, Uwe. 2016. "From global agenda-setting to domestic implementation: successes and challenges of the global health network on tobacco control." *Health Policy and Planning* 31(Supplement 1): i74–i86.

Goldberg, Pinelopi Koujianou. 2009. "Intellectual property rights protection in developing countries: the case of pharmaceuticals." Alfred Marshall Lecture, European Economic Association, Barcelona, Spain. August 27. http://www.econ.yale.edu/~pg87/Goldberg_Marshall.pdf (accessed February 19, 2019).

Goodman, Neville M. 1971. *International Health Organizations and Their Work*. London: Churchill Livingstone.

Goryakin, Yevgeniy, Lorenzo Rocco, and Marc Suhrcke. 2017. "The contribution of urbanization to non-communicable diseases: evidence from 173 countries from 1980 to 2008." *Economics and Human Biology* 26: 151–63.

Gostin, Lawrence O. 2014. *Global Health Law*. Cambridge: Harvard University Press.

Gostin, Lawrence O., and Rebecca Katz. 2016. "The International Health Regulations: the governing framework for global health security." *Milbank Quarterly* 94(2): 264–313.

Gould, Deborah B. 2009. *Moving Politics: Emotion and ACT UP's Fight Against AIDS*. Chicago: University of Chicago Press.

Gould, Deborah B. 2012. "ACT UP, racism, and the question of how to use history." *Quarterly Journal of Speech* 98(1): 54–62.

Graham, Erin R. 2015. "Money and multilateralism: how funding rules constitute IO governance." *International Theory* 7(1): 162–94.

Graham, Erin R. 2017. "Follow the money: how trends in financing are changing governance at international organizations." *Global Policy* 8(S5): 15–25.

Grebe, Eduard. 2011. "The Treatment Action Campaign's struggle for AIDS treatment in South Africa: coalition-building through networks." *Journal of Southern African Studies* 37(4): 849–68.

Greenwood, Brian. 2009. "Can malaria be eliminated?" *Transactions of the Royal Society of Tropical Medicine and Hygiene* 103(S1): S2–S5.

Gregory, Sean. 2016. "Zika fears cause American Olympians to scramble." *Time*, April 25. http://time.com/4257124/zika-fears-cause-american-olympians-to-scramble/ (accessed February 19, 2019).

Grépin, Karen A., Katherine Leach-Kemon, Matthew Schneider, and Devi Sridhar. 2012. "How to do (or not to do) . . . tracking data on development assistance for health." *Health Policy and Planning* 27(6): 527–34.

Gros, Jean-Germain. 2016. *Healthcare Policy in Africa: Institutes and Politics from Colonialism to the Present*. Lanham, MD: Rowman & Littlefield.

Grzymala-Busse, Anna, and Pauline Jones Luong. 2002. "Reconceptualizing the state: lessons from post-communism." *Politics and Society* 30(4): 529–54.

Guidry, John A., Michael D. Kennedy, and Mayer D. Zald. 1999. "Globalizations and social movements." In *Globalizations and Social Movements*, John A. Guidry, Michael D. Kennedy, and Mayer D. Zald (eds.), 1–32. Ann Arbor: University of Michigan Press.

Guillemin, Jeanne. 2005. *Biological Weapons: From the Invention of State-Sponsored Programs to Contemporary Bioterrorism*. New York: Columbia University Press.

Guillen, Mauro F. 2001. "Is globalization civilizing, destructive, or feeble? A critique of five key debates in the social science literature." *Annual Review of Sociology* 27: 235–60.

Gulliford, Martin. 2003. "Commentary: epidemiological transition and socioeconomic inequalities in blood pressure in Jamaica." *International Journal of Epidemiology* 32(2): 408–09.

Hafner, Tamara, and Jeremy Shiffman. 2013. "The emergence of global attention to health systems strengthening." *Health Policy and Planning* 28(1): 41–50.

Hall, John J., and Richard Taylor. 2003. "Health for All by 2000: the demise of the Alma-Ata Declaration and primary health care in developing countries." *Medical Journal of Australia* 178(1): 17–20.

Hameiri, Shahar. 2014. "Avian influenza, 'viral sovereignty,' and the politics of health security in Indonesia." *The Pacific Review* 27(3): 333–56.

Hameiri, Shahar, and Lee Jones. 2015. "The political economy of non-traditional security: explaining the governance of avian influenza in Indonesia." *International Politics* 52(4): 445–65.

Hamel, Liz, Jamie Firth, and Mollyann Brodie. 2014. "Kaiser Health Policy News index: special focus on Ebola." October 16. https://www.kff.org/global-health-policy/poll-finding/kaiser-health-policy-news-index-special-focus-on-ebola/ (accessed February 19, 2019).

Harman, Sophie. 2012. *Global Health Governance*. London: Routledge.

Harman, Sophie. 2016. "The Bill and Melinda Gates Foundation and legitimacy in global health governance." *Global Governance* 22(3): 349–68.

Harman, Sophie, and Sara E. Davies. 2018. "President Donald Trump as global health's displacement activity." *Review of International Studies*. https://doi.org/10.1017/S02602105180027X.

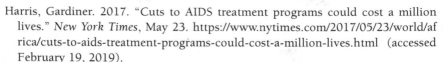

Harris, Gardiner. 2017. "Cuts to AIDS treatment programs could cost a million lives." *New York Times*, May 23. https://www.nytimes.com/2017/05/23/world/africa/cuts-to-aids-treatment-programs-could-cost-a-million-lives.html (accessed February 19, 2019).

Harris, Joseph. 2017. *Achieving Access: Professional Movements and the Politics of Health Universalism.* Ithaca: Cornell University Press.

Harris, Lisa H., Neil S. Silverman, and Mary Faith Marshall. 2016. "The paradigm of paradox: women, pregnant women, and the unequal burdens of the Zika virus pandemic." *American Journal of Bioethics* 16(5): 1–4.

Harris, Richard. 2014. "Smallpox virus found in unsecured NIH lab." NPR, July 8. https://www.npr.org/sections/health-shots/2014/07/08/329847454/smallpox-virus-found-in-unsecured-nih-freezer (accessed February 19, 2019).

Harrison, Mark. 2012. *Contagion: How Commerce Has Spread Disease.* New Haven: Yale University Press.

Harteveld, Eelco, Andrej Kokkonen, and Stefan Dahlberg. 2017. "Adapting to party lines: the effect of party affiliation on attitudes toward immigration." *West European Politics* 40(6): 1177–97.

Harvey, David. 2007. *A Brief History of Neoliberalism.* Oxford: Oxford University Press.

Hatch, Steven. 2017. "How the Ebola crisis helped launch Donald Trump's political career." *Mother Jones*, April 3. https://www.motherjones.com/politics/2017/04/trump-ebola-tweets/ (accessed February 19, 2019).

Hawkes, Corinna, Sharon Friel, Tim Lobstein, and Tim Lang. 2012. "Linking agricultural policies with obesity and noncommunicable diseases: a new perspective for a globalizing world." *Food Policy* 37(3): 343–53.

Hawkesworth, Mary. 2006. *Globalization and Feminist Activism.* Lanham, MD: Rowman & Littlefield.

Hayden, Erika Check. 2017. "Ebola survivors still immune to virus after 40 years." *Nature*, December 14. https://www.nature.com/articles/d41586-017-08664-w (accessed February 19, 2019).

Held, David, Anthony McGrew, David Goldblatt, and Jonathan Perraton. 1999. *Global Transformations: Politics, Economics, and Culture.* Stanford: Stanford University Press.

Helmke, Gretchen, and Steven Levitsky. 2004. "Informal institutions and comparative politics: a research agenda." *Perspectives on Politics* 12(4): 725–40.

Henderson, Donald A. 1997. "Edward Jenner's vaccine." *Public Health Reports* 112(2): 116–21.

Henderson, J. Vernon. 2005. "Urbanization and growth." In *Handbook of Economic Growth, Volume 1, Part B*, Philippe Aghion and Steven N. Durlauf (eds.), 1543–91. Amsterdam: Elsevier.

Heymann, David L. 2006. "SARS and emerging infectious diseases: a challenge to place global solidarity above national sovereignty." *Annals of the Academy of Medicine of Singapore* 35(5): 350–53.

Heymann, David L., and Alison West. 2015. "Emerging infections: threats to health and economic security." In *The Routledge Handbook of Global Health Security*, Simon Rushton and Jeremy Youde (eds.), 92–104. New York: Routledge.

Heymann, David L., Abraham Hodgson, Amadou Alpha Sall, David O. Freedman, J. Erin Staples, Fernando Althabe, Kalpana Baruah, Ghazala Mahmud, Nyoman Kundun, Pedro F.C. Vasconcelos, Silvia Bino, and K.U. Menon. 2016. "Zika virus and microcephaly: why is this situation a PHEIC?" *Lancet* 387(10020): 719–21.

Heywood, Anita E., and Rogelio Lopez-Velez. 2018. "Reducing infectious disease inequities among migrants." *Journal of Travel Medicine*. https://doi.org/10.1093/jtm/tay131.

Heywood, Mark. 2009. "South Africa's Treatment Action Campaign: combining law and social mobilization to realize the right to health." *Journal of Human Rights Practice* 1(1): 14–36.

Heywood, Mark, and Dennis Altman. 2000. "Confronting AIDS: human rights, law, and social transformation." *Health and Human Rights* 5(1): 149–79.

Hills, Kelly. 2016. "Rejecting quarantine: a frozen-in-time reaction to disease." In *Ebola's Message: Public Health and Medicine in the Twenty-First Century*, Nicholas G. Evans, Tara C. Smith, and Maimuna S. Majumder (eds.), 217–31. Cambridge: MIT Press.

Hinterberger, Amy, and Natalie Porter. 2015. "Genomic and viral sovereignty: tethering the materials of global biomedicine." *Public Culture* 27(2): 361–86.

Hintjens, Helen. 2009. "Social movements." In *Globalization and Security: An Encyclopedia, Volume 2: Social and Cultural Aspects*, G. Honor Fagan and Ronaldo Munck (eds.), 369–86. Santa Barbara, CA: ABC-CLIO.

Hirst, Paul, and Grahame Thompson. 1999. *Globalization in Question: The International Economy and the Possibilities of Governance*, second edition. Cambridge: Polity.

Hodal, Kate. 2017. "Bill Gates: don't expect charities to pick up the tab for Trump's sweeping aid cuts." *The Guardian*, September 13. https://www.theguardian.com/global-development/2017/sep/13/bill-gates-foundation-dont-expect-pick-up-the-bill-for-sweeping-aid-cuts-trump (accessed February 19, 2019).

Hoffman, Steven J., and Sarah L. Silverberg. 2018. "Delays in global disease outbreak responses: lessons from H1N1, Ebola, and Zika." *American Journal of Public Health* 108(3): 329–33.

Holbrooke, Richard, and Laurie Garrett. 2008. "'Sovereignty' that risks global health." *Washington Post*, August 10. https://www.washingtonpost.com/wp-dyn/content/article/2008/08/08/AR2008080802919.html (accessed February 19, 2019).

Holmes, Dave, Stuart J. Murray, Amelie Perron, and Genevieve Rail. 2006. "Deconstructing the evidence-based discourse in health sciences: truth, power, and fascism." *International Journal of Evidence Based Healthcare* 4(1): 180–86.

Holsti, Kalevi J. 2004. *Taming the Sovereigns: Institutional Change in International Politics*. Cambridge: Cambridge University Press.

Hooker, L. Claire, Christopher Mayes, Chris Degleling, Gwendolyn L. Gilbert, and Ian H. Kerridge. 2014. "Don't be scared, be angry: the politics and ethics of Ebola." *Medical Journal of Australia* 201(6): 352–54.

Hooton, Christopher. 2014. "'The ISIS of biological agents?': CNN is asking the stupid Ebola questions." *Independent*, October 7. https://www.independent.co .uk/news/world/americas/the-isis-of-biological-agents-cnn-is-asking-the-stupid -ebola-questions-9779584.html (accessed February 19, 2019).

Hooton, Christopher. 2017. "Game of Thrones is the most torrented show six years running." *Independent*, December 29. https://www.independent.co.uk/arts -entertainment/tv/news/game-of-thrones-torrents-streaming-2017-watch-online -hbo-season-7-a8133036.html (accessed February 19, 2019).

Hopkins, Jack W. 1989. *The Eradication of Smallpox: Organizational Learning and Innovation in International Health.* Boulder: Westview Press.

Horner, Jed, James G. Wood, and Angela Kelly. 2013. "Public health in/as 'national security': tuberculosis and the contemporary regime of border control in Australia." *Critical Public Health* 23(4): 418–31.

Howard, Jacqueline. 2016. "The truth about 'Patient Zero' and HIV's origins." *CNN*, October 29. http://edition.cnn.com/2016/10/27/health/hiv-gaetan-dugas -patient-zero/ (accessed February 19, 2019).

Howard-Jones, Norman. 1975. *The Scientific Background of the International Sanitary Conferences, 1851–1938.* Geneva: World Health Organization.

Huang, Kristin. 2017. "Why Taiwan cares so much about getting an invitation to the World Health Assembly." *South China Morning Post*, May 8. http://www .scmp.com/news/china/policies-politics/article/2093407/why-taiwan-cares-so -much-about-getting-invitation-world (accessed February 19, 2019).

Huang, Yanzhong. 2003. "The politics of China's SARS crisis." *Harvard Asia Quarterly* 7(4): 9–16.

Huang, Yanzhong. 2004. "The SARS epidemic and its aftermath in China: a political perspective." In *Learning from SARS: Preparing for the Next Disease Outbreak: Workshop Summary*, Stacey Knobler, Adel Mahmoud, Stanley Lemon, Alison Mack, Laura Sivitz, and Katherine Oberholtzer (eds.), 116–36. Washington: National Academies Press.

Hudson, Valerie M., Bonnie Ballif-Spanvill, Mary Caprioli, and Chad F. Emmett. 2012. *Sex and World Peace.* New York: Columbia University Press.

Huet, Natalie, and Carmen Paun. 2017. "Meet the world's most powerful doctor: Bill Gates." *Politico*, May 5. https://www.politico.eu/article/bill-gates-who-most -powerful-doctor/ (accessed February 19, 2019).

Hughes, Robert G., and Mark A. Lawrence. 2005. "Globalization, food, and health in Pacific Island countries." *Asia Pacific Journal of Clinical Nutrition* 14(4): 298–306.

Hull, Gordon, and Frank Pasquale. 2018. "Toward a critical theory of corporate wellness." *BioSocieties* 13(1): 190–212.

Hung, Ho-fung. 2004. "The politics of SARS: containing the perils of globalization by more globalization." *Asian Perspective* 28(1): 19–44.

Huynen, Maud M. T. E., Pim Martens, and Henk B. M. Hilderink. 2005. "The health impacts of globalization: a conceptual framework." *Globalization and Health* 1: 14.

Imperato, Pascal James. 2016. "The convergence of a virus, mosquitoes, and human travel in globalizing the Zika epidemic." *Journal of Community Health* 41(3): 674–79.

Institute for Health Metrics and Evaluation. 2013. *Financing Global Health 2012: The End of the Golden Age?* Seattle: Institute for Health Metrics and Evaluation.

Institute for Health Metrics and Evaluation. 2017. *Financing Global Health 2016: Development Assistance, Public and Private Health Spending for the Pursuit of Universal Health Coverage.* Seattle: Institute for Health Metrics and Evaluation.

Institute for Health Metrics and Evaluation. 2018. *Financing Global Health 2017: Funding Universal Health Coverage and the Unfinished HIV/AIDS Agenda.* Seattle: Institute for Health Metrics and Evaluation.

Intergovernmental Panel on Climate Change. 1998. *The Regional Impacts of Climate Change: An Assessment of Vulnerability.* Cambridge: Cambridge University Press.

International Organization for Migration. 2017. *World Migration Report 2018.* Geneva: International Organization for Migration.

Irwin, Rachel. 2010. "Indonesia, H5N1, and global health diplomacy." *Global Health Governance* 3(2): 1–21.

Islam, Sheikh Mohammed Shariful, Tina Dannemann Purnat, Nguyen Thi Anh Phuong, Upendo Mwingira, Karsten Schacht, and Günter Fröschl. 2014. "Noncommunicable diseases (NCDs) in developing countries: a symposium report." *Global Health* 10: 81.

Jackson, David. 2016. "Donald Trump targets globalization and free trade as job-killers." *USA Today*, June 28. https://www.usatoday.com/story/news/politics/elections/2016/06/28/donald-trump-globalization-trade-pennsylvania-ohio/86431376/ (accessed February 19, 2019).

Jackson, Robert. 2007. *Sovereignty.* Cambridge: Polity.

Jennings, Michael. 2005. "Chinese medicine and medical pluralism in Dar es Salaam: globalization or glocalization?" *International Relations* 19(4): 457–473.

Jennings, Ralph. 2017. "Taiwan rejection from WHO assembly further strains relations with China." *Voice of America*, May 10. https://www.voanews.com/a/taiwan-rejection-from-who-assembly-further-strains-relations-with-china/3845764.html (accessed February 19, 2019).

Jiang, Shibo, Lu Lu, and Lanying Du. 2012. "Development of SARS vaccines and therapeutics is still needed." *Future Virology* 8(1): 1–2.

Johnson, Candace. 2017. "Pregnant woman versus mosquito: a feminist epidemiology of Zika virus." *Journal of International Political Theory* 13(2): 233–50.

Joint United Nations Program on HIV/AIDS (UNAIDS). 2016. *Global AIDS Update 2016.* Geneva: UNAIDS.

Joint United Nations Program on HIV/AIDS (UNAIDS). 2017. *UNAIDS Data 2017*. Geneva: UNAIDS.

Joint United Nations Program on HIV/AIDS (UNAIDS). 2018. *Fact Sheet—World AIDS Day 2017*. http://www.unaids.org/sites/default/files/media_asset/UNAIDS _FactSheet_en.pdf (accessed February 19, 2019).

Kahn, Laura H., Bruce Kaplan, and James H. Steele. 2007. "Confronting zoonoses through closer collaboration between medicine and veterinary medicine (as 'one medicine')." *Veterinaria Italiana* 43(1): 5–19.

Kaiser Family Foundation. 2019. "The U.S. President's Emergency Plan for AIDS Relief (PEPFAR)." January 31. https://www.kff.org/global-health-policy/fact -sheet/the-u-s-presidents-emergency-plan-for/ (accessed February 19, 2019).

Kaiser, Jocelyn. 2005. "Pandemic or not, experts welcome Bush flu plan." *Science* 310(5750): 952–53.

Kamps, Bernd Sebastian, and Christian Hoffmann. 2003. *SARS Reference*. http:// www.sarsreference.com (accessed February 19, 2019).

Kamradt-Scott, Adam. 2015. *Managing Global Health Security: The World Health Organization and Disease Outbreak Control*. New York: Palgrave Macmillan.

Kamradt-Scott, Adam, and Kelley Lee. 2011. "The 2011 Pandemic Influenza Pre-paredness Framework: global health secured or a missed opportunity?" *Political Studies* 59(4): 831–47.

Kamradt-Scott, Adam, and Colin McInnes. 2012. "The securitization of pandemic influenza: framing, security, and public policy." *Global Public Health* 7(Supplement 2): S95–S110.

Kamradt-Scott, Adam, and Simon Rushton. 2012. "The revised International Health Regulations: socialization, compliance, and changing norms of global health security." *Global Change, Peace, and Security* 24(1): 57–70.

Kapstein, Ethan B., and Joshua W. Busby. 2013. *AIDS Drugs for All: Social Movement and Market Transformations*. Cambridge: Cambridge University Press.

Karesh, William B., and Robert A. Cook. 2005. "The human/animal link." *Foreign Affairs* 84(4): 38–50.

Kaspar, Bradley J. 2014. "Legislating for a new age in medicine: defining the tele-medicine standard of care to improve healthcare in Iowa." *Iowa Law Review* 99(2): 839–66.

Katz, Rebecca, and Scott F. Dowell. 2015. "Revising the International Health Regula-tions: call for a 2017 review conference." *Lancet Global Health* 3(7): e352–e353.

Kaul, Inge. 2012. "Global public goods: explaining their underprovision." *Journal of International Economic Law* 15(3): 729–50.

Kavanagh, Matthew M. 2014. "The politics and epidemiology of transition: PEP-FAR and AIDS in South Africa." *Journal of Acquired Immune Deficiency Syndromes* 65(3): 247–50.

Keck, Margaret, and Kathryn Sikkink. 1998. *Activists Beyond Borders: Advocacy Networks in International Politics*. Ithaca: Cornell University Press.

Ketelaars, Pauline, Stefaan Walgrave, and Ruud Wouters. 2014. "Degrees of frame alignment: comparing organizers' and participants' frames in 29 demonstrations in three countries." *International Sociology* 29(6): 504–24.

Khayatzadeh-Mahani, Akram, Arne Ruckert, and Ronald Labonté. 2017. "Could the WHO's Framework on Engagement with Non-State Actors (FENSA) be a threat to tackling childhood obesity?" *Global Public Health* 13(9): 1337–40.

Kindhauser, Mary Kay, Tomas Allen, Veronika Frank, Ravi Shankar Santhana, and Christopher Dye. 2016. "Zika: the origin and spread of a mosquito-borne virus." *Bulletin of the World Health Organization* 94(9): 675–686C.

Kinney, Elvin L. 1981. "Smallpox in Provincetown, Massachusetts, 1872–73." *Journal of the History of Medicine and Allied Sciences* 36(3): 334–36.

Klotz, Audie. 2002. "Transnational activism and global transformations: the anti-apartheid and abolitionist experiences." *European Journal of International Relations* 8(1): 49–76.

Knecht, G. Bruce. 2006. *Hooked: A True Story of Pirates, Poaching, and the Perfect Fish*. London: Allen and Unwin.

Kobrin, Stephen. 1997. "The architecture of globalization: state sovereignty in a networked global economy." In *Governments, Globalization, and International Business*, John Harry Dunning (ed.), 146–71. Oxford: Oxford University Press.

Koch, Tom. 2016. "Zika is the price we pay for globalization." *Global and Mail*, May 16. https://www.theglobeandmail.com/opinion/zika-virus-is-the-price-we-pay-for-globalization/article28544681/ (accessed February 19, 2019).

Koon, Adam D., Benjamin Hawkins, and Susannah H. Mayhew. 2016. "Framing and the health policy process: a scoping review." *Health Policy and Planning* 31(6): 801–16.

Koplow, David A. 2003. *Smallpox: The Fight to Eradicate a Global Scourge*. Berkeley: University of California Press.

Koplow, David A. 2004. "Deliberate extinction: whether to destroy the last smallpox virus." *Suffolk University Law Review* 37(1): 1–50.

Krasner, Stephen D. 1999. *Sovereignty: Organized Hypocrisy*. Princeton: Princeton University Press.

Krebs, Ronald R., and Patrick Thaddeus Jackson. 2007. "Twisting tongues and twisting arms: the power of political rhetoric." *European Journal of International Relations* 13(1): 35–66.

Kreuder-Sonnen, Christian, and Bernhard Zangl. 2015. "Which post-Westphalia? International organizations between constitutionalism and authoritarianism." *European Journal of International Relations* 21(3): 568–94.

Kristof, Nicholas D. 1997. "For Third World, water is still a deadly drink." *New York Times*, January 9. https://www.nytimes.com/1997/01/09/world/for-third-world-water-is-still-a-deadly-drink.html (accessed February 19, 2019).

Kuehn, Bridget M. 2010. "Human, animal, ecosystem health all key to curbing emerging infectious diseases." *Journal of the American Medical Association* 303(2): 117–18.

Lancet. 2007. "Global solidarity needed in preparing for pandemic influenza." 369(9561): 532.

Langmuir, Alexander D. 1963. "The surveillance of communicable diseases of national importance." *New England Journal of Medicine* 268(4): 182–92.

Lapinski, Maria Knight, Julie A. Funk, and Lauren T. Moccia. 2015. "Recommendations for the role of social science research in One Health." *Social Science and Medicine* 129: 51–60.

Latif, Asad. 2004. "Singapore: surviving the downside of globalization." *Southeast Asian Affairs* 2004: 225–38.

Lau, Max S. Y., Benjamin Douglas Dalziel, Sebastian Funk, Amanda McClelland, Amanda Tiffany, Steven Riley, C. Jessica E. Metcalf, and Bryan T. Grenfel. 2017. "Spatial and temporal dynamics of superspreading events in the 2014-2015 West Africa Ebola epidemic." *Proceedings of the National Academy of Sciences of the United States of America* 114(9): 2337–42.

Ledford, Heidi. 2008. "Gates and Bloomberg team up to tackle tobacco epidemic." *Nature*, July 23. https://www.nature.com/news/2008/080723/full/news.2008.980.html (accessed February 19, 2019).

Lee, Kelley. 2009. *The World Health Organization.* New York: Routledge.

Lee, Kelley, and Zabrina L. Brumme. 2013. "Operationalizing the One Health approach: the global governance challenges." *Health Policy and Planning* 28(7): 778–85.

Leitenberg, Milton. 2002. "Biological weapons and bioterrorism in the first years of the twenty-first century." *Politics and the Life Sciences* 21(2): 3–27.

Leon, Joshua K. 2015. *The Rise of Global Health: The Evolution of Effective Collective Action.* Albany: SUNY Press.

Leong, Russell C. 2003. "Chaos, SARS, yellow peril: virulent metaphors for the Asian American experience?" *Amerasia Journal* 29(1): v–viii.

Lerner, Henrik, and Charlotte Berg. 2015. "The concept of health in One Health and some practical implications for research and education: what is One Health?" *Infection Ecology and Epidemiology* 5(1): 25300.

Lim, Louisa. 2007. "Air pollution grows in tandem with China's economy." NPR, May 17. http://www.npr.org/templates/story/story.php?storyId=10221268 (accessed February 19, 2019).

Linn, Johannes. 2018. "Recent threats to multilateralism." *Global Journal of Emerging Market Economies* 9(1-3): 86–113.

Lisk, Franklyn, Annamarie Bindenagel Sehovic, and Sharifah Sekalala. 2015. "Health and human rights: a wrinkle in time or a new paradigm?" *Contemporary Politics* 21(1): 25–39.

Litonjua, M. D. 2008. "The socio-political construction of globalization." *International Review of Modern Sociology* 34(2): 253–78.

Lloyd-Williams, Ffion, Martin O'Flaherty, Modi Mwatsama, Christopher Birt, Robin Ireland, and Simon Capewell. 2008. "Estimating the cardiovascular mortality burden attributable to the European Common Agricultural Policy on dietary saturated fats." *Bulletin of the World Health Organization* 86(7): 535–41.

Lowe, Celia. 2010. "Preparing Indonesia: H5N1 influenza through the lens of global health." *Indonesia* 90: 147–70.

Lowndes, Vivien, and Mark Roberts. 2013. *Why Institutions Matter: The New Institutionalism in Political Science*. New York: Palgrave Macmillan.

Lugar, Richard, and Barack Obama. 2005. "Grounding a pandemic." *New York Times*, June 6. https://www.nytimes.com/2005/06/06/opinion/grounding-a-pandemic.html (accessed February 19, 2019).

Lukes, Steven. 2005. *Power: A Radical View, Second Edition*. New York: Palgrave Macmillan.

Lyon, David. 1991. "Bentham's panopticon: from moral architecture to electronic surveillance." *Queen's Quarterly* 98(3): 596–617.

Mahajan, Manjari. 2018. "Philanthropy and the nation-state in global health: the Gates Foundation in India." *Global Public Health* 13(10): 1357–68.

Maher, Dermot, Anthony D. Harries, Rony Zachariah, and Don Enarson. 2009. "A global framework for action to improve the primary care response to chronic non-communicable diseases: a solution to a neglected problem." *BMC Public Health* 9: 355.

March, James G., and John P. Olsen. 2006. "Elaborating the 'new institutionalism.'" In *The Oxford Handbook of Political Institutions*, R. A. W. Rhodes, Sarah A. Binder, and Bert A. Rockman (eds.), 3–20. Oxford: Oxford University Press.

Marrero, Shannon L., David E. Bloom, and Eli Y. Adashi. 2012. "Noncommunicable diseases: a global health crisis in a new world order." *Journal of the American Medical Association* 307(19): 2037–38.

Marston, Barbara J., E. Kainne Dokubo, Amanda van Steelandt, Lise Martel, Desmond Williams, Sara Hersey, Amara Jambai, Sakoba Keita, Tolbert G. Nyenswah, and John T. Redd. 2017. "Ebola response impact on public health programs, West Africa, 2014–2017." *Emerging Infectious Diseases* 23(13): S25–S32.

Mathiason, Nick. 2001. "South Africa fights AIDS drug apartheid." *The Guardian*, January 14. https://www.theguardian.com/business/2001/jan/14/aids.theobserver1 (accessed February 19, 2019).

Mathiesen, Karl. 2015. "What is the Bill and Melinda Gates Foundation?" *The Guardian*, March 16. https://www.theguardian.com/environment/2015/mar/16/what-is-the-bill-and-melinda-gates-foundation (accessed February 19, 2019).

McCoy, David, and Linsey McGoey. 2011. "Global health and the Gates Foundation— in perspective." In *Partnerships and Foundations in Global Health Governance*, Simon Rushton and Owain D. Williams (eds.), 143–63. New York: Routledge.

McGoey, Linsey. 2015. *No Such Thing as a Free Gift: The Gates Foundation and the Price of Philanthropy*. London: Verso.

McGrew, Andrew. 2014. "The logics of economic globalization." In *Global Political Economy*, fourth edition, John Ravenhill (ed.), 225–54. Oxford: Oxford University Press.

McInnes, Colin, and Kelley Lee. 2012. *Global Health and International Relations.* Cambridge: Polity.

McKee, Martin, and Michael J. Galsworthy. 2016. "Brexit: a confused concept that threatens public health." *Journal of Public Health* 38(1): 3–5.

McKie, Robin. 2017. "Scientists trace 2002 SARS virus to colony of cave-dwelling bats in China." *The Guardian*, December 10. https://www.theguardian.com/world/2017/dec/10/sars-virus-bats-china-severe-acute-respiratory-syndrome (accessed February 19, 2019).

McMichael, Anthony J. 2013. "Globalization, climate change, and human health." *New England Journal of Medicine* 368(14): 1335–43.

McNamara, Lucy A., Ilana J. Schafer, Leisha D. Nolen, Yelena Gorina, John T. Redd, Terrence Lo, Elizabeth Ervin, Olga Henao, Benjamin A. Dahl, Oliver Morgan, Sara Hersey, and Barbara Knust. 2016. "Ebola surveillance—Guinea, Liberia, and Sierra Leone." *Morbidity and Mortality Weekly Report* 65(3): 35–43.

McNeil, Donald G., Jr. 2009. "U.S. declares public health emergency over swine flu." *New York Times*, April 26. https://www.nytimes.com/2009/04/27/world/27flu.html (accessed February 19, 2019).

McNeil, Donald G., Jr. 2016a. "Delay pregnancy in areas with Zika, WHO suggests." *New York Times*, June 9. https://www.nytimes.com/2016/06/10/health/zika-virus-pregnancy-who.html (accessed February 19, 2019).

McNeil, Donald G., Jr. 2016b. "HIV arrived in the US long before 'Patient Zero.'" *New York Times*, October 26. https://www.nytimes.com/2016/10/27/health/hiv-patient-zero-genetic-analysis.html (accessed February 19, 2019).

McNeill, William H. 1998. *Plagues and Peoples.* New York: Anchor Books.

McVeigh, Karen. 2018. "'Uber for blood': how Rwandan delivery robots are saving lives." *Guardian*, January 2. https://www.theguardian.com/global-development/2018/jan/02/rwanda-scheme-saving-blood-drone (accessed February 19, 2019).

Meltzer, Martin I., Charisma Y. Atkins, Scott Santibanez, Barbara Knust, Brett W. Petersen, Elizabeth D. Ervin, Stuart T. Nichol, Inger K. Damon, and Michael L. Washington. 2014. "Estimating the future number of cases in the Ebola epidemic—Liberia and Sierra Leone, 2014–2015." *Morbidity and Mortality Weekly Report* 63(3): 1–14.

Merolla, Jennifer, Laura B. Stephenson, Carole J. Wilson, and Elizabeth J. Zechmeister. 2005. "Globalization, globalizacion, globalisation: public opinion and NAFTA." *Law and Business Review of the Americas* 11(3): 573–96.

Miles, Steven H. 2015. "Kaci Hickox: public health and the politics of fear." *American Journal of Bioethics* 15(4): 17–19.

Miljkovic, Dragan, Saleem Shaik, Silvia Miranda, Nikita Barabanov, and Anais Liogier. 2015. "Globalization and obesity." *The World Economy* 38(8): 1278–94.

Miller, David, and Claire Harkins. 2010. "Corporate strategy, corporate capture: food and alcohol lobbying and public health." *Critical Social Policy* 30(4): 564–89.

Mirowski, Philip. 2014. *Never Let a Serious Crisis Go to Waste: How Neoliberalism Survived the Financial Meltdown*. London: Verso.

Mittelman, James H. 1996. "The dynamics of globalization." In *Globalization: Critical Reflections*, James Mittelman (ed.), 1–19. Boulder: Lynne Rienner.

Molyneux, David, and Dieudonne P. Sankara. 2017. "Guinea worm eradication: progress and challenges—should we beware of the dog?" *PLoS Neglected Tropical Diseases* 11(4): e0005495.

Moon, Suerie, and Ellen F.M. 't Hoen. Forthcoming. "The global politics of access to medicines: from 1.0 to 2.0." In *The Oxford Handbook of Global Health Politics*, Kelley Lee, Colin McInnes, and Jeremy Youde (eds.). New York: Oxford University Press.

Morand, Olivier. 2004. "Economic growth, longevity, and the epidemiological transition." *European Journal of Health Economics* 5(2): 166–74.

Mullin, Emily. 2015. "Turing Pharma says Daraprim availability will be unaffected by Shkreli arrest." *Forbes*, December 21. https://www.forbes.com/sites/emilymullin/2015/12/21/turing-pharma-says-daraprim-availability-will-be-unaffected-by-shkreli-arrest/#31372c5d21ee (accessed February 19, 2019).

Mullis, Kenan. 2009. "Playing chicken with bird flu: 'viral sovereignty,' the right to exploit natural resources, and the potential human rights ramifications." *American University International Law Review* 24(5): 943–67.

Munck, Ronaldo. 2008. "Globalization, governance, and migration: an introduction." *Third World Quarterly* 29(7): 1227–46.

Murphy, Tom. 2015. "$100 million contingency fund launched by World Health Organization." *Humanosphere*, May 19. http://www.humanosphere.org/global-health/2015/05/100-million-contingency-fund-launched-by-world-health-organization/ (accessed February 19, 2019).

Murugesu, Jason. 2018. "The science behind why the sugar tax is a good idea." *New Statesman*, April 6. https://www.newstatesman.com/politics/health/2018/04/science-behind-why-sugar-tax-good-idea (accessed February 19, 2019).

Narula, Svati Kirsten. 2016. "Thanks for mutton, New Zealand: your fatty meat products are making Tonga obese." *Quartz*, January 21. https://qz.com/597669/thanks-for-the-mutton-new-zealand-your-fatty-meat-products-are-making-tonga-obese/ (accessed February 19, 2019).

Neiderud, Carl-John. 2015. "How urbanization affects the epidemiology of emerging infectious diseases." *Infection Ecology and Epidemiology* 5(1): 27060.

Nelson, Thomas. 2011. "Issue framing." In *The Oxford Handbook of American Public Opinion and the Media*, George C. Edwards III, Lawrence R. Jacobs, and Robert Y. Shapiro (eds.), 189–203. New York: Oxford University Press.

Nestle, Marion. 2013. *Food Politics: How the Food Industry Influences Health and Nutrition*. Berkeley: University of California Press.

Neustadt, Richard E., and Harvey Fineberg. 1982. *The Epidemic That Never Was: Policy-Making and the Swine Flu Affair*. New York: Vintage Books.

The New York Times. 2017. "Planet Fat." https://www.nytimes.com/series/obesity-epidemic (accessed February 19, 2019).

Nguyen, Vinh-Kim. 2010. *The Republic of Therapy: Triage and Sovereignty in West Africa's Time of AIDS*. Durham, NC: Duke University Press.

Nielson, Daniel L. and Michael J. Tierney. 2003. "Delegation to international organizations: agency theory and World Bank environmental reform." *International Organization* 57(2): 241–76.

Nixon, Laura, Pamela Meija, Andrew Cheyne, and Lori Dorfman. 2015. "Big Soda's long shadow: news coverage of local proposals to tax sugar-sweetened beverages in Richmond, El Monte, and Telluride." *Critical Public Health* 25(3): 333–47.

O'Brien, Timothy L., and Stephanie Saul. 2006. "Buffett to give bulk of his fortune to Gates charity." *New York Times*, June 26. https://www.nytimes.com/2006/06/26/business/26buffett.html (accessed February 19, 2019).

Oduwole, Jumoke, and Akinola Akintayo. 2017. "The rights to life, health, and development: the Ebola virus and Nigeria." *African Human Rights Law Journal* 17(1): 194–217.

Ogunsola, Folasade. 2015. "How Nigeria beat the Ebola virus in three months." *The Conversation*, May 13. https://theconversation.com/how-nigeria-beat-the-ebola-virus-in-three-months-41372 (accessed February 19, 2019).

Oldstone, Michael B. A. 2010. *Viruses, Plagues, and History: Past, Present, and Future*. Oxford: Oxford University Press.

O'Manique, Colleen. 2015. "Gender, health, and security." In *Routledge Handbook of Global Health Security*, Simon Rushton and Jeremy Youde (eds.), 48–59. New York: Routledge.

Omran, Abdel R. 1971. "The epidemiologic transition: a theory of the epidemiology and population change." *Milbank Quarterly* 49(4): 509–38.

One Health Initiative Task Force. 2008. *One Health: A New Professional Imperative*. Washington: American Veterinary Medical Association.

Oni, Tolu, John S. Yudkin, Sharon Fonn, Philip Adongo, Margaret Kaseje, Ademola Ajuwon, Lesley Doyal, and Leslie London. 2019. "Global public health starts at home: upstream approaches to global health training." *Lancet Global Health* 7(3): e301–e302.

Osterholm, Michael T., and Mark Olshaker. 2017. *Deadliest Enemy: Our War Against Killer Germs*. New York: Little, Brown, and Company.

Osterholm, Michael T., and John Schwartz. 2000. *Living Terrors: What America Needs to Know to Survive the Coming Bioterrorist Catastrophe*. New York: Delta.

Ostrom, Vincent, and Elinor Ostrom. 2015. "Public goods and public choices." In *Elinor Ostrom and the Bloomington School of Political Economy, Volume 2, Resource Governance*, Daniel H. Cole and Michael D. McGinnis (eds.), 3–36. Lanham, MD: Lexington Books.

Packard, Randall M. 2016. *A History of Global Health: Interventions into the Lives of Other Peoples*. Baltimore: The Johns Hopkins University Press.

Pan American Health Organization. 2015. "Neurological syndrome, congenital malformations and Zika virus infection. Implications for public health in the Americas—Epidemiological Alert." December 1. https://www.paho.org/hq/index .php?option=com_content&view=article&id=11484%3A1-december-2015 -neurological-syndrome-zika-virus-infection-americas-epidemiological -alert&catid=2103%3Arecent-epidemiological-alerts-updates&Itemid =42346&lang=en (accessed February 19, 2019).

Parekh, Bhikhu. 2003. "Cosmopolitanism and global citizenship." *Review of International Studies* 29(1): 3–17.

Parry, Jane. 2004. "WHO queries culling of civet cats." *BMJ* 328: 128.

Parry, Jane. 2010. "Pacific Islanders pay heavy price for abandoning traditional diet." *Bulletin of the World Health Organization* 88(7): 484–85.

Patterson, Amy S. 2011. *The Church and AIDS in Africa: The Politics of Ambiguity.* Boulder: First Forum Press.

Patterson, Amy S. 2018. *Africa and Global Health Governance: Domestic Politics and International Structures.* Baltimore: The Johns Hopkins University Press.

Pauly, Louis W. 1997. *Who Elected the Bankers? Surveillance and Control in the World Economy.* Ithaca: Cornell University Press.

Payne, Rodger. 2001. "Persuasion, frames, and norm construction." *European Journal of International Relations* 7(1): 37–61.

Payne, Rodger. 2017. "Laughing off a zombie apocalypse: the value of comedic and satirical narratives." *International Studies Perspectives* 18(2): 211–24.

Pennington, Hugh. 2003. "Smallpox and bioterrorism." *Bulletin of the World Health Organization* 81(10): 762–67.

Petchesky, Rosalind Pollack. 2003. *Global Prescriptions: Gendering Health and Human Rights.* London: Zed Books.

Piot, Peter. 2015. *AIDS Between Science and Politics*, Laurence Garey (trans.). New York: Columbia University Press.

Plumer, Brad. 2016. "One tweet that shows how the Zika virus caught scientists flat-footed." *Vox*, February 12. https://www.vox.com/2016/2/12/10978820/zika -virus-questions-science (accessed February 19, 2019).

Pomfret, John. 2003. "SARS cover-up official policy, say doctors." *Sydney Morning Herald*, April 21. https://www.smh.com.au/articles/2003/04/20/1050777164864 .html (accessed February 19, 2019).

Preston, Richard. 1994. *The Hot Zone.* New York: Doubleday.

Price, Richard. 2003. "Transnational civil society and advocacy in world politics." *World Politics* 55(4): 579–606.

Price-Smith, Andrew T. 2002. *The Health of Nations: Infectious Disease, Environmental Change, and Their Effects on National Security and Development.* Cambridge: MIT Press.

Price-Smith, Andrew T. 2009. *Contagion and Chaos: Disease, Ecology, and National Security in the Era of Globalization.* Cambridge: MIT Press.

Queensland Government. 2017. "Hendra virus infection." http://conditions.health
.qld.gov.au/HealthCondition/condition/14/217/363/hendra-virus-infection (accessed February 19, 2019).

Rabinowitz, Peter, and Lisa Conti. 2013. "Links among human health, animal
health, and ecosystem health." Annual Review of Public Health 34: 189–204.

Rached, Danielle Hanna, and Deisy de Freitas Lima Ventura. 2017. "World Health
Organization and the search for accountability: a critical analysis of the new
Framework of Engagement with Non-State Actors." Cadernos de Saúde Pública
33(6): e00100716.

Reich, Michael R., and Priya Bery. 2005. "Expanding global access to ARVs: the challenges of prices and patents." In The AIDS Pandemic: Impact on Science and Society,
Kenneth H. Maier and H. F. Pizer (eds.), 324–50. New York: Academic Press.

Reubi, David. 2018. "Epidemiological accountability: philanthropists, global
health, and the audit of saving lives." Economy and Society 47(1): 83–110.

Reus-Smit, Christian, and Tim Dunne. 2017. "The globalization of international
society." In The Globalization of International Society, Tim Dunne and Christian
Reus-Smit (eds.), 18–40. Oxford: Oxford University Press.

Reuters. 2017. "Merkel takes aim at US 'winners and losers' policy before G20." July
5. https://www.reuters.com/article/us-g20-germany-merkel-idUSKBN19Q15D
(accessed February 19, 2019).

Ricci, James. 2009. "Global health governance and the state: premature claims of a
post-international framework." Global Health Governance 3(1): 1–18.

Richards, Paul. 2016. Ebola: How a People's Science Helped End an Epidemic. London: Zed Books.

Richardson, D. Russell, Russell Fry II, and Michael Krasnow. 2013. "Cost-savings
analysis of telemedicine use for ophthalmic screening in a rural Appalachian
health clinic." West Virginia Medical Journal 109(4): 52–55.

Richardson, Matt X., Mike M. Callaghan, and Sarah Wamala. 2015. "Globalization
and global health." In The Handbook of Global Health Policy, Garrett W. Brown,
Gavin Yamey, and Sarah Wamala (eds.), 555–76. Malden, MA: Wiley Blackwell.

Richey, Lisa Ann, and Stefano Ponte. 2011. Brand Aid: Shopping Well to Save the
World. Minneapolis: University of Minnesota Press.

Rid, Annette, and Ezekiel J. Emanuel. 2014. "Why should high-income countries help combat Ebola?" Journal of the American Medical Association 312(12):
1297–98.

Riedel, Stefan. 2005a. "Edward Jenner and the history of smallpox and vaccination." Baylor University Medical Center Proceedings 18(1): 21–25.

Riedel, Stefan. 2005b. "Smallpox and biological warfare: a disease revisited." Baylor University Medical Center Proceedings 18(1): 13–20.

Roache, Sarah A., and Lawrence O. Gostin. 2017. "The untapped power of soda
taxes: incentivizing consumers, generating revenue, and altering corporate
behavior." International Journal of Health Policy and Management 6(9): 489–93.

Roberts, Dan. 2014. "US imposes travel restrictions on passengers from west Africa." *The Guardian*, October 22. https://www.theguardian.com/us-news/2014/oct/21/us-limited-ebola-travel-restrictions-west-africa (accessed February 19, 2019).

Robertson, Roland. 1992. *Globalization: Social Theory and Global Culture*. London: Sage.

Robins, Steven, and Bettina von Lieres. 2004. "Remaking citizenship, unmaking marginalization: the Treatment Action Campaign in post-apartheid South Africa." *Canadian Journal of African Studies* 38(3): 575–86.

Ruckert, Arne, and Ronald Labonté. 2014. "The social determinants of health." In *The Handbook of Global Health Policy*, Garrett W. Brown, Gavin Yamey, and Sarah Wamala (eds.), 267–85. Malden, MA: Wiley Blackwell.

Rushing, Wanda. 2004. "Globalization and the paradoxes of place: poverty and power in Memphis." *City and Community* 3(1): 65–81.

Rushton, Simon, and Adam Kamradt-Scott. 2015. "The revised International Health Regulations and outbreak response." In *The Politics of Surveillance and Response to Disease Outbreaks: The New Frontier for States and Non-State Actors*, Sara E. Davies and Jeremy R. Youde (eds.), 23–40. Burlington: Ashgate.

Santos, Boaventura de Sousa. 2004. "A critique of lazy reason: against the waste of experience." In *The Modern World-System in the Longue Dureé*, Immanuel Wallerstein (ed.), 157–98. Boulder: Paradigm.

Santosa, Ailiana, Stig Wall, Edward Fottrell, Ulf Högberg, and Peter Byass. 2014. "The development and experience of epidemiological transition theory over four decades: a systematic review." *Global Health Action* 7(1): 23574.

Sarlio-Lähteenkorva, Sirpa. 2015. "Could a sugar tax help combat obesity? Yes." *BMJ* 351(8019): h4047.

Sassen, Saskia. 1996. *Losing Control? Sovereignty in an Age of Globalization*. New York: Columbia University Press.

Schneider, Jake, and Darrell M. West. 2017. "How the Trump budget harms global health and weakens international stability." *Brookings*, July 27. https://www.brookings.edu/blog/techtank/2017/07/27/how-the-trump-budget-harms-global-health-and-weakens-international-stability/ (accessed February 19, 2019).

Scholte, Jan Aart. 2000. *Globalization: A Critical Introduction*. New York: Palgrave Macmillan.

Sciubba, Jennifer, and Jeremy Youde. 2017. "Puerto Rico's troubles are far from over. The population's health is at risk." *Washington Post*, October 13. https://www.washingtonpost.com/news/monkey-cage/wp/2017/10/13/puerto-ricos-troubles-are-far-from-over-the-populations-health-is-at-risk/?utm_term=.ceccb8731b5b (accessed February 19, 2019).

Scott, James C. 1998. *Seeing Like a State: How Certain Schemes to Improve the Human Condition Have Failed*. New Have: Yale University Press.

Sebrie, Ernesto M., and Stanton A. Glantz. 2007. "Attempts to undermine tobacco control: tobacco industry 'youth smoking prevention' programs to undermine meaningful tobacco control in Latin America." *American Journal of Public Health* 97(8): 1357–67.

Seckinelgin, Hakan. 2009. "Global activism and sexualities in the time of HIV/AIDS." *Contemporary Politics* 15(1): 103–18.

Sedyaningsih, Endang R., Siti Isfandari, Triono Soendoro, and Siti Fadilah Supari. 2008. "Towards mutual trust, transparency, and equity in virus sharing mechanism: the avian influenza case of Indonesia." *Annals Academy of Medicine Singapore* 37(6): 482–88.

Sell, Susan K. 2003. *Private Power, Public Law: The Globalization of Intellectual Property Rights.* Cambridge: Cambridge University Press.

Sell, Susan K. 2004. "The quest for global governance in intellectual property and public health: structural, discursive, and institutional dimensions." *Temple Law Review* 77(2): 363–400.

Sell, Susan K., and Aseem Prakash. 2004. "Using ideas strategically: the contest between business and NGO networks in intellectual property rights." *International Studies Quarterly* 48(1): 143–75.

Sen, G., and P. Östlin. 2008. "Gender inequity in health: why it exists and how we can change it." *Global Public Health* 3(Supplement 1): 1–12.

Senthilingham, Meera. 2015. "How paradise became the fattest in the world." CNN, May 1. https://edition.cnn.com/2015/05/01/health/pacific-islands-obesity/index.html (accessed February 19, 2019).

Sepkowitz, Kent A. 2004. "The 1947 smallpox vaccination campaign in New York City, revisited." *Emerging Infectious Diseases* 10(5): 960–61.

Shawar, Yusra R., and Jeremy Shiffman. 2017. "Generation of global political priority for early childhood development: the challenges of framing and governance." *Lancet* 389(10064): 119–24.

Shendruk, Amanda. 2017. "Funding the United Nations: what impact do US contributions have on UN agencies and programs?" Council on Foreign Relations, September 21. https://www.cfr.org/article/funding-united-nations-what-impact-do-us-contributions-have-un-agencies-and-programs (accessed February 19, 2019).

Shiffman, Jeremy. 2008. "Has donor prioritization of HIV/AIDS displaced aid for other health issues?" *Health Policy and Planning* 23(2): 95–100.

Shiffman, Jeremy. 2009. "A social explanation for the rise and fall of global health issues." *Bulletin of the World Health Organization* 87(8): 608–13.

Shiffman, Jeremy. 2014. "Knowledge, moral claims, and the exercise of power in global health." *International Journal of Health Policy and Management* 3(6): 297–99.

Shiffman, Jeremy, and F. E. Okonofua. 2007. "The state of political priority for safe motherhood in Nigeria." *BJOG: An International Journal of Obstetrics and Gynecology* 114(2): 127–33.

Shiffman, Jeremy, Hans Peter Schmitz, David Berlan, Stephanie L. Smith, Kathryn Quissell, Uwe Gneiting, and David Pelletier. 2016. "The emergence and effectiveness of global health networks: findings and future research." *Health Policy and Planning* 31(Supplement 1): i110–i123.

Shiffman, Jeremy, and Stephanie Smith. 2007. "Generation of political priority for global health initiatives: a framework and case study of maternal mortality." *Lancet* 370(9595): 1370–79.

Shilts, Randy. 1987. *And the Band Played On: Politics, People, and the AIDS Epidemic.* New York: Penguin.

Siedner, Mark J., Edward T. Ryan, and Isaac I. Bogoch. 2018. "Gone or forgotten? The rise and fall of Zika virus." *Lancet Public Health* 3(3): e109–e110.

Sifferlin, Alexandra. 2018. "Do I still need to worry about Zika?" *Time*, April 17. http://time.com/5241521/zika-virus-pregnancy/ (accessed February 19, 2019).

Siplon, Patricia D. 2002. *AIDS and the Policy Struggle in the United States.* Washington: Georgetown University Press.

Sipress, Alan. 2009. *The Fatal Strain: On the Trail of Avian Flu and the Coming Pandemic.* New York: Penguin.

Skolnik, Richard. 2016. *Global Health 101*, third edition. Burlington, MA: Jones and Bartlett.

Smith, Frank L., III. 2012. "Insights into surveillance from the influenza virus and benefit sharing controversy." *Global Change, Peace, and Security* 24(1): 71–81.

Smith, Raymond A., and Patricia D. Siplon. 2006. *Drugs into Bodies: Global AIDS Treatment Activism.* Westport, CT: Praeger.

Snow, David A., E. Burke Rochford, Jr., Steven K. Worden, and Robert D. Benford. 1986. "Frame alignment processes, micromobilization, and movement participation." *American Sociological Review* 51(4): 464–81.

So, Alvin Y., and Ngai Pun. 2004. "Introduction: globalization and anti-globalization of SARS in Chinese societies." *Asian Perspectives* 28(1): 5–17.

Sparke, Matthew, and Dimitar Anguelov. 2012. "H1N1, globalization, and the epidemiology of inequality." *Health and Place* 18(4): 726–36.

Speed, Ewen, and Russell Mannion. 2017. "The rise of post-truth populism in pluralist liberal democracies: challenges for health policy." *International Journal of Health Policy and Management* 6(5): 249–51.

Spencer, Craig. 2015. "Having and fighting Ebola—public health lessons from a clinician turned patient." *New England Journal of Medicine* 372(12): 1089–91.

Spencer, James H. 2015. *Globalization and Urbanization: The Global Urban Ecosystem.* Lanham, MD: Rowman & Littlefield.

Statista. 2018. "Sales of the leading alkaline battery brands in the United States in 2016 (in million US dollars)." https://www.statista.com/statistics/309871/sales-of-the-leading-alkaline-battery-brands-in-the-us/ (accessed February 19, 2019).

STAX Group. 2018. "Sugar, tobacco, and alcohol taxes to achieve the SDGs." *Lancet* 391(10138): 2400–01.

Steele, Brent J., and Jacque L Amoureux. 2006. "NGOs and monitoring genocide: the benefits and limits to human rights panopticism." *Millennium* 34(2): 403–32.

Stephenson, Niamh. 2011. "Emerging infectious disease/emerging forms of biological sovereignty." *Science, Technology, and Human Values* 36(5): 616–37.

Stevenson, Michael A., and Andrew F Cooper. 2009. "Overcoming constrains of state sovereignty: global health governance in Asia." *Third World Quarterly* 30(7): 1379–94.

Stevenson, Michael A., and Michael Moran. 2015. "Health security and the distortion of the global health agenda." In *The Routledge Handbook of Global Health Security*, Simon Rushton and Jeremy Youde (eds.), 328–38. New York: Routledge.

Stiglitz, Joseph. 2002. *Globalization and Its Discontents*. New York: W.W. Norton and Company.

Stoto, Michael A. 2014. "Biosurveillance capability requirements for the Global Health Security Agenda: lessons from the 2009 H1N1 pandemic." *Biosecurity and Bioterrorism: Biodefense Strategy, Practice, and Science* 12(5): 225–30.

Strange, Carolyn. 2007. "Postcards from Plaguetown: SARS and the exoticization of Toronto." In *Medicine at the Border: Disease, Globalization, and Security, 1850 to the Present*, Alison Bashford (ed.), 219–39. New York: Palgrave Macmillan.

Su, Shuo, Gary Wong, Yingxia Liu, George F. Gao, Shoujun Li, and Yuhai Bi. 2015. "MERS in South Korea and China: a potential outbreak threat?" *Lancet* 385(9985): 2349–50.

Sun, Lena H. 2016. "150 experts say Olympics must be moved or postponed because of Zika." *Washington Post*, May 27. https://www.washingtonpost .com/news/to-your-health/wp/2016/05/27/125-experts-say-olympics-must-be -moved-or-postponed-because-of-zika/?utm_term=.83f28a3e7b08 (accessed February 19, 2019).

Supari, Siti Fadilah. 2007. *It's Time for the World to Change: In the Spirit of Dignity, Equity, and Transparency*. Jakarta: Penerbit Lentera.

't Hoen, Ellen, Jonathan Berge, Alexandra Calmy, and Suerie Moon. 2011. "Driving a decade of change: HIV/AIDS, patents, and access to medicines for all." *Journal of the International AIDS Society* 14(1): 15.

Tarrow, Sidney, and Charles Tilly. 2007. "Contentious politics and social movements." In *The Oxford Handbook of Comparative Politics*, Charles Boix and Susan C. Stokes (eds.), 435–60. Oxford: Oxford University Press.

Tarwater, Patrick M., and Clyde F. Martin. 2001. "Effects of population density on the spread of disease." *Complexity* 6(6): 29–36.

Taylor, Allyn L. 1997. "Controlling the global spread of infectious diseases: toward a reinforced role for the International Health Regulations." *Houston Law Review* 33(5): 1327–62.

Tejera, Valentina. 1999. "Tripping over property rights: is it possible to reconcile the Convention on Biological Diversity with Article 27 of the TRIPS Agreement?" *New England Law Review* 33(4): 967–88.

Telegraph. 2018. "Historic non-stop flight between Australia and UK takes off." March 24. https://www.telegraph.co.uk/news/2018/03/24/historic-non-stop -flight-australia-uk-ready-take/ (accessed February 19, 2019).

Tesh, Sylvia Noble. 1989. *Hidden Arguments: Political Ideology and Disease Prevention Policy*. New Brunswick, NJ: Rutgers University Press.

Theves, C., P. Biagni, and E. Crubezy. 2014. "The rediscovery of smallpox." *Clinical Microbiology and Infection* 20(3): 210–18.

Thomas, Rebekah, and Veronica Magar. 2018. "Mainstreaming human rights across WHO." In *Human Rights in Global Health: Rights-Based Governance for a Globalizing World*, Benjamin Mason Meier and Lawrence O. Gostin (eds.), 133–53. New York: Oxford University Press.

Thomas, Zoe, and Tim Swift. 2017. "Who is Martin Shkreli, 'the most hated man in America'?" *BBC*, August 4. https://www.bbc.com/news/world-us-canada-343 31761 (accessed February 19, 2019).

Thompson, Avery. 2017. "It's astonishingly easy to bring back smallpox." *Popular Mechanics* 8 July. https://www.popularmechanics.com/science/health/a27217/ easy-to-bring-back-smallpox/ (accessed February 19, 2019).

Thornton, Jacqui. 2018. "The UK has introduced a sugar tax, but will it work?" London School of Hygiene and Tropical Medicine, June. https://www.lshtm .ac.uk/research/research-action/features/uk-sugar-tax-will-it-work (accessed February 19, 2019).

Thun, Eric. 2014. "The globalization of production." In *Global Political Economy*, fourth edition, John Ravenhill (ed.), 283–304. Oxford: Oxford University Press.

Tomasevski, Katarina, Sofia Gruskin, Zita Lazzarini, and Aart Hendriks. 1992. "AIDS and human rights." In *AIDS in the World*, Jonathan M. Mann, Daniel J. M. Tarantola, and Thomas W. Netter (eds.), 537–73. Cambridge: Harvard University Press.

Trump, Donald. 2017a. "Remarks by President Trump to the 72nd session of the United Nations General Assembly." September 19. https://www.whitehouse.gov/ briefings-statements/remarks-president-trump-72nd-session-united-nations -general-assembly/ (accessed February 19, 2019).

Trump, Donald. 2017b. "Remarks by President Trump at working lunch with African leaders." September 20. https://www.whitehouse.gov/briefings-statements/ remarks-president-trump-working-lunch-african-leaders/ (accessed February 19, 2019).

Tucker, Jonathan B. 2001. *Scourge: The Once and Future Threat of Smallpox*. New York: Grove Press.

Tversky, Amos, and Daniel Kahneman. 1981. "The framing of decisions and the psychology of choice." *Science* 211(4481): 453–58.

UCL-Lancet Commission on Migration and Health. 2018. "The UCL-Lancet Commission on Migration and Health: the health of a world on the move." *Lancet* 392(10164): 2606–54.

Ulijaszek, Stanley J. 2002. "Modernization and the diet of adults on Rarotonga, the Cook Islands." *Ecology of Food and Nutrition* 41(3): 203–28.

United Nations. 1948. *Universal Declaration of Human Rights*. http://www.un.org/en/universal-declaration-human-rights/ (accessed February 19, 2019).

United Nations. 1985. *Siracusa Principles on the Limitation and Derogation Provisions in the International Covenant on Civil and Political Rights*, UN Document E/CN.4/1985/4, Annex. https://www.icj.org/wp-content/uploads/1984/07/Siracusa-principles-ICCPR-legal-submission-1985-eng.pdf (accessed February 19, 2019).

United Nations. 2000. "Goal 5: improve maternal health." http://www.un.org/millenniumgoals/maternal.shtml (accessed February 19, 2019).

United Nations Children's Fund. 2018. "Maternal health: current status and progress." https://data.unicef.org/topic/maternal-health/maternal-mortality/ (accessed February 19, 2019).

United Nations Conference on Trade and Development. 2009. *World Investment Report 2009: Transnational Corporations, Agricultural Production, and Development*. Geneva: UNCTAD.

United Nations Conference on Trade and Development. 2012. *World Investment Report 2012: Towards a New Generation of Investment Policies*. Geneva: UNCTAD.

United Nations Development Programme. 2018. "Goal 3 targets." http://www.undp.org/content/undp/en/home/sustainable-development-goals/goal-3-good-health-and-well-being/targets/ (accessed February 19, 2019).

University College London. N.d. "Auto-Icon." https://www.ucl.ac.uk/bentham-project/who-was-jeremy-bentham/auto-icon (accessed February 19, 2019).

University of Washington. 2017. "Bill and Melinda Gates Foundation boosts vital work of UW's Institute for Health Metrics and Evaluation." January 25. https://www.washington.edu/news/2017/01/25/bill-melinda-gates-foundation-boosts-vital-work-of-the-uws-institute-for-health-metrics-and-evaluation/ (accessed February 19, 2019).

Vezzani, Simone. 2010. "Preliminary remarks on the envisaged World Health Organization Pandemic Influenza Preparedness Framework for the sharing of viruses and access to vaccines and other benefits." *Journal of World Intellectual Property* 13(6): 675–96.

Vogel, Gretchen. 2016. "WHO ends Zika designation as international public health emergency." *Science*, November 18. http://www.sciencemag.org/news/2016/11/who-ends-zika-designation-international-public-health-emergency (accessed February 19, 2019).

Wade, Robert. 2009. "Is the globalization consensus dead?" *Antipode* 41(S1): 142–65.

Wald, Patricia. 2008. *Contagious: Cultures, Carriers, and the Outbreak Narrative*. Durham: Duke University Press.

Wallinga, Jacco, and Peter Teunis. 2004. "Different epidemic curves for severe acute respiratory syndrome reveal similar impacts of control measures." *American Journal of Epidemiology* 160(6): 509–16.

Watts, Jonathan. 2003. "China takes drastic action over SARS threat." *The Lancet* 361(9370): 1708–09.

Weir, Lorna. 2015. "Inventing global health security, 1994–2005." In *Routledge Handbook of Global Health Security*, Simon Rushton and Jeremy Youde (eds.), 18–31. New York: Routledge.

Weir, Lorna, and Eric Mykhalovskiy. 2010. *Global Public Health Vigilance: Creating a World on Alert*. New York: Routledge.

Wenham, Clare. 2017. "What we have learnt about the World Health Organization from the Ebola outbreak." *Philosophical Transactions of the Royal Society Biology B: Biological Sciences* 372(1721): 20160307.

Whiteside, Alan, and Nicholas Zebryk. 2015. "Ebola and AIDS in Africa." *Canadian Journal of African Studies* 49(2): 409–19.

Whitley, Richard J. 2003. "Smallpox: a potential agent of bioterrorism." *Antiviral Research* 57(1-2): 7–12.

Wilkinson, Claire. 2007. "The Copenhagen School on tour in Kyrgyzstan: is securitization theory usable outside Europe?" *Security Dialogue* 38(1): 5–25.

Wilson, Kumanan, John S. Brownstein, and David P. Fidler. 2010. "Strengthening the International Health Regulations: lessons from the H1N1 pandemic." *Health Policy and Planning* 25(6): 505–09.

Wilson, Reid. 2018. "How Ebola entered the American consciousness: a Trump tweet." *The Hill*, May 8. http://thehill.com/homenews/state-watch/386616-how -ebola-entered-the-american-consciousness-a-trump-tweet (accessed February 19, 2019).

Wirtz, Veronika J., Hans V. Horgerzeil, Andrew L. Gray, Maryam Bigdeli, Cornelis P. de Joncheere, Margaret A. Ewen, Martha Gyansa-Lutterodt, Sun Jing, Veera L. Luiza, Regina M. Mbindya, Helene Moller, Corrina Moucheraud, Bernard Pécoul Lembit Rago, Arash Reshidan, Dennis Ross-Degnan, Peter N. Stephens, Yot Teerawattananon, Ellen F.M. 't Hoen, Anita K. Wagner, Prashant Yadav, and Michael R. Reich. 2017. "Essential medicines for universal health coverage." *Lancet* 389(10067): 403–76.

Wolfe, Caitlin M., Esther L. Hamblio, Jacqueline Schulte, Parker Williams, Augustine Koryon, Jonathan Enders, Varlee Sanor, Yatta Wapoe, Dash Kwayon, David J. Blackley, Anthony S. Laney, Emily J. Weston, Emily K. Dokubo, Gloria Davies-Wayne, Annika Wendland, Valerie T.S. Daw, Mehboob Badini, Peter Clement, Nuha Mahmoud, Desmond Williams, Alex Gasasira, Tolbert G. Nyenswah, and Mosoka Fallah. 2017. "Ebola virus disease contact tracing activities, lessons learned, and best practices during the Duport Road outbreak in Monrovia, Liberia, November 2015." *PLoS Neglected Tropical Diseases* 11(6): e0005597.

Wolff, Jonathan. 2012. *The Human Right to Health*. New York: W.W. Norton.

Wong, Oscar. 2004. "Severe acute respiratory syndrome (SARS): wild game chefs and healthcare workers." *Occupational and Environmental Medicine* 61(1).

Wong, Gary, Wenjun Liu, Yingxia Liu, Boping Zhou, Yuhai Bi, and George F. Gao. 2015. "MERS, SARS, and Ebola: the role of super-spreaders in infectious disease." *Cell Host and Microbe* 18(4): 398–401.

World Cancer Research Fund International. 2018. *Building Momentum: Lessons on Implementing a Robust Sugar-Sweetened Beverage Tax.* London: World Cancer Research Fund International.

World Health Organization. N.d. *Designation/Establishment of National IHR Focal Points.* http://www.who.int/ihr/English2.pdf (accessed February 19, 2019).

World Health Organization. 1948. *Constitution of the World Health Organization.* Geneva: World Health Organization. http://www.who.int/governance/eb/who _constitution_en.pdf (accessed February 19, 2019).

World Health Organization. 2003a. "Summary of probable SARS cases with onset of illness from 1 November 2002 to 31 July 2003." http://www.who.int/csr/sars/ country/table2004_04_21/en/ (accessed February 19, 2019).

World Health Organization. 2003b. "WHO issues a global alert about cases of atypical pneumonia." March 12. http://www.who.int/mediacentre/news/re leases/2003/pr22/en/ (accessed February 19, 2019).

World Health Organization. 2010. "Pandemic (H1N1) 2009—update 100." May 14. http://www.who.int/csr/don/2010_05_14/en/ (accessed February 19, 2019).

World Health Organization. 2014a. "Are the Ebola outbreaks in Nigeria and Senegal over?" October 14. http://www.who.int/mediacentre/news/ebola/14 -october-2014/en/ (accessed February 19, 2019).

World Health Organization. 2014b. *Programme Budget 2014-2015.* Geneva: World Health Organization. http://www.who.int/about/resources_planning/PB14-15 _en.pdf (accessed February 19, 2019).

World Health Organization. 2015. *Global Status Report on Road Safety 2015.* Geneva: World Health Organization.

World Health Organization. 2016a. "Framework of engagement with non-State actors." http://www.who.int/about/collaborations/non-state-actors/A69_R10 -FENSA-en.pdf?ua=1 (accessed February 19, 2019).

World Health Organization. 2016b. *International Health Regulations (2005),* third edition. Geneva: World Health Organization.

World Health Organization. 2016c. "Top 10 causes of death." http://www.who .int/gho/mortality_burden_disease/causes_death/top_10/en/ (accessed November 8, 2018).

World Health Organization. 2016d. "WHO statement on the first meeting of the International Health Regulations (2005) Emergency Committee on Zika virus and observed increase in neurological disorders and neonatal malformations." February 1. http://www.who.int/news-room/detail/01-02-2016-who-statement -on-the-first-meeting-of-the-international-health-regulations-(2005)-(ihr-2005) -emergency-committee-on-zika-virus-and-observed-increase-in-neurological -disorders-and-neonatal-malformations (accessed February 19, 2019).

World Health Organization. 2017a. "Cumulative number of confirmed human cases of avian influenza A(H5N1) reported to WHO." June 15. http://www.who.int/influenza/human_animal_interface/2017_06_15_tableH5N1-corrected.pdf (accessed February 19, 2019).

World Health Organization. 2017b. "Human papillomavirus vaccines: WHO position paper, 2017." *Weekly Epidemiological Record* 92(19): 241–68.

World Health Organization. 2017c. "Obesity and overweight." http://www.who.int/en/news-room/fact-sheets/detail/obesity-and-overweight (accessed February 19, 2019).

World Health Organization. 2017d. *Programme Budget 2018-2019.* http://www.who.int/about/finances-accountability/budget/PB2018-2019_en_web.pdf?ua=1 (accessed February 19, 2019).

World Health Organization. 2017e. *Seventieth World Health Assembly Resolutions and Decisions.* http://apps.who.int/gb/ebwha/pdf_files/WHA70-REC1/A70_2017_REC1-en.pdf#page=30 (accessed February 19, 2019).

World Health Organization. 2017f. *World Malaria Report 2017.* Geneva: World Health Organization.

World Health Organization. 2018a. "Contingency Fund for Emergencies (CFE) contributions and allocations." http://www.who.int/emergencies/funding/contingency-fund/allocations/en/ (accessed February 19, 2019).

World Health Organization. 2018b. "Countries." http://www.who.int/countries/en/ (accessed February 19, 2019).

World Health Organization. 2018c. "Ebola virus disease." February 12. http://www.who.int/news-room/fact-sheets/detail/ebola-virus-disease (accessed February 19, 2019).

World Health Organization. 2018d. "Non-state actors in official relations with WHO." http://www.who.int/about/collaborations/non-state-actors/in-official-relations/en/ (accessed February 19, 2019).

World Health Organization. 2018e. "Social determinants of health." http://www.who.int/social_determinants/en/ (accessed February 19, 2019).

World Health Organization. 2018f. "Tuberculosis." http://www.who.int/news-room/fact-sheets/detail/tuberculosis (accessed February 19, 2019).

World Intellectual Property Organization. N.d. *What Is Intellectual Property?* Geneva: World Intellectual Property Organization.

Worobey, Michael, Thomas D. Watts, Richard A. McKay, Marc A. Suchard, Timothy Granade, Dirk E. Teuwen, Beryl A. Koblin, Walid Heneine, Phillippe Lemey, and Harold W. Jaffe. 2016. "1970s and 'Patient 0' HIV-1 genomes illustrated early HIV/AIDS history in North America." *Nature* 539(7627): 98–101.

Wulfhorst, Ellen, and David Morgan. 2014. "US CDC says returning Ebola medical workers should not be quarantined." Reuters, October 27. https://www.reuters.com/article/us-health-ebola-usa-newyork-idUSKBN0IG12920141027 (accessed February 19, 2019)

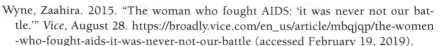

Wyne, Zaahira. 2015. "The woman who fought AIDS: 'it was never not our battle.'" *Vice*, August 28. https://broadly.vice.com/en_us/article/mbqjqp/the-women-who-fought-aids-it-was-never-not-our-battle (accessed February 19, 2019).

Yahuda, Michael. 1996. "The international standing of the Republic of China on Taiwan." *The China Quarterly* 148: 1319–39.

Yahya, Maryam. 2007. "Polio vaccines—'no thank you!' Barriers to polio eradication in northern Nigeria." *African Affairs* 106(423): 185–204.

Yin, Mo, and Paul Anantharajah Tambyah. 2015. "The 2009 influenza pandemic and the Ebola crisis: what are the lessons learnt?" *Future Virology* 10(4): 335–39.

Youde, Jeremy. 2008a. "Is universal access to antiretroviral drugs an emerging international norm?" *Journal of International Relations and Development* 11(4): 415–40.

Youde, Jeremy. 2008b. "Who's afraid of a chicken? Securitization and avian flu." *Democracy and Security* 4(2): 148–69.

Youde, Jeremy. 2009a. "Ethical consumerism or reified neoliberalism? Product (RED) and private funding for public goods." *New Political Science* 31(2): 201–20.

Youde, Jeremy. 2009b. "From resistance to receptivity: transforming the HIV/AIDS crisis into a human rights issue." In *The International Struggle for New Human Rights*, Clifford Bob (ed.), 68–82. Philadelphia: University of Pennsylvania Press.

Youde, Jeremy. 2010. *Biopolitical Surveillance and Public Health in International Politics*. New York: Palgrave Macmillan.

Youde, Jeremy. 2011a. "The Clinton Foundation and global health governance." In *Partnerships and Foundations in Global Health Governance*, Simon Rushton and Owain David Williams (eds.), 164–83. New York: Palgrave Macmillan.

Youde, Jeremy. 2011b. "Mediating risk through the International Health Regulations and biopolitical surveillance." *Political Studies* 59(4): 813–30.

Youde, Jeremy. 2012a. "Biosurveillance, human rights, and the zombie plague." *Global Change, Peace, and Security* 24(1): 83–93.

Youde, Jeremy. 2012b. *Global Health Governance*. Cambridge: Polity.

Youde, Jeremy. 2013a. "Cattle scourge no more: the eradication of rinderpest and its lessons for global health campaigns." *Politics and the Life Sciences* 32(1): 43–57.

Youde, Jeremy. 2013b. "The Rockefeller and Gates Foundations in global health governance." *Global Society* 27(2): 139–58.

Youde, Jeremy. 2015. "Biosurveillance, human rights, and the zombie plague." In *The Politics of Surveillance and Response to Disease Outbreaks: The New Frontier for States and Non-State Actors*, Sara E. Davies and Jeremy Youde (eds.), 57–69. Burlington: Ashgate.

Youde, Jeremy. 2016. "Private actors, global health, and learning the lessons of history." *Medicine, Conflict, and Survival* 32(3): 203–20.

Youde, Jeremy. 2017. "Covering the cough: memory, remembrance, and influenza amnesia." *Australian Journal of Politics and History* 63(3): 357–68.

Youde, Jeremy. 2018. *Global Health Governance in International Society*. Oxford: Oxford University Press.

Zhang, Sarah. 2016. "Zika is no reason to cancel the Olympics. Here's why." *Wired*, June 4. https://www.wired.com/2016/06/zika-no-reason-cancel-olympics/ (accessed February 19, 2019).

Zirulnick, Ariel. 2014. "Nigeria contains Ebola—and US officials want to know more." *Christian Science Monitor*, October 6. https://www.csmonitor.com/World/Africa/2014/1006/Nigeria-contains-Ebola-and-US-officials-want-to-know-more (accessed February 19, 2019).

Zurleck-Brown, Sarah, Holly Newby, Doris Chou, Nobuko Mizoguchi, Lale Say, Emi Suzuki, and John Wilmoth. 2013. "Understanding global trends in maternal mortality." *International Perspectives on Sexual and Reproductive Health* 39(1): 32–41.

INDEX

About the Author

Jeremy Youde is dean of the College of Liberal Arts and professor of political science at the University of Minnesota Duluth and an internationally recognized expert on global health politics. His research focuses on questions of global health governance and global health politics. He is the author of four previous books and co-editor of three recent volumes. He is also chair of the Global Health Section of the International Studies Association. He earned his BA in political science and global development studies at Grinnell College and his MA and PhD in political science at the University of Iowa. Prior to assuming his current position, he taught at San Diego State University, Grinnell College, and the Australian National University.

GLOBALIZATION
Series Editors
Manfred B. Steger
*University of Hawai'i at Mānoa
and Western Sydney University*
and
Terrell Carver
University of Bristol

"Globalization" has become the buzzword of our time. But what does it mean? Rather than forcing a complicated social phenomenon into a single analytical framework, this series seeks to present globalization as a multidimensional process constituted by complex, often contradictory interactions of global, regional, and local aspects of social life. Since conventional disciplinary borders and lines of demarcation are losing their old rationales in a globalizing world, authors in this series apply an interdisciplinary framework to the study of globalization. In short, the main purpose and objective of this series is to support subject-specific inquiries into the dynamics and effects of contemporary globalization and its varying impacts across, between, and within societies.

Globalization and Sovereignty, 2nd ed.
John Agnew

Globalization and War
Tarak Barkawi

Globalization and Human Security
Paul Battersby and Joseph M. Siracusa

Globalization and the Environment
Peter Christoff and Robyn Eckersley

Globalization and American Popular Culture, 4th ed.
Lane Crothers

Globalization and Migration
Eliot Dickinson

Globalization and Militarism, 2nd ed.
Cynthia Enloe

Globalization and Law
Adam Gearey

Globalization and Feminist Activism, 2nd ed.
Mary E. Hawkesworth

Globalization and Postcolonialism
Sankaran Krishna

Globalization and Media, 3rd ed.
Jack Lule

Globalization and Social Movements, 2nd ed.
Valentine M. Moghadam

Globalization and Terrorism, 2nd ed.
Jamal R. Nassar

Globalization and Culture, 4rd ed.
Jan Nederveen Pieterse

Globalization and Democracy
Stephen J. Rosow and Jim George

Globalization and International Political Economy
Mark Rupert and M. Scott Solomon

Globalization and Citizenship
Hans Schattle

Globalization and Money
Supriya Singh

Globalization and Islamism
Nevzat Soguk

Globalization and Urbanization
James H. Spencer

Globalisms, 3rd ed.
Manfred B. Steger

Rethinking Globalism
Edited by Manfred B. Steger

Globalization and Labor
Dimitris Stevis and Terry Boswell

Globaloney 2.0
Michael Veseth

Globalization and Health
Jeremy Youde

 Supported by the Globalization Research Center at the University of Hawai'i, Mānoa